A Career Handbook for TV, Radio, Film, Video & Interactive Media

2nd edition

Written by SHIONA LLEWELLYN
and SUE WALKER

A & C Black • London

Second edition 2003
Reprinted 2005
A & C Black Publishers Limited
37 Soho Square
London W1D 3QZ
www.acblack.com

First edition published 2000

© 2003, 2000 *Skillset*

ISBN 0–7136–6320–0

A CIP catalogue record for this book is
available from the British Library.

Every effort has been made to ensure that the
information contained in this book is correct at the
time of going to press.

A & C Black uses paper produced with elemental
chlorine-free pulp, harvested from managed
sustainable forests.

Typeset in $9^{3}/_{4}$/13pt Utopia

Contents

Contents

iii

Foreword

Everyone needs a helping hand at the start of their career, whatever they decide to do. I know I certainly did. Traditionally, there has not been an awful lot of help available to those wishing to enter the UK media industry. Persistence, tenacity and a thick skin have been necessary attributes of those brave spirits who have embarked on the great adventure.

Let's face it, if you want to work in the media industry in this country you have to be prepared for some tough times. Yes, it can be momentarily glamorous, yes it is often quite exciting, but it is also hard work and it can be very difficult to get a break. But, it is worth persevering, as the personal satisfaction can be enormous.

This book genuinely is one of a kind as it is the only publication to cover the whole industry in such detail. It gives useful background information, helpful tips and advice, and is not afraid to pull punches in telling it like it is. It's an invaluable resource if you are planning to work in the industry, or even if you already do and just want help to move your career along.

One of the biggest problems facing people wishing to enter the industry is how to plan your entry strategy. This book guides you through this process in a no-nonsense way, and in doing so gives you a real head-start. It is also an invaluable resource for careers advisors, teachers and parents as it provides detailed information on the jobs, the entry requirements, the background experience and the progression routes available.

Importantly, this book gives information about the education and training decisions and routes you may wish to consider to give yourself the best possible start. Furthermore, it makes it clear that learning is something that we must *all* do throughout our lives. As we face up to challenges such as the inevitable development of new technologies, we must keep our skills up-to-date so that *all* of us in the industry you now wish to enter, can remain competitive.

I am delighted that *Skillset*, as the voice of education and training in the industry, has been able to produce this definitive guide. No-one else would be able to access the unrivalled information and support from within the industry which makes this book unique. My close association as the organisation's patron could leave me open to the charge of being biased. But I can honestly say that this publication is the most important book on this subject ever to have emerged anywhere. I am delighted that this second edition, by way of a substantial reprint of the first, has been so comprehensively revised and updated to secure its position as the leading publication in this field.

If you are serious about wanting to develop and succeed in this industry, this book could be the key to unlock your future career. Read it, absorb it and use it. Oh, and good luck!

Lord Puttnam of Queensgate CBE

Acknowledgements

The research, writing, editing and eventual publication of this book has been a massive task. The collation and checking of facts, the writing and re-writing of chapters, the verification and industry endorsement of the advice, and the editing and proofing of copy has involved a large number of *Skillset* staff and leading industry professionals.

It has been a process which has been both time consuming and labour intensive, but it is this process which makes this publication so unique. This is not a book which expresses the views, opinions or perceptions of an individual author. It is a book written in conjunction with the industry it sets out so definitively to describe. For this reason it is owned and endorsed by the industry in a way that no other publication can claim.

Establishing exactly the right team is what makes this collaboration such a success. The knowledge and unrivalled expertise of Shiona Llewellyn, the author of the first edition, has ensured strength and depth to this edition. This has been supplemented by the time, energy, enthusiasm and knowledge of the amazing Sue Walker, without whom you would not be reading this publication.

It is also important to acknowledge and thank the following, who have all contributed an enormous amount of their time and expertise so willingly and freely: Penny Bance, Helen Boyes, Tom Campbell, Andrew Craske, Paula Moses, Denise Feeney, Neil Flintham, Mike Foley, Catherine Godward, Hilary Irving, Colin Kirkpatrick, Ingrid Lewis, Ann Pointon, Clare Thalman, Carol Varlaam, Ilka Walkley and last, but not least, the team at A & C Black. Our sincerest thanks to all of them.

We hope that you enjoy reading and using this book.

Gary Townsend
Communications Director – *Skillset*

Preface

Welcome to the second edition of the *Skillset Careers Handbook*, which has been researched and written with help from across the TV, Radio, Film, Video and Interactive Media industries. Many professionals have contributed advice and information with the aim of providing an up-to-date, comprehensive resource for anyone that is interested in this fascinating and fast-changing industry. Feedback on the first edition – which sold out after a few months and had to be reprinted – indicated that the content provided was of value to a diversity of individuals and organisations, and not just job seekers. However, its primary purpose is to help anyone who hopes to get into – or on in – this tough and competitive world.

This book is often to be found on the business shelves of bookshops, squeezed between software manuals, legal texts and accountancy syllabuses. This is wholly appropriate, as the opportunities available in this industry are many and diverse with numerous prospects for people with IT, financial, analytical or legal skills throughout the industry.

There are lots of obvious and less obvious opportunities for people with all kinds of other skills too; people from every kind of educational background build interesting careers in an industry which is still more interested in how well you perform in a job, rather than a multitude of paper qualifications. This is one of the reasons for the success of the *Skillset* Professional Qualifications (described later in the book), which are now well regarded across the industry.

This book aims to give everyone access to the type of information that, until now, was only available to a privileged few. It provides an introduction to the real industry, which is often rather different from what is portrayed in careers office brochures. We hope it will encourage you to explore areas of work that you may not have considered. There are many employment areas (ironically often the 'newer' areas) which still offer excellent long-term career opportunities in an industry that is well known for its reliance on short-term contracts.

Another initiative – jointly sponsored by *Skillset* and BECTU, the union which represents technical and production staff in TV, Radio, Film, Video and Interactive Media – is already changing the face of careers guidance, information and advice for these industries. *skillsformedia* offers an on- and off-line service to individuals who work – or want to work – in this industry. Described later in the handbook, it offers a range of services, which complement the information we provide.

For this second edition, we have been given invaluable help in updating – sometimes rewriting – specialist chapters, to reflect the changes that have taken place in the individual sectors over the past couple of years. Each contributor is credited for their work, but we would also like to offer our thanks to all of them for helping us produce such a high-quality product.

By reading this book, you should gain an understanding of 'how the jigsaw fits together'. There are similarities between the individual sectors (for example film and TV), but there are also significant differences, which only serve to underline the need for well-thought-out research and career planning.

Making a good, well-planned start to your career can improve your chances of success. There is plenty of advice within this book about choosing courses that should help you, applying for (and doing) work experience, and understanding what industry employers look for in candidates. Many people who have recently crossed these hurdles have shared their experiences to help you.

Once you have made a start, *Skillset* standards and professional qualifications may help your development and employability, especially if you target one of the skills shortage areas. A significant feature of this industry is that some jobs are hugely over-subscribed and others are so under-subscribed that skilled practitioners can virtually name their price.

There are no magic wands to be waved. If you do decide to try and establish a career in this industry, the content of this book will only be part of what you will be expected to offer. You will need a range of sought-after skills (including IT, interpersonal and business related skills), considerable drive, and a passion for your chosen area of work. Contacts won't go amiss either.

Busy professionals from every aspect of the industry have given their time and experience to write this book. Without exception, they wanted to offer positive help to people at the start of their careers. Many contributors have said: 'I wish there had been a resource like this when I was setting out...'

Shiona Llewellyn

Introduction

Skillset is the Sector Skills Council for the audio-visual industries, which include television, radio, film, video and interactive media. It works with all parts of the industry (employers, trade associations, unions, industry bodies, individuals and training and education providers) as well as government and its public agencies in Scotland, Northern Ireland, Wales and England to:

- Find out what skills issues exist, and what needs to be done to address them
- Encourage industry and government to invest in training programmes that can tackle most issues
- Set industry standards for training and education providers
- Check, approve and monitor training providers and higher/ further education institutions to make sure that they are meeting those standards
- Develop qualifications which people working in the industry can complete as evidence of the skills that they have learned
- Provide industry-based careers information, advice and guidance
- Encourage and support diversity
- Promote skills for business throughout the industry and advise on UK education and training policy.

This book is just one in a series of *Skillset* initiatives designed to help the people who contribute to some of our most exciting, creative industries to meet the challenges and opportunities provided by a 'high-tech', global marketplace. The industry needs a broad cross-section of talented, highly motivated individuals who are passionate about the work they do. Much of the statistical information contained in this handbook has been taken from current *Skillset* research at the time of writing – refer to the website www.skillset.org to find the up-to-date details, and to read the full reports.

an increasingly important area

The audio-visual industries are an exciting and growing part of the economy, providing employment for more than 200,000 people. In addition to contributing very positively to the UK's balance of trade, they promote British talent all over the world. Characterised by the need for high-level craft, technical and creative skills, they offer a broad cross-section of career opportunities.

Improve your chances

People have always been interested in working 'in the media', and the growth of relevant university and college courses has hugely increased, as has the number of 'hopefuls' who approach employers for work – or work experience – each year. During the research for this book, recruiters throughout the industry have been consulted; their advice should help any reader improve their chances of gaining a foothold in this competitive industry. One piece of information should be of particular interest to many career starters or changers and their advisors: that there are many areas of skills shortage in a generally oversubscribed sphere of work.

a springboard for further research

Although this is a big book, packed with information, it could be considerably bigger: every industry area could justify a publication of its own. The chapters are intended to provide a sound foundation to get you started. If you are serious about establishing a career in any of the areas described, potential employers will expect you to be proactive in gaining additional information, relevant experience – and of course, contacts.

'What's in it for me?'

This book contains a mixture of relevant careers guidance, to help people from a diversity of educational and cultural backgrounds explore the possibilities of working in an environment that is almost too attractive. Every year, many thousands of wasted applications are made by individuals who have a false picture of the real world of TV, radio, film, video and interactive media. By reading this book, you should be in a position to answer the all-important careers question: 'Is it really for me?'

Where are the jobs?

As the industry grows, and technology continues to develop, the pattern of employment changes. Recent *Skillset* research indicates that more people are now employed in the sectors of interactive media, computer games and web design than in the whole of the television industry. Each employment area includes a number of large companies, but the majority of jobs – especially for people at the start of their careers – will be in small or medium sized enterprises (SMEs) which in general employ fewer than 20–25 people on a full-time basis.

Interactive media and games

This sector combines computer and communications technology with 'traditional' media communications, to enable the end-user to make choices about the information that they receive and the ways in which they receive it. Companies in this area of employment may be involved in:

- Internet and web-based content production and generation
- The games sector
- Interactive TV and radio
- CD-ROM and DVD
- Streaming video production

Although the sector is dominated by a few large international companies, thousands of smaller players employ 10–20 people each.

Television

Most people still apply to the BBC, ITV or C4 for jobs, and yet, although these are still the largest employers in terrestrial television, there are well over 1000 other potential employers, ranging from BSkyB to a multitude of small independent production companies. Around 24,000 people work in the TV industry.

Radio

Each week, people in the UK spend more time listening to the radio than watching TV. Although the BBC still dominates the airwaves, commercial radio has been a great success story, with four large companies owning many local licences. The growth of digital stations is likely to increase employment opportunities for a sector which currently employs around 23,000 people.

The film industry

Film production levels in the UK are constantly fluctuating in what is often referred to as a 'boom and bust' cycle. At the time of publication, film production is currently at a relatively low level, but a diversity of individuals do gain employment – usually as free-lancers – across the sector. Most companies are SMEs, with 91% of businesses employing fewer than 10 people on regular contracts. Cinema-going is at its highest level for many years. The Film Council, which was established in 2000, is working hard to create a sustainable and profitable national industry.

The animation sector

UK animation is admired throughout the world. In addition to feature films and 'shorts', the sector provides specialist services to the TV, commercials and games sector. About 1500 people are employed, mainly in small companies based in the four centres of excellence around London, Bristol, Manchester and Cardiff. Large numbers of freelancers supply this sector, which is very labour-intensive and requires a mix of high-level creative and techno-logical skills.

The facilities sector

Supporting independent TV and film production, as well as major broadcasters, are specialist facilities houses which offer equip-ment, studio facilities and highly skilled staff. Mainly based in the London area, the majority are very specialised, providing expertise in areas such as editing, animation, computer graphics and sound effects. A major source of employment for technical people, the sector (which is dominated by SMEs) also uses many freelancers.

Corporate production – the non-broadcast sector

More money is spent on corporate production each year than on the whole European film industry. 'Non-broadcast' business-to-business communications are commissioned, often with very high budgets, to fulfil a diversity of specific purposes from launching a new global brand to charity fund-raising and professional development. Companies specialise in audio-visual presentation equipment, video conferencing, film and video production, live events and some aspects of the interactive media sector. There are many small and medium sized employers, with core teams of 10–25 people who call in freelance help when required.

Commercials

Often referred to as 'mini-feature films', the makers of UK commercials are among the best in the world. High budgets allow the use of specialist techniques and effects, often at the cutting edge of technology and creativity. Employers usually operate with small core teams, complemented by highly experienced free-lancers. This sector, which is especially hard to break into, can attract high-profile feature film directors.

Written on behalf of the industry

This book has been paid for by a cross-section of industry organisations. Every chapter has been read and approved by current industry practitioners and employers. Their suggestions and amendments have been included to ensure that the information provided paints a real picture of the different elements of this complex business.

Written for anyone interested in the media

As the title suggests, this is essentially a careers book – written to assist anyone who is considering a first or second job within the media industry. But many people currently working within the different parts of the industry have commented on its broader educational value. It's likely that anyone who enjoys any aspect of the output of this industry will be interested to 'go behind the scenes' to gain an understanding of how 'the jigsaw fits together'.

Using this book

Although some dedicated individuals will read this book from start to finish, the majority of readers are more likely to 'dip' into sections of particular interest. Consequently, each chapter has been designed to stand alone, supported by cross-references. Because of this, there is some inevitable repetition of key cross-sectoral issues, for example the listing of sought-after skills.

An introduction to working styles

A key feature of the book is its realistic approach to employment issues. Many employers have commented on the lack of consideration applicants tend to give to the patterns of employment which affect the lives and lifestyles of people throughout certain areas of the industry. The majority of individuals who work in the 'creative' areas will never have what many people in this country still consider to be a 'proper job' with a regular income. Making a conscious decision to enter an employment area where short-term contracts are the norm requires serious thought. Hopefully, this book will help you plan the beginning of a career that 'fits'.

Finding out more

There is always more to learn, especially within industries that are changing as quickly as the ones described in this book. The final chapter of this book is a treasure-trove of information sources, giving details of the relevant trade associations and useful magazines, journals and books. These are kept up-to-date through the *Skillset* website: www.skillset.org. You can also consult www.skillsformedia.com for further invaluable career-related information.

Working in the TV, Radio, Film, Video and Interactive Media Industry

Most people who plan to work 'in the media' are firmly focused on the traditional areas of employment. A recent survey of under-graduates put the BBC as the most desirable place to work in the UK, and every large organisation across the industry will receive hundreds – even thousands – of speculative applications every year. And yet, at the beginning of the 21st century, more than half the jobs in this exciting sector are in the 'new' media areas of interactivity, computer games and web design. Occupational profiles increasingly require a mix of competencies, including IT skills, with many previously distinct roles broadening. Individuals who can offer a combination of analytical, technical, interpersonal and creative skills will have a previously unforeseen range of career opportunities. Within this chapter, we hope to provide a 'taster' of those opportunities to help you identify a possible career pathway; later in the handbook, we give some advice on the practicalities of identifying vacancies, and actually getting jobs.

An area of opportunity

Recent research indicates that employment in the audio-visual industries remains stable, despite numerous reports of cutbacks. *Skillset* and the Department for Culture, Media and Sport (DCMS) estimate that around 200,000 people are now working within this 'knowledge-based' contributor to the UK economy.

The impact of new technology has been huge – influencing

every element of the media communications business. In particular, the growth of digitalisation has changed the way in which films and television programmes are made. In an increasingly competitive global market, where remote working (often with people based in different countries) has become commonplace, employers are seeking people with a mix of technical, creative and business skills. Language skills are also sought-after by many companies. Much of the work offered is likely to be 'interdisciplinary', crossing many traditional boundaries. Interestingly, this creates real opportunities for career-changers. Some of the most successful people in new media have 'bolted on' their technical and information-technology skills and knowledge to a non-technical base.

Feast and famine

Every Monday the *Media Guardian* is a 'must buy' for most people who are actively job hunting in the media industry. Advertisements for 'conventional' jobs, for example for researchers or assistant producers, often attract hundreds of applications, while the 'New Media' section of the same paper contains adverts which may only attract a handful of suitable people. Deciding how to plan your job-hunting strategy is key to establishing a satisfying career. Understanding what the different jobs involve, and building a realistic picture of your own strengths and interests, will help you to do this.

Within this chapter, we aim to give you an insight into the range of skills and experience that are employed within the different sectors. The job profiles given are deliberately brief, and intended only to kick-start your personal research. The *Skillset* website www.skillset.org provides considerably more detail. If you are serious about finding a job in parts of this industry, you will need to spend a lot of time researching possible areas of opportunity for entry-level jobs and the subsequent pathways which may develop from each one.

You will almost certainly be surprised by the range of profiles that we have included. Many people find that the reality of working in this industry is not quite what they expected – it's certainly not just about making programmes or films. Throughout the industry, departments and small companies are run on increasingly tough commercial principles, with each job classified in terms of cost or potential profitability to the employing organisation. Each team-member will be expected to provide measurable value for money. 'Multi-skilling' and 'multi-tasking' are now commonplace; many people work cross-sectorally; and professionals across the sectors are constantly discovering ways of reducing budgets through creative use of technology or resources.

Maximising potential

In independent TV companies, advertisers and sponsors are wooed, and licensing and merchandising deals struck, to produce maximum exploitation – for example, by arranging for linked products to be released alongside, or subsequent to, the pro-grammes. Books, magazines, videos and associated merchandise may all 'add value' to the worth of the original production. Some programmes – for example, *Who Wants to be a Millionaire* – have become brands in their own right. Archives are being viewed as marketable resources. New channels are expected to offer new opportunities for broadcasters to make money, and related 'phone-ins' can cover all the production costs of an expensive entertainment show. Interactivity – which eventually is expected to contribute significant income – is well established. *Pop Idol* attracted many millions of votes and launched a number of lucrative spin-offs.

As a result, people with proven business and audience-aware-ness skills are sought throughout the industry. At the senior level, many decision-makers now join the industry from other business areas and MBAs are increasingly visible. It's a tough, and increasingly global, marketplace; the high rewards – and they can be very high – will go to individuals who can make a positive contribution to the success of their organisation.

The UK film world is also changing. Traditionally a 'cottage industry', where companies were formed to make a production and then disbanded on completion, there is now active government support to encourage a system which is more closely related to the US industry. Detailed in Chapter 4, *The Film Industry*, this new approach will create a wide range of new business-related opportunities.

Types of employment

Terms and conditions of employment

Different types of employment contracts are described in some detail in Chapter 10, *Getting in and Getting on in the TV, Radio, Film, Video and Interactive Media Industry* (*see* pp. 269–272). They do vary widely, and it is important to understand the implications of each on your life in general.

Working freelance – the Skillset freelance survey

This fascinating study published in January 2002 gives a valuable insight into the employment of freelancers across the traditional industry. As the new media world employs fewer freelancers, response to the survey was heavily biased towards the traditional industry. Major findings included:

The employment picture

* A total of 44,000 freelancers are estimated to be working in key sectors of the audio-visual industries on a given day – accounting for 35% of the active workforce on that day.
* Around one-third of freelancers are women (33%) – a slight drop from 37% in 1993.
* 7.6% are of minority ethnic origin – a considerable increase from 3.0% in 1993.
* The average age of the freelance workforce is 39. Six per cent are aged under 25, and 7% over 55. The age-profile of women is much lower than that of men – 56% are aged 35 or under compared with 36% of men.
* Over one-quarter of freelancers hold an undergraduate degree in media studies as a highest qualification; one-quarter hold a degree in another subject; and 15% hold a postgraduate degree in a media-related subject.
* Over one-third of freelancers earned less than £20,000 in the year leading up to the survey.
* Male freelancers earn considerably more than women. For example, 10% of men had earned £50,000 in the previous year, but just 2% of women; 50% had earned less than £20,000 per year compared with 38% of men. This is almost certainly related to the younger age-profile of women freelancers.

* The majority of freelancers (60%) live in London or the South East. This compares with the census estimate that 65.5% of the total workforce (including employees) were working in London or the South East on 19th May 2000.

The survey also enquired about how people got their first job, and concluded that 'by far the most common means of securing current posts are through people previously worked with (47%) and directly from employers (35%). Only 4% of those surveyed had obtained their current work through responding to advertisements'. The next survey will be carried out later in 2003. Watch *Skillset*'s website (www.skillset.org) for all new research, as and when it becomes available.

Could I be a successful freelancer in TV, film, video or radio?

If you would like to work in production this is a very important question. It is estimated that around 50% of the people who work (in any capacity) in TV and film production are self-employed freelancers – although, at the time of writing, there seemed to be indications that this figure may be beginning to fall as more employers offer contracts and staff jobs. Industry observers will tell you that about one-quarter of freelancers have far too much work, and are sought-after by many potential employers. The majority of freelancers, in contrast, will 'get by' but not always be in employment, and another significant proportion will barely get any work. To improve your chances of being a member of a sought-after team, you will need to exhibit a range of skills and personality factors, including the following:

Personal marketing

Until you have a proven track record, people will not be approaching you with job offers – and so it will be up to you to 'market' yourself to potential employers. This means making direct approaches – by letter and CV, through showreels, on the phone, in conversation – to let people know that you exist and have useful skills or qualifications to offer. It is this aspect of working freelance that many people find hard and off-putting. Some people find that, once they have a track record, an agent will take over this marketing role for a percentage fee.

administrative ability

Successful freelancers are well organised, keeping records of established and potential contacts, information about what's going on in the industry, and who is involved. A well-managed diary is essential. You are unlikely to be offered repeat work if you are late or go to the wrong address. The most employed freelancers are talented, reliable individuals who provide a cost-effective service. Some people find that subscribing to a 'diary service' is a worthwhile investment.

Team skills

When a freelance crew comes together, it is expected to function effectively in a very short time. The ability to 'get on' and work with a wide range of people is therefore an essential attribute. You will be expected to fit in quickly; there is little room for bad tempers or ego trips on a busy set or shoot.

Financial awareness

As a freelancer, you will be self-employed, responsible for your own tax and National Insurance contributions. Once established, you may also be expected to cope with expenses and bills that have to be dealt with immediately. You will need to negotiate your fee and make sure that you get paid. A lesson that many freelancers learn is that no-one will ever phone to say, 'You haven't invoiced.' If you are to build a freelance career you will need to manage your money effectively. It will help to have some basic accounting skills, or to employ the services of someone who can help to keep your finances in order. Get to know your bank manager – *before* he or she demands to see you!

Extending your skills

It will help your freelance career and financial stability if you can do more than one job. Taking advantage of any opportunity to develop additional skills will show ability and commitment. Computer literacy and word-processing skills are needed for all kinds of jobs within the industry, and they may also be useful during enforced 'resting' periods.

Something to fall back on

Unless you are very well connected, brilliant, or just lucky, you will need to earn money outside the industry periodically. It is useful to plan for this and not wait until the money has run out. People do lots of different jobs, from lecturing in media studies to data management or stacking supermarket shelves... you will need to develop a marketable skill, and useful contacts for this work, too.

The traditional industry is a tough business, beneath the glamorous exterior. People work very hard – and often spend long hours getting a job finished in uncomfortable surroundings. Any employer will be concerned about your ability to fit in with the team, and at the beginning of a career, this – in combination with your enthusiasm and passion for the industry – is probably as important as any formal qualification you may bring with you. Most of the opportunities available to new entrants in the next decade will be within the independent sector – and in small teams, everyone has to mix well and contribute several skills.

Summing up

To sum up, as a freelancer you will have to:

- Accept responsibility for getting – and doing – your own work
- Make your own (sometimes difficult) decisions
- Cope with the 'downtimes'
- Be strategic and personally organised
- Be enthusiastic about your work
- Be a genuine team player.

You will be *responsible for your own development and training*, and will need to:

- Adapt to change, responding to market trends and needs
- Learn to develop and apply new skills
- Keep up with relevant technology.

You will be advised to *decide what your 'core business' should be* by:

- Analysing the existing and potential competition
- Finding out if people are interested in paying for what you offer
- Being flexible in response to a changing industry.

You will have to decide *what to charge* for your work by:

- Finding out about the opportunities – some employers may want a Rolls Royce but only be prepared to pay Mini rates, and many actually want a Mini and will not pay for more
- Understanding the different market sectors
- Taking into consideration your overheads, and the fact that you may wait months for a cheque.

You will need to *be organised* – in effect, you will be running a business. So, you'll need to:

- Decide about effective marketing techniques
- Get your finances well organised, including planning for tax, National Insurance and VAT payments and allowable expenses
- Get advice on the legal and 'intellectual property' issues, if you are a Producer
- Decide if you need a base away from home, and find the most productive working environment for you
- Explore local sources of help and support for small businesses.

You will need to *keep in touch with a network of people and service providers who may be useful to you:*

- Build a contacts list
- Join industry associations
- Attend relevant training courses.

And finally…

Continue to invest in your future

Once you have established a freelance career, you will be encouraged to further develop competence in your chosen area(s) of work by gaining *Skillset* Professional Qualifications. These are qualifications that have been especially constructed for the TV, radio, film, video and interactive media industry, and they are all assessed by practitioners from within the relevant sectors. *See* Chapter 9, *Training and Education for the Industry* for an introduction to the training opportunities and funding available for freelancers.

A changing world

Very few programme commissions are now accepted without firm plans to exploit all the possibilities for interactivity. Websites abound, and everyone talks about 'convergence'. However, there are also many other specialist suppliers to the industry, often facilitated by high-level technology.

Consult a directory such as *The Knowledge* or *The Production Guide* (*see* Chapter 11, *Finding Out More*) which is used as a source of reference by producers and production managers throughout the industry, and you will almost certainly be surprised by the number and diversity of specialist services that are now available. All manner of production and post-production services are on offer, from providers of trained animals to work-permit 'fixers'. Facilities houses – offering specialist skills such as animation, digital editing or special effects – are contracted by producers from across the industry to supply a specific service for an often tightly negotiated price. The successful companies in this competitive sector do not just provide excellent facilities and skilled staff – they 'add value' to the business relationships they develop by being very client-focused and pleasant to work with, thus putting an emphasis on good interpersonal skills for technical staff. Although considerable numbers of people work in this sector, individual companies are usually small and vacancies occur infrequently. Most individuals will start their careers as a 'runner', being generally useful as an extra pair of hands, or as a very junior member of a specialist team.

Financial decision-making in TV and film

Experienced producers will tell you that in the past, before the accountants moved into TV in a big way, a programme would be commissioned on the basis of a 'good idea'; and that, once agreed, the money would be found from somewhere. It's certainly not like that now. Before a programme or series is commissioned, a business case has to be put up for consideration. This is true for in-house producers as well as independents who are pitching in competition. A number of factors will be taken into consideration, including:

- Expected audience (size and demographics)
- Cost
- Production time
- Possibility of international sales
- Opportunities for licensing and marketing exploitation

Programmes will usually be commissioned to a specific duration, to fit a particular schedule 'slot'. 'Strands' – which have a particular 'brand image' – may actually be made by many different production teams. Only when a producer has clinched the deal will he or she be in a position to build the team.

In the film world, money is even more of an issue. A producer may pitch the concept to many potential backers before – if ever – a decision is made. Corporate productions use research and development information to reassure their clients that their investment is likely to achieve its agreed aims. More information about making corporate videos, short films and feature films can be found in the relevant chapters.

The influence of technology

Obviously, technology dominates all the 'new media' elements of the industry, where computers are the standard tools of trade. However, developments in technology have affected the working practices across the traditional media industries.

A single individual can now record and report on a news story, by carrying their own, relatively light-weight equipment. Some jobs are actually done by machines now, and in general, today's sophisticated and easy-to-use technology has reduced the need for large numbers of highly qualified people. Engineers have been worst hit (although there is now a skills shortage of some specialised engineers), but they are certainly not alone: for example, graphic designers and film and TV editors have found that a good proportion of their work is now supported by computers.

In other cases, one person may be employed to operate a range of equipment, in response to the needs of the production. Known as 'multi-skilling', this is one of the most significant changes which has occurred within the traditional industry. Originating in local radio, where talented people work in often very small teams to fill a great deal of airtime, it is now evident throughout the production processes of the more traditional employers.

Multi-skilling has many advantages – in financial and also in personnel terms, since it can provide individuals with much more varied jobs. Much of the work now on offer is 'interdisciplinary', requiring a mix of technical, creative and business skills. However, some industry professionals feel that there will always be opportunities for highly skilled and focused experts, which may explain the increasing interest in specialised postgraduate courses and high level NVQs.

The development of the *Skillset* Professional Qualifications (*see* Chapter 9, *Training and Education for the Industry*) has established standards for a broad range of employment areas – thus opening up possibilities for individual accreditation in more than one skill area. Every job in broadcast, film, video and interactive media has an association with technology. Whether your ambition is to be a TV director, a games producer, a cameraperson or an administrator, you will need to be computer literate, and willing to develop new skills when required by your work.

What are the jobs?

Understanding the essential and desirable skills, experience and personality factors required by the type of work you want to do is crucial to effective career planning. Recruiters tell us that the majority of applicants – especially for very popular types of work – are unaware of the requirements of the job that they say they can do. Make sure this doesn't happen to you!

Jobs in this industry can be divided into five broad categories:

- Specialist IT jobs for new media and the audio-visual industry
- Administration, management and business development
- Programme- or film-making
- Technical and craft areas
- Journalists and presenters

In the traditional media areas some jobs are required at every stage of a production – or even when nothing is actually in production – but the majority of people will concentrate their work during one phase of programme- or film-making:

- Pre-production
- Production
- Post-production

Freelancers will be contacted to work when – and only when – needed.

Skillset *Occupational Map and Job Profiles*

After extensive consultation with industry practitioners, *Skillset* has produced an invaluable resource known as an Occupational Map. This contains job profiles, which describe in detail the vast majority of jobs in the various sections of the audio-visual industry.

For the purposes of the Map, job groups have been broken down into six sections, depending on the work areas:

Section One – The Creative Roles

Covers occupations in the areas of Animation, Art and Design, Costume, Interactive Media, Make-up and Hairdressing, Set Crafts and Special Effects, Animal Department, and Computer Games.

Section Two – The Technical Roles

Covers occupations in the areas of Camera, Exhibition, Lighting, Riggers, Grips and Cranes, Sound and Technical and Studio Operations, Production Sound, and Post-production Sound.

Section Three – The Writing and Production Roles

Covers occupations in the areas of Journalism, Producing, Post-production and Script Writing.

Section Four – The Programming and Broadcasting Roles

Covers occupations in the areas of Broadcast Engineering, Commissioning and Scheduling, Library/Archives, Media Access and Programme Distribution.

Section Five – The Office Roles

Covers occupations in the areas of Administration and Secretarial, Finance, General Management, Human Resources, Information Technology, Legal, Press and Public Relations, and Sales and Marketing.

Section Six – Health & Safety

Covers Health & Safety responsibilities, legislation and professionals, including the roles of Health & Safety Advisors and the responsibilities of employers.

A full list of job profiles contained in the Occupational Map can be found on *Skillset's* website at www.skillset.org. Look under 'Careers'.

Below is a representative sample of jobs that can be found there, to help inform you about some of the most asked-about jobs. Please note that these are edited descriptions; for full versions, please refer to the Skillset *website.*

1. The Creative Roles

animation
Sample occupations found in this area:

animator
Animators work with a range of media including celluloid, two-dimensional and three-dimensional models or puppets to create animated images, which are then photographed in sequence to produce a film. Animators may also use computers to produce the required image. They may draw cartoons of characters in different positions to coincide with movement in a given direction, and synchronise lip movements with words, and action with music and sound effects.

Creativity and artistic qualities are a must, along with patience and attention to detail. A feel for movement and timing is required to produce a smooth animation sequence. Computer skills, including the use of graphics, painting and animation software, are also essential.

animation assistant
Assistant Animators focus on specific details of an animated sequence, as directed by other animators. They may be required to interpret rough drawings, develop characters or flesh-out movement in animated sequences.

Must be able to follow directions quickly and accurately, and be able to work effectively both independently and as part of a team. Must be computer literate and familiar with relevant graphics and animation software. Artistic abilities and attention to detail are a must.

Other occupations in this area include Cel Painter, Animation Producer, Character Designer and Cartoonist.

ART AND DESIGN

Sample occupations found in this area:

Production Designer

The Production Designer is the Head of the Art Department and acts as the visual co-ordinator of every aspect of a production. They will work from the first stages of pre-production through to the end of filming and are responsible for the visual look of all sets and locations.

Strong visual awareness and design skills are required. Production management and team leadership skills, and the ability to prioritise and meet deadlines, are also necessary. Excellent communication and presentation skills are needed, as well as the ability to give direction and work effectively as part of a team. An ability to inspire and motivate the creative team towards a common aesthetic is essential. Must have thorough knowledge of Health & Safety regulations.

Art Director

The Art Director is the Production Designer's assistant in the area of location and set design. Art Directors are responsible for the day-to-day running of the Art Department and its budget, keeping the Production Designer informed at all times. It is their job to realise the environmental vision of the Production Designer in the construction of sets and scenes utilising the production requirements.

Visual awareness and excellent communication and presentation skills are necessary. Organisational ability, creativity and attention to detail are essential. Must be able to visualise and conceptualise images into a final product. Artistic and creative abilities along with design, drawing and practical skills are a must, as are project management experience and an ability to work under pressure. Knowledge of budgeting also required.

Graphics/Graphic Designer

Graphics use a variety of print, electronic and film media to create designs to meet clients' needs. Graphics for film and television use film and latest video and computer technology to produce opening titles, credits and programme information sequences that embrace a variety of visual styles. Graphics for television also help to brand the channel through animated station idents and on-screen promotion of programmes.

Must be artistic and constantly generate ideas. The ability to think imaginatively and logically to combine image with sound is essential. Good computer skills and a knowledge of different graphics packages are also required. The ability to manage resources and work effectively both independently and as a member of a team is also necessary.

Props Master/Mistress
The Props Master/Mistress is responsible for the procurement, upkeep, monitoring and maintenance of all props for a particular production in a timely manner within budgetary limits.

Practical and organisational skills are essential. Excellent written and oral communication and presentation skills required. Financial skills and the ability to work within a budget also necessary. Must have the confidence to negotiate with suppliers. Research skills and computer literacy are also useful.

Art Department Runner
This is the entry-level job for the Art Department. Duties include cleaning, making coffee, photocopying, developing film, picking up and dropping off various items as necessary, running between set, office and location as required. Usually, Art Department Runners will also be training in their selected area along the way, shadowing those higher up the scale.

Enthusiasm and a willingness to do anything (within reason) is required. Must have excellent communication and organisational skills, and be willing to accept direction. The ability to use initiative and solve problems quickly and efficiently is essential. A current driving licence is usually required.

Other occupational roles in this area include Sketch Artist, Graphics Technician, Draughtsperson and Scenic Operative.

COSTUME/WARDROBE
Sample occupations in this area:

Wardrobe Master/Mistress/Costume Design Assistant
A Wardrobe Master/Mistress co-ordinates the buying and/or making of costumes for television, film and stage productions.

Must be prepared to work long and irregular hours. Good communication, organisation and time management skills are necessary. The ability to work as part of a team and to give and accept direction is essential. Must have a thorough knowledge of fashion and historical or culturally specific costuming, as well as pattern-making and sewing skills, and creative flair. Excellent interpersonal skills and the ability to put people at their ease are essential.

Wardrobe Assistant
The Wardrobe Assistant works closely with the Costume Designer and Wardrobe Master/Mistress, assisting in the making, ordering, or adaptation of costumes and accessories required.

Must have good communication and organisational skills. Good sewing skills are required, plus a knowledge of period costume. Must be able to work within strict time and budget constraints.

Other jobs in this area may include Costume Stylist, Dress Maker, Costume Stock Operative and Costume and Wig Stores Assistant.

INTERACTIVE MEDIA
At this stage it remains difficult to define 'Interactive Media', and much work is still to be done before a comprehensive set of job profiles can be produced. For more on this fast-developing area, *see* Chapter 8.

MAKE-UP AND HAIRDRESSING
Sample occupations in this area:

Make-up Artist/Make-up and Hair
Make-up Artists apply make-up to actors and other performers involved in stage, film and television productions. Due to an increase in multi-skilling the majority of Make-up Artists are now

also expected to successfully style, trim, blow-dry and spray-dye hair in addition to their make-up duties. They may also order and design wigs according to production needs.

Must have artistic skills and creative flair for the application and adaptation of make-up products and effects. Good colour perception and familiarity with different make-up products and application techniques. Patience, tact and good communication skills to be able to put people at ease. Knowledge of Health & Safety in this area is required to deal with different substances, materials and skin reactions.

Make-up Effects/Prosthetics

Make-up Effects Artists are responsible for specialist make-up techniques, including direct applied effects, materials and prosthetics. These may include latex, moulding, ageing, scarring, bruising and prosthetic limbs.

Creative flair and an ability to turn abstract design ideas into practical applications are essential. A thorough knowledge of Health & Safety is required to deal with different substances, materials and skin reactions, as is familiarity with different make-up products, effects and techniques. Good communication skills are essential.

Make-up Assistant/Make-up Trainee

The Make-up Assistant keeps the make-up room clean and tidy, assists with the purchase of supplies, and may be given responsibility for making-up extras and some of the artistes. They will work both on set and on location, standing by to maintain artistes' make-up between takes as required. They will usually be expected to do some basic hair work too.

Good communication skills and the ability to put people at ease are essential, as is attention to detail to ensure continuity throughout the production. Fitness for bending, standing and coping with long hours is also a must.

Other occupational roles in this area may include Make-up Lab/Workshop Technician, Wigmaking Assistant, Make-up Stores Assistant and Specialist Make-up Advisors.

SET CRAFTS

Sample occupations in this area:

Painter

Painters and Decorators apply paint, varnish, wallpaper and other finishes to props, scenery and set.

Must have excellent Health & Safety knowledge and awareness. Must be comfortable with working at heights, have good balance and be physically fit. Must have good knowledge of colour, shade and texture. Excellent communication skills required, as well as creative flair and attention to detail.

Carpenter

Carpenters and Joiners construct, erect, install and repair wooden structures and fittings used in internal and external sets, and cut, shape, fit and assemble wood to make props, furniture, decorative objects and scenic equipment.

Must have a good sense of balance and be comfortable working at heights. Knowledge of Health & Safety requirements when working with tools is essential. Must be aware of the strengths and weaknesses of different wood types and their uses. Communication skills and an ability to work well in a team are also necessary.

Plasterer

Plasterers apply plaster and cement mixtures to walls and ceilings, fix fibrous sheets and cast and fix ornamental plasterwork. They may also be required to carry out textured work and moulding casting, and to fix glass-reinforced plastic.

Must be able to do neat and accurate work, often unsupervised. Good communication skills required. Familiarity with different surface materials and preparation techniques is essential. Good health and stamina, and an awareness of Health & Safety issues, are also required.

Other jobs in this area may include Master Plasterer, Drapes Assistant, Chargehand and Wood Working Assistant.

SPECIAL EFFECTS

Sample occupations in these areas:

Special Physical Effects:

Special Effects Technician

It is the responsibility of the Special Effects Technician to produce models and effects in line with client specifications and production requirements. They will assist the Special Effects Supervisor and Senior Technician in the preparation, construction and execution of all models and effects, in accordance with technical specifications and Health & Safety regulations.

Health & Safety awareness is paramount, as is lateral thinking and the ability to make things work in a safe and controlled way. Communication and presentation skills are essential, along with an ability to give and accept direction as required. Must be familiar with all special effects equipment and materials, including safe operation and use.

Special Effects Trainee

Special Effects Trainees assist other special effects personnel in the construction and operation of special physical effects. They will be expected to learn about the various equipment and materials used in the construction and operation of special physical effects, and will need to keep an accurate record of their work experience for the Special Effects Supervisor.

Enthusiasm and a willingness to do anything (within reason) is required. Must have excellent written and oral communication and organisational skills, and be willing to accept direction. The ability to use initiative and solve problems quickly and efficiently is essential. Must have a thorough knowledge of Health & Safety regulations, along with common sense and attention to detail.

2. The Technical Roles

CAMERA

Sample occupations in this area:

Director of Photography

The Director of Photography (DoP), or Cinematographer, usually works on features, dramas, commercials and sometimes light entertainment. He or she works in close partnership with the Director and Production Designer, interpreting their ideas and turning them into a visual reality. It is a largely creative role and they will usually work in close partnership with the Lighting team to ensure the correct 'look' and 'feel' of a shot.

Creativity and attention to detail is essential. Must have good colour vision and a thorough knowledge of cameras and lighting, including lenses, mounts, heads, accessories and their assembly. Good communication skills and the ability to give and accept direction are required. A knowledge of camera mechanics is also essential. Must have considerable experience in the industry and excellent Health & Safety awareness.

Lighting Cameraman

The Lighting Cameraman essentially performs the same role as the Director of Photography, but will more usually work on documentaries, arts programmes, current affairs and some light entertainment.

Must be artistic and possess extensive technical knowledge of cameras, stock and lights. The ability to manage a team and communicate well with others is essential. Creative flair is needed as well as technical skill. Must be aware of Health & Safety risks.

Camera Operator

Camera Operators set up, position and operate camera equipment in studios or on location to shoot required scenes. Tasks will vary considerably depending on whether they are working in film or in television, and on single or multi-camera shoots.

Must be prepared to work long and irregular hours. Organisational skills and the ability to work under pressure are essential. Must be able to give and accept direction. Patience and attention to detail are also required, as is the ability to work effectively both independently and as part of a team. Health & Safety awareness is also necessary.

First Assistant Cameraman (Focus Puller)

All shooting requires that the correct focus be maintained; but it is usually only on features, drama, commercials and sometimes light entertainment that a 1st Assistant Cameraman (AC) forms part of the camera crew.

Must have a thorough understanding of camera assemblies. Must be meticulous and pay close attention to detail. Good vision and knowledge of light, shading and focus required. Must be able to accept direction, and have excellent communication skills. The ability to manage others is also necessary.

Second Assistant Cameraman (Clapper Loader)

Working mainly in film, the 2nd Assistant Cameraman (AC) is responsible for loading the film into the camera magazines and unloading the exposed film stock. They operate the clapperboard, which provides a visual and audible identification for each shot to help the cutting room run sound and picture in synchronisation.

Must have a thorough understanding of camera mechanics. Organisational and communication skills are necessary, along with a willingness to accept direction. Must be physically fit with good Health & Safety awareness.

Camera Assistant

The Camera Assistant is the junior member of the camera team. On a tape shoot they may label the tapes and keep records of what has been recorded on each one, and will make sure that there are sufficient tapes available for each day's recording. They will also assist with the movement and assembly of camera equipment, rig monitors, and ensure that cables do not get in the way of camera movement.

A good working knowledge of cameras and their accessories is necessary. Must be willing to work long, irregular hours. Must be physically fit with good Health & Safety awareness. Good communication skills also required.

Other occupations in this area may include Video Assistant, Film Camera Assistant and Rostrum Camera Operator.

LIGHTING
Sample occupations in this area:

Gaffer
Gaffers are responsible for the operation and maintenance of lighting equipment for film productions. They report directly to the Lighting Director or DoP and manage the team of electricians.

Physical agility and a good head for heights are required for rigging and positioning equipment. Technical knowledge of different types of lighting equipment and effects is a must, along with Health & Safety awareness. Good communication skills and the ability to accept direction and work as part of a team are also essential requirements.

Best Boy
The Best Boy is chargehand to the Gaffer and is responsible for the ordering and co-ordination of the supply of lighting equipment. They are responsible for setting up and positioning lighting equipment, and for connecting and arranging cables and wiring to approved Health & Safety standards. They may also assist with the maintenance and repair of electrical lighting equipment and cables. For Health & Safety reasons the Best Boy is usually a qualified electrician, who will assist the Gaffer in co-ordinating the work of other electricians working on the production.

Thorough knowledge of Health & Safety standards and practice is essential – as are good technical knowledge of lighting equipment and electrical supply, along with the ability to accept direction and work as part of a team.

RIGGERS, GRIPS AND CRANES
This area has developed from a number of other occupational groups, due to the considerable Health & Safety risks involved.

Sample occupations in this area:

Crane Operator

The Crane Operator is responsible for the setting up and safe operation of cranes used in a production. They may work with camera cranes, whether used remotely or with personnel riding on the system, or they may work with 'Cherry Pickers' for lighting. All camera cranes require at least a two-man operation, so in camera they are assisted by the Grip(s).

Excellent Health & Safety knowledge is required, along with technical and systems knowledge of a variety of camera and/or lighting equipment. Must have excellent communication skills and the ability to work effectively both independently and as part of a team. Physical strength, co-ordination and flexibility are also necessary.

Rigger

Riggers assemble and install rigging gear such as scaffolding, cables, ropes, pulleys, winches, lifting equipment and specialised access equipment for all trades and departments on productions. They will lift, lower, move or position machinery and structures for set and scenery. They may also rig lighting and camera equipment, including erecting camera and crane rostrums as directed by the Director of Photography.

Should have excellent Health & Safety knowledge and awareness, and be capable of conducting risk assessments on set and on location. Must be physically fit and comfortable working at heights. Must be able to manage a large workforce and communicate effectively at all levels of the production. The ability to work effectively both independently and as part of a team, and taking into account all foreseeable risks, is essential. Financial and technical skills are important as the Rigger may be responsible for a wide variety of equipment. Must also be numerate and capable of keeping accurate records.

Grip

The Grip handles the equipment that enables a camera to move and elevate during a shot. There may be many pieces of equipment available, depending on the desired effect. The Grip operates this equipment after discussion with the Camera Operator or Supervisor to work out which type of movement is required. They may lay tracks and operate a dolly (a moveable camera platform) to ensure the smooth movement of the camera, or they may be required to operate camera cranes when high shots are required.

Must have excellent Health & Safety awareness and a good knowledge of camera equipment, scaffolding and construction. Engineering understanding and problem-solving skills are also an advantage. Excellent communication skills and the ability to work effectively both independently and as part of a team are essential. Physical strength, co-ordination and flexibility are also necessary. Should be able to come up with innovative concepts to achieve the required shots both safely and effectively.

Other occupations in this area may include: Stagehand, Fork Lift Operator, Scissor Lift Operator, Studio Runner, and Scaffolder.

SOUND
Sample occupations in these areas:

Production Sound:

Production Mixer/Sound Recordist
Production Mixers record sound on location or in a studio, usually in synchronisation with the camera, to ensure that 'real' sound of the highest quality is recorded at the time of filming/recording. They are also responsible for setting up talkback communication between production, presenters and artistes, etc., as well as other communication such as 'live' links by land line, microwave link or satellite.

Must be computer literate with a good knowledge of sound recording, playback and editing equipment and lighting techniques. Must have thorough Health & Safety awareness. Good hearing and attention to detail required, as are patience and stamina for working long hours. An excellent sense of timing and good communication and presentation skills are necessary, as are diplomacy and tact when working with artistes and other members of the crew. The ability to give and accept direction is also essential.

Boom Operator

The Boom Operator works closely with the Production Mixer or Sound Recordist, and is responsible for achieving the best quality sound recording. They will operate the long 'boom arm', either hand-held or dolly-mounted, with the microphone attached, manoeuvring it as close to the 'action' as possible without getting it in shot. They will usually have to learn the script in order to anticipate lines and move the boom arm accordingly.

Excellent hearing and attention to detail are essential. A good knowledge of microphone characteristics, lighting techniques and camera-lens angles is necessary. A good memory is essential for learning the script, and excellent timing skills for anticipating lines and moving the boom accordingly. Good communication skills are required, along with diplomacy and tact when working with artistes and other members of the crew. Must be able to put people at their ease, as many artistes may be nervous when having microphones fitted. Physical fitness and balance are also important. Must have thorough Health & Safety awareness.

Sound Assistant

The Sound Assistant works with the Boom Operator and Production Mixer or Sound Recordist, helping them to record sound in the studio or on location. They may be responsible for the assembly and maintenance of sound recording equipment, setting up communication and public address systems, and the placing of microphones. They may also play-in music from tape, CD, computer or in a live situation, operating sound effects as necessary under the direction of the Director and Sound Supervisor.

Good knowledge of Health & Safety standards and practice is necessary as are physical fitness and balance. Some technical knowledge may be required for the operation and maintenance of equipment. Good communication skills and the ability to accept direction are also important. Excellent hearing and attention to detail are essential. Must be able to put people at their ease, as many artistes may be nervous when having microphones fitted.

Post-production Sound:

Re-recording Mixer/Dubbing Mixer

Re-recording Mixers work with dialogue, music and sound effects. They will generally work as part of a team to combine, balance and adjust a film or television programme's audio elements, including original production sound, dialogue, effects, and music into a soundtrack using work of the various Sound Editors and the Sound Designer.

Must be computer literate and have a good working knowledge of sound recording, playback, editing and mixing equipment. Experience with various soundtrack delivery systems is a distinct advantage. Excellent hearing and a good sense of timing are required, as are good communication skills.

Sound Editor

The Sound Editor creates the soundtrack by cutting and synchronising to the picture, sound elements such as production wild tracks, dialogue tracks, library material and Foley, in analogue or digital form. They then present these to the Re-recording Mixer for the final sound balance.

Must be familiar with the operation and use of digital and analogue recording, playback and editing equipment. Excellent hearing, sense of timing and attention to detail are required. Patience and a sense of humour are also necessary.

Foley Artist (Sound Effects)

The Foley Artist creates and performs replacement sound effects in a recording studio to supplement any missing synchronised sounds or to enhance action on screen. These may include body movements, weapon-handling noises, individuals' footsteps on a variety of surfaces, body blows, glass put-downs, clothing and properties' noises, paper movement, doors creaking, dogs scratching, etc.

Perfect timing, lateral thinking, dexterity and imagination are key skills for this area. Excellent hearing and attention to detail are essential.

Other occupations in this area include Music Mixer, Assistant Dubbing Mixer and Sound Engineer.

TECHNICAL AND STUDIO OPERATIONS

Sample occupations in this area:

Vision Mixer

Working closely with the Director in a studio control room (sometimes known as the 'gallery') or outside broadcast unit, the Vision Mixer selects and controls which images to use from a number of sources (e.g. multi-camera shoots) to build the programme. They will operate vision mixing consoles and associated digital video effect devices and picture stores.

Must have excellent timing, co-ordination and quick reactions. Excellent communication skills required, plus the ability to handle stress and concentrate for long periods of time. Patience and attention to detail are also required.

Technical Operators

Technical Operators may perform a variety of multi-skilling tasks in a studio environment, including key gallery functions. Tasks may include: preparing broadcast and video hardware and software for use; operating and monitoring the function of specified broadcast and video software and hardware; preparing and maintaining vision control equipment and environments; monitoring and controlling picture quality during recordings and transmission; vision mixing; operating studio remote cameras; rigging equipment; recording specified video and audio materials to a range of formats; supporting the recording of video materials; and composing static video images.

Excellent communication skills are required, as is the ability to deal tactfully and diplomatically with artists, customers and the public. The ability to work without supervision and in a team is also necessary. Must be able to remain calm under pressure. Computing and engineering skills are essential, as is technical and operational knowledge of a variety of equipment.

Videotape (VT) Operator

The Videotape Operator is responsible for setting up and operating videotape-recording equipment; and for recording and playing back what the camera records during takes, for review on set or location. They may also be responsible for airing programming, commercial playback, and recording satellite feeds. They will report to the VT Engineer and will assist them with first-line maintenance of studio and technical equipment where necessary.

Must be able to set priorities, budget time and interface with co-workers. Must be able to identify problems and correct errors quickly and smoothly. Good communication skills required, together with basic computer skills.

Other occupations in this area include Autocue Operator and Vision Controller.

3. The Writing and Production Roles

JOURNALISM

Sample occupations in this area:

Journalist

Journalists work across a range of factual, news and current affairs programming for radio and television, generating and reporting on local, national and international stories. This is done by researching and writing reports via personal and telephone interviews, visits and library research.

An eye for a story and a focus on the reader, viewer or listener are paramount. A good command of language and the ability to meet deadlines and work well under pressure are essential skills. A journalist needs to be inquisitive and have an interest in all people and events. Excellent communication skills are a necessity. Must be able to write clearly and concisely and have good information technology skills. A clear and distinct voice is needed for broadcasting; self-confidence and an ability to face criticism is important. Must also have an up-to-date knowledge of ethical principles, standards and the law, particularly copyright, as it affects the media. Excellent Health & Safety knowledge is also paramount, as journalists will usually have to conduct risk assessments on location.

Reporter

Reporters develop contacts and enterprising stories, and may be responsible for gathering information, writing, producing and presenting a story. They will contribute story ideas to editorial meetings, research and develop new stories, and assist the Producer in preparing broadcasts. Television Reporters may also go out on location with a crew, direct the crew, conduct interviews, and record pieces to camera.

Must be a creative storyteller with strong ethics and judgement skills, to ensure the best stories and features. Must also have an up-to-date knowledge of ethical principles, standards and the law, particularly copyright, as it affects the media. Research and organisational skills are essential, along with excellent written and oral communication and presentation skills. Must be able to think and write quickly and keep calm in a crisis. Strong journalistic skills and a good memory are required. A clear voice is necessary for broadcasting.

Presenter

Presenters introduce, present and host productions for radio or television. Depending on the production, they may introduce programmes, host shows, read news, interview people, report on issues and events, research and write scripts, attend production meetings and/or find guests to appear in a production.

Excellent communication skills are required. Must be able to follow instructions and direction, memorise facts and ad-lib as necessary. Skills in planning and organisation, performance and presentation are also required. Must be quick-thinking and flexible, with sound judgement skills and an excellent sense of timing. Must also have an up-to-date knowledge of ethical principles, standards and the law as it affects the media. Confidence and enthusiasm with a clear voice for broadcasting are tools of the trade.

PRODUCING/PRODUCTION

Sample occupations in this area:

Producer

The Producer 'manages' the production and brings together all the elements to make a film or programme work, such as finance, cast and crew. Some Producers are more creative and 'hands on', developing the initial concepts and commissioning Writers and Directors, sometimes doing their own script editing and becoming involved with casting decisions. Others come from a more business-oriented background, such as finance or law.

Must have a thorough knowledge of the industry and a good understanding of everyone's role. Needs research, writing and editing skills, and a thorough knowledge of compliance, media law and copyright. Communication skills are paramount, plus patience and stamina. May work very long hours, so dedication is a must. The ability to generate original ideas and inspire others is also important. Health & Safety awareness is paramount.

Director

The Director takes overall responsibility for the creative, visual and audio effect of a production. Directors are involved in both pre- and post-production. Responsibilities include: managing the shooting throughout the production, and managing both human and technical resources at a shoot.

Must be creative with a vivid imagination and the ability to visualise the final product. Must be a good communicator and decision-maker. It is important to have an understanding of, and respect for, other people's roles in the making of a programme or film. Storyboarding skills are essential. The Director is often under a huge amount of pressure, so an ability to keep calm and think straight is required. Health & Safety awareness is paramount.

Assistant Producer

The Assistant Producer is responsible for managing a specific subset of production, as defined by the Producer, as well as filling-in for the Producer in his or her absence. They may be called upon by designers to ensure that production requirements are being met.

The Assistant Producer will also undertake project management and scheduling tasks, reporting to the Producer on progress or problems. They may also be required to do some basic directing. Depending on the size of the production, an Assistant Producer may also take on the role of Researcher.

Must have excellent written and oral communication skills. Organisational and planning abilities, along with managerial and research skills, are necessary – as is a thorough knowledge of compliance, media law and copyright. Must be able to give and take direction and instruction. The ability to work as part of a team as well as independently, and the ability to meet deadlines, is also essential. Health & Safety awareness is paramount.

Production Manager

As budgets get tighter, Production Managers have an increasingly important role. Overseeing the Production Assistant and the Production Co-ordinator, the Production Manager has a large financial responsibility and works closely with the Production Accountant to ensure that the production gets made on time and on budget.

Experience of the whole production process and an appreciation of other people's roles are important. Must have sound financial ability and organisational skills. Must also have a thorough awareness of Health & Safety regulations, particularly when booking locations. Should also be calm and patient.

Floor Manager

In TV studios, the Floor Manager co-ordinates and manages everything that happens during a rehearsal or production, from cueing actors to organising props and overseeing an audience.

Must be organised and have the ability to work under pressure. Excellent communication and interpersonal skills are required, along with the ability to give and accept direction as required. Health & Safety awareness is paramount.

Location Manager

Location Managers are involved at every stage in a production, from finding locations to making sure that they are left in a satisfactory condition when 'handed back' to the owner. At the pre-production stage they will prepare a photographic storyboard of all suggested locations, for display in the production office. They are responsible for liaising with residents and businesses in the front-line of filming; they will quiet noise sources (where possible) during shooting; and they may work ahead of the crew in setting up the next location.

Must be well organised and a good communicator, with persuasive powers when it comes to obtaining the location that the Director has set his or her heart on. Administrative and organisational skills are also useful. Excellent Health & Safety knowledge is required.

Script Supervisor/Continuity

Also called Continuity, the Script Supervisor is responsible for pre-timing the script (important when a programme has been commissioned for an exact slot). They will also prepare a shooting breakdown and continuity notes, to be used by all departments during shooting. During the shooting/filming the Script Supervisor watches for any continuity errors, noting any that occur and passing them on to the Director for action.

Attention to detail is essential, as is a clear, concise mind. Must have an excellent sense of timing, and be able to write detailed notes quickly and efficiently. Good interpersonal skills are required for dealing with the Director and other departments. Must have stamina and patience as they could be standing by the camera watching the action for hours on end.

Researcher

Researchers are responsible for all the behind-the-scenes information used in TV programmes and films, and may also offer specialist medical, legal or script-writing advice. Depending on the size of the production, a Researcher may also perform the role of Assistant Producer.

Must be well motivated and a constant source of ideas. Must also have an up-to-date knowledge of ethical principles, standards and the law, particularly copyright, as it affects the media. Should be credible and good at putting people at their ease. Excellent communication skills are required, as well as confidence and patience.

Production Co-ordinator

The Production Co-ordinator works closely with the Production Assistant and the Line Manager/Production Manager to ensure that all the necessary paperwork is generated and distributed, accommodation and transport arrangements made, equipment booked and all artist and crew contracts arranged.

First-class administrative skills and a calm, friendly and extremely efficient manner are needed. Patience, tact and the ability to deal effectively and politely with any problems or complaints are essential. Organisational skills are also a must.

Production Assistant

An essential part of the production team, PAs provide vital administrative support. A wealth of material is generated by a production office – such as scripts, call sheets and daily reports – and the Production Assistant will be involved in creating these, as well as booking hotels, hiring equipment and sorting travel arrangements in the absence of a Production Co-ordinator. A PA's role may vary greatly depending on whether they are working on film, drama, documentary or light entertainment, etc. The size of the production will also play a large part in determining their duties.

Many Radio Production Assistants will also have some technical duties, such as operating studio machinery or editing tape.

Communication and administrative skills are vital, as is the ability to keep calm in a crisis. Hard work and sheer stamina are a must as the production office team is usually the first to arrive in the morning and the last to leave at night. Must be able to bar count if working on music programmes, and pay attention to detail and timing for film and television. Organisational skills are also a necessity. Musical appreciation and a knowledge of copyright, contracts, union rates, and all production processes and equipment are essential. Mental arithmetic skills are also required when working in a 'live' studio environment.

First Assistant Director

The 1st AD is the right-hand person to the Director of a feature film or television programme, but also answers to the Producer. In pre-production the 1st AD usually compiles the list of props and background artistes, and works out the production schedule. Whilst shooting, it is their responsibility to drive the production forwards, making sure that the film or programme is on schedule.

Excellent Health & Safety knowledge is essential, together with strong communication skills. A degree of tact and diplomacy is also required for working with other members of the production team, cast and crew. Must be patient, clear-headed and concise. Must be authoritative, without being rude or getting annoyed. Organisational and timing skills are also necessary.

Second Assistant Director

The 2nd AD is responsible for organising the daily call sheet (a document for all crew, detailing who needs to be on set and at what time, transport arrangements, extras required, etc.). They will provide information on artistes' timings, etc. to the Production Co-ordinator for the progress report. They are responsible for making sure that actors are in make-up and wardrobe at the correct time and on set when needed, and will ensure that artistes are well looked after on set. They may also be responsible for finding extras (no easy task when you need 400 people in two days' time!).

Must be meticulous and good at dealing with people, employing tact and diplomacy to put people at their ease. Excellent communication skills, patience and common sense are key traits. Organisational skills are also required.

Third Assistant Director

The 3rd AD is the right-hand person to the 1st AD. Their duties are not usually as clearly defined as in other profiles, and they may have to assist with a variety of tasks depending on the production. They are usually responsible for getting extras on set and keeping them there; and on location, they may be required to stop traffic and keep members of the public out of shot.

Must be good-natured and patient, with excellent interpersonal skills. Common sense and enthusiasm are important. Good time-keeping and organisational skills are also an asset.

Location Assistant/Assistant Location Manager

The Location Assistant reports directly to the Location Manager and assists them in their work. They may be responsible for hiring locations, ensuring that all cast and crew know where they need to be and where the dressing rooms and green rooms are, and making sure that the location(s) is/are clean and tidy before and after use.

Communication skills and confidence in dealing with others is essential. A clean and tidy nature and some organisational abilities will also help.

Runner

A Runner basically runs around getting everything in place. They have to know exactly what is needed on a film or television set and get it there as quickly and efficiently as possible – whether it's a cup of coffee for the star or a vital prop gone missing.

Must be efficient and pleasant. Excellent communication and organisational skills are also required. Must be prepared to work very long hours. Enthusiasm, stamina and initiative are the vital traits.

Other occupations in this area include Audience Manager, Production Supervisor and Floor Assistant.

POST-PRODUCTION

Sample occupations found in this area:

Post-production Supervisor/Co-ordinator

The Post-production Supervisor/Co-ordinator oversees all aspects of post-production to ensure that the final version of the film or programme meets production requirements, is suitable for on-air broadcast if applicable, and satisfies the correct duration requirements.

Must be computer literate with an excellent working knowledge of analogue and digital editing equipment and techniques. Good communication skills are required, as is the ability to give and accept direction. Attention to detail is paramount to achieve satisfactory final productions.

Film Editor/Offline Editor

The Film Editor uses digital non-linear editing equipment to combine selected shots for each scene in sequence and also combines sequences, to form a logical and smooth-running story. They are responsible for balancing the picture for photography, performance, consistency and timing. In addition, they will usually have to prepare digitally edited material for the laboratories, and may be responsible for negative cutting and auto conforming. They may also be required to integrate temporary sounds from a sound library to help 'hold' the picture together during picture editing.

Must have a thorough knowledge of laboratory procedures in handling negatives and prints for picture and sound. Attention to detail and good sense of timing are required to match shots and scenes. Computer literacy and a familiarity with analogue and digital recording and editing equipment are essential. Imagination, an aptitude for storytelling and analytical ability are also useful.

Assistant Film Editor

The Assistant Film Editor organises the editing room and co-ordinates schedules for the Film Editor. They are responsible for loading the DV tapes onto a non-linear editing system such as Avid or Lightworks, and may also have to digitise analogue videotapes. They may also perform remedial editing tasks on digital non-linear editing equipment, depending on their level of experience and under the supervision of the Film Editor.

Computer literacy and a knowledge of editing systems and software are necessary. Must be able to accept direction and perform tasks quickly and efficiently. Organisation and communication skills are also required.

SCRIPTWRITING

Sample occupations found in this area:

Scriptwriter

Scriptwriters work to produce scripts for a variety of radio, TV or film productions. Tasks may include: choosing themes for written work; conducting research into the subject; assembling background material and obtaining necessary data; planning and organising material and writing the work; revising or editing the work and ensuring coherence of style; proper development of theme, plot and characterisation; and correct referencing where applicable. They may also adapt other people's work for productions, for example, turning a book into a screenplay.

Good knowledge of story structure is important, along with the ability to produce fresh and original ideas. Good communication skills and a willingness to accept criticism and implement changes are key skills. An excellent understanding of English, particularly grammar and spelling, is also vital. Creative flair and the ability to realise other people's ideas are also essential when doing commissioned work. Must be self-motivated and able to work to deadlines.

Script Editor

A Script Editor is responsible for checking the story structure, pacing and characters to ensure that production requirements are being met, and for helping to spot and resolve problems in a script.

An excellent command of English is a must, together with an understanding of story structure, the principles of storytelling and genres. Must be able to forge strong relationships with Scriptwriters and Producers and possess a great deal of tact.

Other occupations in this area may include Script Reader, Writer, Author, and Screenplay Writer.

4. The Programming and Broadcasting Roles

BROADCAST ENGINEERING
Sample occupations in this area:

Engineering Manager

An Engineering Manager is responsible for establishing procedures for maintaining high standards of quality, reliability and safety.

Excellent Health & Safety knowledge is required, together with good communication skills. Must be confident and able to lead a team. Technical knowledge and managerial skills are also necessary.

Studio Engineer

Studio Engineers are responsible for operating all the equipment necessary for the production of a programme within a studio. This includes studio cameras, audio consoles, studio lighting, video switches, character generators and electronic still-storage graphics display equipment.

Technical, operational and systems knowledge is required. Good communication skills and the ability to work both independently and as part of a team are also necessary. Computer skills and problem-solving abilities are required. Must be prepared to work long hours. Awareness of broadcast critical delivery is a must.

Transmission Engineer

Transmission Engineers are responsible for the inspection and testing of transmission equipment, and the repair and maintenance of transmission systems for radio and television. It is their responsibility to troubleshoot and repair any damaged equipment in the transmission system, to make recommendations for improvements and to thoroughly document their work.

Must be computer literate, with good technical knowledge of transmission systems, including both analogue and digital. Project management experience and the ability to work both independently and as part of a team are essential. Good communication skills are also required.

Other occupations in this area include Post-production Engineer, Supervisory Engineer, Communication/Links Engineer, Project Design Engineer, Projects Engineer, Maintenance Engineer, Production Engineer, Contribution/Distribution Engineer and Broadcast Technologist.

COMMISSIONING and SCHEDULING

Sample occupations in this area:

Commissioning Editor

A Commissioning Editor commissions independent producers to make specific programmes to an agreed brief and budget. They are responsible for selecting and developing programmes that anticipate viewers' demands, often with a specific target audience and scheduled transmission in mind.

Must understand the needs of the commissioning organisation and its target audiences, together with programming trends. Should be able to spot and nurture talent both on and off the screen and be able to communicate ideas with programme-makers. Requires editorial, analytical and decision-making skills, business acumen and resilience. Excellent communication skills and the confidence to negotiate with others are required, together with the courage to take risks.

Scheduler

A Scheduler is responsible for generating the long-term programme strategy, as well as building the current schedule for transmission.

Must have a thorough understanding of editorial compliance issues. Good communication and negotiation skills are required, together with a logical and analytical mind. Schedulers should also have a genuine curiosity about human behaviour, and understand how programme schedules can affect viewing. Excellent planning and organisational abilities are essential.

Other occupational roles in this area may include Planning Assistant, Development Assistant, Network Assistant, Planner and Deputy Scheduler.

LIBRARY/ARCHIVES

Sample occupations in this area:

Archivist

Archivists analyse and document records, and plan and organise systems and procedures for the safekeeping of records and historically valuable documents.

Good oral and written communication skills are required for liaison with production and research personnel. Must be able to work without supervision and accurately manage records and resources. Organisational skills and attention to detail essential. Must be computer literate.

Librarian

Librarians design, develop, and manage collections of recorded material and the delivery of information services to production personnel. They are responsible for assisting production and research personnel in locating, obtaining and using data, information and resources, and assisting with identifying and interpreting information.

Must have excellent communication and interpersonal skills. Organisation, planning and administrative skills are essential for managing resources. Must be computer literate and have a firm grasp of database software packages.

Library Assistant

Library Assistants and Clerks classify, sort and file publications, documents, audio-visual and computerised material in libraries and offices. Library Assistants will also assist Librarians with information enquiries, inspect returned items for damage and carry out minor repairs where necessary, and input data into any databases required.

Must have good communication and organisational skills, with a practical and logical approach.

Other occupations in this area include Acquisitions Assistant, Archive Librarian, Film Librarian, Music Librarian, Videotape Librarian and Archive Administrator.

MEDIA ACCESS

Media Access includes areas such as Subtitling, Signing and Audio Description, and is designed to provide audio-visual access to those with vision and hearing impairments. It is an important area, promoting equal opportunity and allowing the UK's hard of hearing, deaf, blind and visually impaired population access to film and television – something most of us take for granted. For descriptions of these specialised job groups, see the Occupational Map and job profiles on *Skillset*'s website, www.skillset.org.

PROGRAMME DISTRIBUTION
Sample occupations in this area:

Sales Director

The Sales Director is responsible for developing and executing marketing strategies, and for managing sales staff and accounts.

Must be able to meet and exceed goals. Confidence, enthusiasm, persistence and perseverance are essential. Should have excellent communication and presentation skills and must be organised and determined. Should be able to make important decisions on the spot and deal with any problems that arise quickly and efficiently. Financial skills are also a must.

Acquisitions Assistant

The Acquisitions Assistant orders, tracks and co-ordinates the receipt of all programmes and documents. They are responsible for resolving any problems with orders, channelling materials to appropriate departments, and keeping a record of all programmes, products and documents received.

Must have a good knowledge of computer systems. Organisation and planning abilities are a must, together with good communication skills. Attention to detail and problem-solving skills also required.

5. The Office Roles

A number of office support roles can be found within all sectors of the audio-visual industries, ranging from prominent managerial positions to secretarial and administrative staff.

The sub-divisions within this group are described below. For job roles and descriptions in these areas, refer to the job profiles on *Skillset*'s website at www.skillset.org.

General Management

Job-holders within this occupational group plan, organise, manage and direct the financial, personnel, training and industrial relations policies of organisations and companies.

Sales and Marketing

Sales and Marketing personnel are responsible for planning, organising and implementing an organisation's marketing and sales policies to increase financial gain.

Human Resources

Human Resources personnel are responsible for the effective recruitment and training of staff. They may prepare job descriptions, draft advertisements, interview candidates, monitor employee performance and provide training courses.

Finance

Finance personnel plan, organise, direct and co-ordinate financial information and advise on company financial policy.

Legal

Legal department personnel are responsible for providing legal advice to companies and organisations. They may draft and negotiate contracts on behalf of employers or clients; advise employers and departments on aspects of law and the legislative implications of any decisions made; advise on the legalities of issues such as copyright and compliance law and plagiarism; and represent organisations in court as necessary.

Press and Public Relations

Press and Public Relations personnel are responsible for the public image of productions and companies. It is their responsibility to promote films, television programmes, radio productions and other products, ensuring that the desired image is portrayed for maximum effect and profit.

6. Health & Safety

Health & Safety legislation places primary responsibility for Health & Safety at work on the employer. In the audio-visual industries this may be a broadcaster, producer, production company or studio. It is the responsibility of every employer to ensure that employees are competent to carry out work safely. In order to do this they must produce a Health & Safety Policy in the form of a Production Safety Plan.

Although all personnel are required to take reasonable care of their own, and others', health and safety in the workplace, employers may also hire additional staff to carry out risk assessments and provide Health & Safety training as necessary. These occupations are described in detail in the job profiles on *Skillset*'s website www.skillset.org. Look under 'Careers'.

In summary

The job profiles have been selected by *Skillset* to give you a broad overview of jobs within the audio-visual industries. We hope that they have made interesting and stimulating reading, and that you have developed ideas about jobs of particular interest. Many of the jobs described will not be offered to candidates (however ambitious) right at the beginning of their careers. In order to be taken seriously for such jobs, you will need to have proved yourself at a more junior level, and gained a reputation for being 'good to work with'. These industries depend on teamwork, where individuals share their talents to achieve an aim – often within a very tight timescale. Especially at the beginning of a career, you will benefit from being flexible, cheerful, highly motivated and willing to learn. The Head of Physical Production for a major film company advised, 'You have to make yourself indispensable.' Once you have made a positive start, there is plenty of help around, much of which is highlighted in this book, to help you develop your career.

So... be strategic – and helpful!

2

The Television Industry

Broadcast television is the largest sector of the industry; with a workforce of around 24,000, it contributes in the region of £12 billion to the UK economy, including exports of about £440 million. Dominated by the BBC, the broadcasters are the 15 ITV licence holders, the network breakfast station GMTV, Channel 4, and *five*. In addition, there are over 1000 independent production companies who make, but do not transmit, programmes. The fastest growing element of the industry – cable and satellite – provides a multichannel environment which is made up of platform operators, who run the distribution networks, and channel providers, who supply the content. BSkyB is the largest supplier, dominating the UK market with 5.7 million digital subscribers.

(adapted from the *Skillset* workforce development plan 2000)

An introduction

Broadcast television employs many thousands of talented people to produce, and to exploit, a diversity of intellectual property within a global marketplace. Although the household names of the BBC, ITV, C4 and *five* continue to dominate our screens, the success of BSkyB has provided food for thought for many senior executives. These are the major players (although *five* employs only about 250 people), but there are over 1000 companies all concerned with using talent and technology to develop effective communications or entertainment for an increasingly sophisticated and difficult-to-reach range of target audiences. New Media is a major contributor to the modern industry, and there will continue to be increasing convergence between IT and programme-making all aimed at 'adding value' for the viewer.

In addition to the broadcasters, there is a thriving independent production sector which is responsible for some of our best-known programmes. These range from highly successful international players, employing more than 200 people, to a multitude of 'one-man-bands' who sell their ideas and build teams whenever they persuade a commissioner that they will do the best job. It is a highly competitive, dynamic business, which can offer interesting and rewarding (but not always highly paid) careers to a diversity of individuals each year.

Within this chapter, we aim to paint a 'big picture' of the modern TV industry, which is likely to give you a better overview than many insiders. We hope that it will inspire you to research further, to identify career areas that may provide real opportunities for you.

Very much a business

Throughout this chapter you will notice references to 'revenue', 'budgets' and 'profits'. It comes as a big shock to some new entrants that despite all the fun and glamour (and whatever you are told, it is more fun than many career areas), television is a very tough business. Nowadays, everyone working in this industry needs an awareness of customers, budgets, audiences and ratings. Decisions as to which programmes to include in a schedule may be based on detailed statistics about the predicted audience. The days of programmes being made on the basis of a 'good idea' alone have all but gone from the major channels. However, ideas are still the currency of this business, and decisions are not all made by the accountants.

Working styles

Working in TV is all about teamwork. The ability to 'establish and maintain good working relationships' is a key element of the well-regarded *Skillset* Professional Qualifications, particularly since at least half of the workforce are self-employed freelancers. As such, they effectively run as small businesses, pitching for work, billing when it's done, and saving enough to pay the taxman. So a major consideration, if you are hoping to build a programme-making career, is your suitability for this style of working.

The regular jobs – in both large and small companies – will be in areas where there is a constant need for particular skills or knowledge, often in management, administration or business-support areas. In larger companies, a diversity of individuals will be employed on fixed-term or 'rolling' contracts, which may be for anything from one month to many years.

The money

The broadcast 'Rich List' – published every August – shows that a small minority of people still make a vast amount of money out of the TV industry. But most people will not be earning a great deal. In many ways, it is a question of supply and demand: people get paid more for specialist jobs that are hard to fill, and less for sought-after jobs where there is always someone prepared to work for less. Many freelancers will earn less than £20,000 (less than classroom teachers) in a year. When you start to make career decisions, find out as much as possible about the average rates of pay for your areas of interest.

The output

There is considerable opportunity for programme-makers and new media specialists to produce the huge output which is required to fill all the space provided. The different elements of the industry tend to specialise in particular types of work, although some will operate between sectors – perhaps making a range of broadcast and non-broadcast shows, or mixing animation with interactive games. Most will have a clear strategic plan to produce one or more of the following:

- Broadcast television, for terrestrial, satellite or cable channels
- Television commercials – 'mini feature films'
- Pop promos
- Multimedia education and entertainment
- Interactive television

Most companies will employ a core team supplemented by freelancers who increasingly move between sectors.

audience-focused

Directly or indirectly, the money for programmes is almost always linked to the audiences they are expected to (or actually do) attract. The BBC has to be seen to satisfy all its licence-payers, and ITV, C4 and *five* receive the bulk of their incomes from advertising revenue. Thus 'customer focus' is an essential element of the modern industry. Huge amounts of time and money are spent trying to understand and predict audiences. Many companies invest heavily in research and development prior to production, and producers have been known to 'change the ending' following a research exercise. However, whatever the expected audience (either in size or demographic mix), the different elements of the industry still work to:

- Entertain
- Educate
- Inform or train
- Market or advertise

or

- Provide a community service

In a world that has changed significantly over the past decade, the industry still manages to deliver all of these things in a creative way.

an abundance of talent – and a shortage of skills

One of the ironies of the modern industry is that some areas of work are so overpopulated, with numerous 'qualified' individuals chasing every opportunity, that rates of pay have been eroded. Some people will even work for free, to gain experience in their chosen area. The majority of freelancers are only employed for around half of any one year.

And yet, other aspects of the industry have been identified as 'skills shortage areas'. These range from traditional 'set craft' roles – for example, carpenters, fibrous plasterers, scenic painters – through script editing, to management roles such as production accounting, compliance and rights management. Broadcast and transmission engineers are in seriously short supply, as an ageing workforce starts to retire...

So when you start to consider your options, it's a good idea to think 'beyond the obvious', and also to consider the type of lifestyle you hope to have. People who succeed in a skills shortage area can expect to earn considerable amounts of money. Career changers may also be interested to fully explore their options – for example, lawyers and accountants who can communicate effectively with programme-makers are in a highly paid minority – especially if they also have foreign language skills.

a Global Marketplace

Later in this chapter, you will see references to 'territories' across the world. Satellite and cable technology has opened up the whole world as a potential marketplace, providing opportunities that range from international sales and rights negotiations to co-producing programmes.

The MEDIA programme – based at the Film Council in London and funded by the European Union – offers a range of support services to help TV, film and interactive media businesses break into and succeed in Europe. (Further details are included in Chapter 11, *Finding Out More*.)

The major TV companies are all involved with a multitude of overseas projects – from modifying formats for a different audience, to supplying footage of the Premier League to a huge Far Eastern audience, or 'reworking' *Banzai* for the Japanese market – and this is a trend which will certainly grow. And current and archive programmes are sold – in whole or in part – for use around the world, bringing significant earnings to their owners.

So individuals with a good knowledge of different cultures and languages and strong business skills are likely to be spoilt for choice.

The economics of television

Modern television is big business, closely watched by shareholders and City analysts. Accountants and programme finance specialists abound, and are involved in every aspect of pre-production, production, post-production and the continuing exploitation of assets. Everyone who wants to establish and build a career in the industry will need an awareness – and preferably an interest – in budget development and control, audience demographics and ratings. Fundamental decisions about what programmes to make may be based on detailed statistics about the cost per predicted target viewer; good ideas are no longer made into good programmes without business justification. A dramatic fall in advertising revenue, coupled with the losses incurred by the recently closed ITV Digital, have concentrated the minds of managers and programme-makers within Granada and Carlton, and there are few cable and satellite companies who are making the profits that they originally predicted. Despite these changes of fortune, ITV, Channel 4 and *five* reported a slight increase in programme investment in the last financial year. But at the time of writing, the BBC finances are a source of envy for many people in the industry: the licence fee, increasing revenue from commercial activities, and the stated aim of the Director General to spend more money on programme-making have combined to produce a range of opportunities for internal and external commissions.

Where does the money come from?

As mentioned, the BBC continues to be funded by the licence fee (£2.53 billion in 2001/2002). Its commercial arm BBC Worldwide produces books, magazines, audio and video tapes, DVDs and a range of programme-related merchandise as well as selling current and archive BBC materials within a global marketplace. In 2001/2002 BBC Worldwide contributed profits of £106 million, and it predicts substantial increases in the future. The World Service also receives a grant from the Foreign Office.

Despite attempts to diversify their revenue sources (especially through digital and broadband), the ITV companies are still primarily reliant on advertising revenue, which has seen a fall in recent times. The reasons for these past falls are complex and involve the increasing fragmentation of the industry. More choice of channels has taken large numbers of viewers from the traditional terrestrial channels, without any of the new channels attracting large enough audiences to 'compensate' – so that traditional 'spot advertising' is of reduced value for brand owners. In addition, advertising budgets have fallen globally, although at the time of writing there is some optimism about increased spending in 2003. The ITV companies have cut overheads, and invested in alternative ways to produce revenue, including sponsorship, licensing and merchandising and the sale of current and archive programme and formats to international broadcasters.

BSkyB changed the face of broadcasting in the UK by introducing the concept of 'pay to view'. Its funding situation is rather different. At the time of writing, approximately 70% of income comes from subscription, 9% from advertising sales, 10% from other Pay TV platforms, 7% from interactive and 5% from other sources. However, many of the money-making options that some people throughout the TV industry are very excited about – such as fully interactive sports coverage, linked with betting and purchasing options – involve massive set-up costs and may take years to build.

Cable and satellite companies sell their channels to a provider – BSkyB, Freeview or NTL – or to overseas owners. Again, initial optimism about revenue as a result of digital audiences has not been fulfilled, and many new contracts are at a lower rate than was originally negotiated.

Going against the trend, regional and local advertising has held up fairly well in this tough climate, and local cable TV is proving quite attractive, gathering income from advertising and sponsorship to help cover costs. Increased interest in the nations and regions may provide a range of career opportunities.

Whatever the primary source of existing revenue, all organisations in the modern TV industry are exploring new ways to exploit their products and brands further into the global marketplace. Programmes are regarded as 'assets on the balance sheet' to be used creatively for years into the future. One company that owns an archive of game shows said that many 10- or even 15-year-old products would sell to Latin American countries, where the population was keen to learn English.

Through business partnerships with the Discovery Channel and Flextech, the BBC is consciously 'showcasing' archive material to new audiences, and other TV companies are also using digital channels as a means of re-showing popular material. There is a hidden cost to this type of initiative: royalties have to be paid for any use beyond that originally agreed.

There are often excellent business insight articles in the trade press, and in the media pages of the broadsheets. Reading these will give you an idea of the challenges facing decision-makers in the modern industry – and may inspire you to qualify as an accountant or lawyer before embarking on a TV career!

The business of news

'It's easy to inform... but to inform entertainingly, so that people listen and engage, is a much bigger challenge.' This attitude has certainly influenced the majority of TV news providers. *Five* started the trend, saying memorably that watching the news 'doesn't have to be like taking cod-liver oil'; and their more accessible approach – including the presenter sitting on, rather than behind a desk – has inspired other producers. About 70% of the UK population gains its daily news information from the television, and large numbers of journalists are employed to ensure 24-hour coverage. BBC News 24, CNN and SkyNews all consume vast amounts of information each day, supplying an audience that 'dips in' and wants immediate, accurate, news. Inevitably, audiences of this magnitude are of considerable interest to advertisers.

This relaxation of style has also affected the choice of news-readers and reporters and there is now considerably more diversity to be seen – and heard – on the small screen. Supplying a potentially very lucrative world audience can raise problems that are less likely to occur when broadcasting in one country. Care has to be taken that content – even style of dress or gestures – does not offend sections of the audience. The challenge for any news organisation is to get it right – time after time. Even the major broadcasters can make mistakes. For example, an allegation was made of an alleged link between the terrorist, Osama Bin Laden and a company, in a news bulletin. The broadcaster admitted an editorial mistake and had to reach a settlement with the company. But the events of September 11th did show the value of rolling news to many sceptics. By 5.00 p.m. in the UK, 15 million people were watching, on a mix of digital and terrestrial channels.

All of these factors are likely to affect the careers of many aspiring broadcast journalists. Some of the rising stars would seem more at home in the 'quality' tabloids or consumer magazines than in the traditional broadsheets. However, in these apparently more relaxed times, it's still essential for journalists to have a professional training – not least in law. The re-negotiation of the supply of news to the ITV Network – where ITN were, for the first time, seriously challenged by SkyNews – resulted in a significant cut in budgets, which is likely to have a series of visible and invisible effects and may reduce the opportunities for traditional broadcast journalists in this high-profile area. Sky News won its first ever BAFTA for its coverage of the events of September 11th, and also high praise from the Independent Television Commission for 'the most comprehensive coverage'.

Formats – and the geese that lay golden eggs

Any contact with industry strategists, especially in the entertainment world, will quickly expose the hot topic of *formats* – who has got what, and what could be developed. Chief executives have challenged creative teams to 'come up with winning formats' and the rights, licensing and merchandising teams are waiting to exploit a winning formula. Basically, everyone wants their own, highly protected, version of *Who wants to be a Millionaire* – generally accepted as the best mass-market TV brand ever devised. Currently licensed to more than 100 territories, and shown in 76, it has spawned a host of spin-offs and made fortunes for its owners – and their lawyers. However, nothing goes on forever. *Millionaire* ratings continued to fall from a peak of 19 million to 8 million by the beginning of 2003, and the ITV network centre was reconsidering its schedule.

Formats are big news. The BBC has set up 'The Format Factory' to develop new ideas; ITV companies have specialist cross-functional 'think tanks' to explore ideas… and it's very difficult. There is a thin line between being inspired by another show, and copying it. Really new ideas are in short supply, especially those that can have instant international appeal, or can be modified for a new audience, such as *The Weakest Link* in the United States. Developing a format requires a thorough knowledge of potential audiences and existing intellectual property rights, an insight into how programmes can be made in an increasingly high-tech world – and a stroke of genius. If you already have ideas, write them down, and then approach TV companies – but don't give away the critical information until a contract is agreed!

The intellectual property debate

'It's safest to assume that everything belongs to someone, and can't be used without permission,' said a senior business affairs spokesperson. Certainly, knowledge of intellectual property law is increasingly important – both in terms of generating profit, and for reducing the risk of litigation from a diversity of sources. Talent drives the industry, and the rights to use, or reuse, material are potentially very valuable assets. The advent of the secondary digital market, together with the convergence of TV with the web, has complicated an already complex area; and there is a real shortage of specialists who can understand and communicate with the various interested parties associated with any decision. For example, a soap star (appearing in a programme which makes money through advertising and sponsorship) may appear on a directly linked chat show on a digital channel, followed by an Internet chat room, both of which encourage profitable phone-in revenue. In such a case, everything has to be negotiated and agreed *before* the event. Similarly, specialists in 'clipsales' – short sequences from archive material – emphasise that only the elements bought and paid for (usually at many hundreds of pounds per minute) should be released to broadcasters, as there is a risk of whole programmes being shown if they are supplied... which can light a legal tinderbox!

Companies that use materials without permission can face expensive legal arguments, sometimes without even being aware that they have transgressed – an increasing problem in a fragmented market. Similarly, owners of intellectual property (including programmes) are having to be extra vigilant, to ensure that their precious material is not being exploited without any 'royalty'. PACT continues its campaign to improve what it sees as the fairness of rights agreements for its members. Check their website for up-to-date information.

New rights agreements are likely to specify:

- All the media to be used, including named digital channels and websites.
- The 'territory' – in the international programme sales market, broadcasters negotiate rights for geographical territories, which each pay a fee. This has been complicated by satellite broadcasting, where some viewers (illegally) can access programmes or channels that have not been licensed for viewing in their territories. A common territory agreement might be 'worldwide, excluding the US'.
- The duration of the contract – e.g. two years. If all the rights have not been used during this period, they will be forfeited.
- The numbers involved – e.g. two UK showings, or 5000 videos.

If you have an analytical mind, and an interest in technology and other cultures, it would certainly be worthwhile to explore opportunities in rights or business affairs. Specialist lawyers who can communicate with producers can earn very large amounts of money.

The branding revolution

Marketing professionals are now evident throughout the strategic management of all the commercial companies and the BBC. Digital channels will often benefit significantly from professional marketing – 'identifying and satisfying a not-always-recognised need'. An article in the *Guardian*, following the heavily marketed and advertised launch of BBC4, included this view: 'The way to build a successful niche channel is good marketing to draw in your target audience and habit-forming scheduling to keep them hooked.' Unfortunately, many digital channels have no budget for such publicity, and have to rely on the curiosity of potential viewers.

Channels now have easily identifiable 'idents' – think of the Channel 4 '4' – and programme 'strands' or genres are publicised to target audiences, using a variety of media including billboards and press advertising. Investment in feature films, for instance by the new in-house Film Four department and BBC Films, may also help to promote the brand to a target audience. ITV was relaunched as ITV1 in 2001 as a single brand, rather than as a group of regional companies. Attracting, satisfying and retaining viewers (and thus the advertising paymasters) is the baseline for a diversity of sophisticated marketing strategies, unheard of a decade ago. On an Electronic Programme Guide (EPG), the main players are only given as much prominence as other content providers, so building the 'value' and 'quality' of the brand in a potential viewer's mind is crucial.

The BBC is far from complacent about the long-term continuation of the licence fee, and has invested large amounts in specialist corporate identity consultants to ensure a consistency of approach – especially when broadcasting to a global market. Channels, programmes and exploitable merchandise are all assets which already are or may be worth money. Managed creatively, they could contribute hugely to the growth of the TV industry throughout the world.

So there will be career opportunities for professional market-eers, and it is expected that cross-media movement will become common. Some companies are already run by marketeers, and the rapid growth of *five* was certainly complemented by effective marketing. As one industry professional says: 'It's all about creating customer loyalty by pushing creative work across a range of different platforms, to attract and retain the broadest possible audience.' If anything, the challenge will continue to grow.

The commissioning process

By law, at least 25% of all non-news or current affairs programmes shown on UK terrestrial TV have to be supplied by independent producers. Some companies – especially C4 – commission a greater proportion of their material from 'indies', and much of the new content aired on satellite or cable channels will be made by external suppliers.

Watch the credits at the end of a TV programme, and you will often see and hear information about the independent company that has made it. Sometimes these will be household names such as Hat Trick or Tiger Aspect (although there are more than 1000 indies, the majority of commissions go to a fairly small number of companies), but you will also notice unfamiliar names, especially outside the prime-time schedule. Surprisingly for many, the major players in the industry also act as independents, competing for commissions from other terrestrial channels. A good example is *The Royle Family*, made for the BBC by Granada.

Getting commissioned is a highly competitive, time-consuming and often expensive process, as independents gather and prepare content to back up their proposals. Theoretically at least, every commission is up for open competition, and the decision-makers often comment that any really professional proposal will be treated seriously.

Throughout the year, the major companies will publish information on their websites, outlining what they are looking for within different genres, e.g.:

- Entertainment
- Arts
- Animation

- Factual
- Drama
- Current affairs
- Religion

– and outlining how much they will be prepared to pay. Programmes are also commissioned specifically for nations and regions.

Companies will submit proposals for shortlisting. Of these, one key commissioner said: 'I look for key sequences, storylines that are fresh and new, practical thoughts about how it will work on TV, information about important contributors/presenters (including their availability) and, sometimes, a commitment to use a particular producer/director or presenter.'

Shortlisted independents will pitch against each other to win the right to make a specific programme. Considerable effort and resources will be put into preparation for these meetings, as the decision will be made by considering a mix of factors above and beyond the 'good idea'– for example:

- Audience awareness for the specific slot
- Relationship with advertisers/sponsors
- Potential for interactivity/adding value to the basic programme
- Potential for intellectual property deals/international sales
- Budget and project management skills of the independent team.

Sometimes – and especially in very expensive areas such as drama or animation – the commissioning company will only provide a proportion of the total budget, requiring the indie to find other income sources, often in the form of co-production investment. No wonder good business managers are so sought-after by the larger independents. To help this situation, Channel 4 has recently agreed to set up new production agreements with key suppliers to establish a more 'grown up' relationship which should result in mutually beneficial long-term partnerships. All aspects of programme finance will be affected – distribution, formats and sales. Many independent producers also want to negotiate a stake in the revenues from exploitation of their programmes.

Cable and satellite companies will also commission new content for their channels; winning a commission for a large, well-established channel such as Discovery may command a generous budget, but the majority of offers will be for low-budget programming. However, the newly launched BBC4 has announced that it will be prepared to pay suppliers between £115,000 to £300,000 per hour 'with about 40% towards the top end' which has been greeted as very good news by arts producers.

The art of scheduling

Attracting and retaining an audience and winning viewers from the competition is so important that huge amounts of time and money are spent in trying to understand and predict the audiences before investing in programme-making. Scheduling – deciding what to show, and when – is a tough and sometimes bloody business. Programmes can be used to manipulate audiences, with schedules carefully constructed (as far as possible) to deliver one audience onto a following show. It can also be used to tempt an audience away from the programme that it 'should' be watching. These 'spoilers' may be introduced at the last minute in the hope of having a detrimental impact on the ratings recorded by the opposition. When BBC4 was launched on BBC2, it recorded 'very satisfactory' figures (for a digital station that is… considering that less people watched the launch than would normally have watched BBC2) – but it lost a significant proportion of its fairly highbrow audience to the temptation of an interview with Victoria Beckham on a rival channel.

Programmes that are 'worthy' or are part of the franchise/licensing agreements – such as religious broadcasting, serious documentary, or specialist arts shows – may be scheduled into 'graveyard slots' against major soaps or movies, or very late at night, thereby satisfying the regulators, but not the programme-makers. Strands of programmes are used to pull in a predicted audience at certain times of the day – for example the BBC2 lifestyle strand between 8.00 p.m. and 9.00 p.m., where programmes will vary in content but will have a broadly similar theme. Audiences become familiar with a schedule, and often resist change. When *Changing Rooms* was moved to 9.00 p.m. it lost more than 10% of its audience, who returned when the show was rescheduled.

So scheduling is, and will remain, a major challenge for companies and programme-makers. Getting shown in a prime-time slot may be a real career development move, but persuading commissioners to risk an unknown product may be almost impossible. For this reason, independent producers may team up with larger companies in order to win a commission and then make a programme for such a visible slot.

ITV, C4, *five* and the satellite and cable companies are all in competition for the spenders of today and tomorrow – particularly the elusive 16–34 year olds. At the time of writing, BBC3, a new digital channel specifically aimed at young people, received the go-ahead from DTI/DCMS in September 2002, with a launch date in February 2003. And the BBC has to show that it provides value-for-money to every segment of its licence-paying population. The media row about Chairman Gavyn Davies' remarks about white, middle-class, well-educated men in the south of England 'taking out more than they put in' to the BBC emphasises that the corporation is exercised to provide an attractive service to a diverse potential and existing audience.

As the choice offered to the audience gets larger, it will become increasingly difficult for schedulers to 'manage' the potential audience – a fact which is bound to affect advertising and sponsor-ship revenue. Numerate people with a fascination for schedules (it's a good exercise to 'deconstruct' a night's viewing and think about why programmes have been placed in particular slots) and the ability to communicate with TV execs and programme-makers could build interesting careers in this area.

a blurring of genres

Ratings of audience-share dominate the minds of programme-makers, and many producers are constantly exploring cost-effective ways of delivering large audiences. This has changed the pattern of what is offered on our screens. For example, 'reality TV' – which some prefer to call 'observational programming' – is used to show 'real' drama at a fraction of the cost required to make traditional drama. Similarly, current affairs producers may aim for higher-than-normal ratings by including celebrity interviews or using high-profile celebrities as presenters. Arts programmes may profile pop stars, and science may feature human interest stories such as the effects of extreme weather. Religious programmes are regularly criticised for not being religious enough… all the genres have been 'extended' in the hope of broadening the audience.

In career terms, this can be quite significant. Nowadays there are more generalist programme-makers who move between related genres. Specialists – for example, serious documentary makers, or arts programmers – face immense competition for a reduced number of opportunities. Similarly, because any major new drama series is likely to be co-produced with one or more English-speaking countries, the production team will also be mixed. Children's TV is being badly affected, although the new BBC digital channels may well have a beneficial effect: ITV dropped plans for a dedicated CITV channel during 2001, and there appeared to be a plethora of bought-in products scheduled.

Some of the winners in this more relaxed environment are teams that can make programmes which will attract the elusive late-teen/early twenties audience. Now, 'drama labs' have been established, making high-quality shows for as little as £35,000 per half-hour (and, although costs can vary widely either way, conventional drama can often be more than £100,000 per hour). Drama labs can keep their costs low by using a range of new media techniques and running parallel stories on the web. In this world, a blurring of the traditional genres, coupled with an interest in applying technology creatively, has provided interesting work for a diversity of individuals.

Gathering the statistics – the ratings

Detailed information is gathered around the clock by BARB – the British Audience Research Bureau – from specialist meters installed in 5100 carefully selected homes across the UK. The residents of these homes communicate with BARB at set intervals through a specially modified handset. BARB is a cross-industry-funded, specialist organisation, with all the main broadcasters holding shares. Thus there is no 'vested interest' and the statistics produced can be accepted as a fair representation of the 'big picture' at any one time. Inevitably, it's not a perfect system – it deals with human beings, after all – but it is generally accepted as probably still the best in the world. The statistics produced by BARB provide the bedrock for decision-making and are the standard currency of the industry. The 'raw' overnight data produced is often used for last-minute scheduling changes. TVRs – television ratings – all have a statistical 'relative standard error', which creates a figure that is '95% sure' that a channel's audience registered between minimum and maximum figures. But – importantly in the multichannel age – the higher the basic audience, the lower the error rate. Some channels which register 0 may in fact be attracting many thousands – or not; but the system is not yet sensitive enough for such small audiences.

To gain an insight into current ratings and trends, look at the back of *Broadcast* magazine. The soaps and drama serials continue to dominate. Sitcoms are no longer the 'appointment TV that they used to be'. At the time of writing, BBC1 dominated prime-time viewing. The 'Top 50' table provides information about viewing in multichannel homes, giving clear evidence that, when people have cable and satellite (perhaps because they have paid to have them?) they watch traditional terrestrial TV far less.

If you are interested in particular areas of programme-making, look at the relevant 'Top 10' table, where ratings information about Factuals, Drama, Sport, Children's and Entertainment shows are listed separately – invaluable for interview preparation.

The influence of advertising

Advertising revenue is the driving force behind ITV, *five* and – increasingly – C4. Inevitably it influences the programmes that are commissioned and scheduled. Indirectly, in the battle for ratings it will also have an effect on BBC programming, as programmes are scheduled to 'win' the audience from the opposition. At the time of writing, there has been a major downturn in the amount of money being spent by advertising agencies, and many programme-makers have felt the impact of stringent budget cuts. To justify spending usually many thousands of pounds on a piece of airtime in which to publicise a product or service, the agencies and their 'commissioners' – the brand marketeers – need to be convinced that the 'spend per head' will be a reasonable investment. Historical audience figures supplied by BARB (British Audience Research Bureau), which provide detailed demographic information, are used to make decisions about the 'best value fit' for a product. Commercials are made for TV often with very high budgets, using feature-film-making techniques, sophisticated post-production skills and specialist teams of programme-makers who are briefed and guided by the TV departments of advertising agencies to satisfy the brief agreed with the clients. Commercials are made to specific durations, and several variations may be produced to fit different slots, or to appeal to the perceived different audiences watching different channels – most will be 10, 20 or 30 seconds. The amount of advertising shown on terrestrial TV is limited and carefully regulated by the ITC to a maximum of 20% in any one-hour period; and schedules may be built around the advertising to retain a sought-after audience.

The main issue facing the TV advertising industry is that the fragmenting marketplace is very difficult to measure using existing techniques. Around 44% of UK homes now have access to multi-channel TV, and viewing patterns have changed forever. BARB figures indicate that in any one week, around 41% of the potential audience are now watching satellite or cable channels – and therefore, not BBC1, BBC2, ITV, C4 or *five*. To further complicate matters, there are now so many channels that few audiences are large enough (except, say, for major sporting events) to register even half a million viewers, and thus be of commercial interest to advertisers. However, the multichannel world does provide real opportunities for 'niche' advertising, not least because very detailed information can be gathered from digital viewers to enable more confident targeting. Advertising in this way will often be in competition with magazines – which will not be giving up their revenue very willingly. As the 'cake' continues to divide, opportunities emerge for creative media analysts, who will take advantage of the varied methods of communicating with an increasingly sophisticated audience. Programme-makers, airtime sales executives and media buyers will also be expected to meet this challenge.

Inevitably, the companies that have relied heavily on advertising revenue are having to explore and develop other sources of income. Pay per view, sponsorship, and involving advertisers in making their own programmes – or even running their own channels – are all possibilities. Sponsorship is already far more evident, and may be used to provide additional revenue for high quality and 'important' programmes which are part of the franchise commit-ment, but which do not always attract a large, advertiser-attractive audience (arts programmes are good examples – the ITC forbids any sponsorship of news or current affairs). Sponsorship may also be used by brands who wish to be associated with well-established popular 'bankers' such as soaps, or sports programmes.

TV is an expensive business, which has to be funded from somewhere – a licence fee, subscriptions, interactive payments or traditional advertising revenue. It will be interesting to observe how the balance shifts over the next few years.

The digital revolution... so far

Advances in technology, and considerable government enthusiasm for a 'switchover' of the UK audience for analogue to digital reception, have fuelled huge investment in the digital platform providers. We were promised a range of tempting goodies, which would enhance our experience of watching TV, including:

- Greater choice
- Greater convenience
- Better quality sound and vision
- Exciting opportunities for interactivity
- Access via mobile phones/PCs, etc.

At the time of writing, most of the public seem quite confused about what – if anything – they really want from this list. About 40% of UK households now have access to digital TV, and some City pundits refer to the sector as a 'mature' market, implying that it is unlikely to grow significantly in the forseeable future. Original ideas about switching off the analogue signal by 2006 were moved back to 2010, and this date has yet to be confirmed as definite.

From a business point, many of the big players in the digital market have lost vast fortunes. On May 1st, 2002, ITV Digital was finally switched off, having failed to renegotiate the cost of football rights with the FA. It is estimated that both Carlton and Granada each lost £100m. The two main cable companies Telewest and NTL have had to restructure massive debts and have both recorded huge losses... and few channels are attracting sufficient viewers to achieve the necessary advertising revenue.

Although the picture is still bleak, there is cause for optimism as to the future of digital television. At the time of writing, a recent survey showed growing consumer interest in new channels offering more choice. During the Christmas week 2002, almost a quarter of the viewing public was watching multichannel programmes including satellite, cable and digital stations. Multi-channel viewing overtook ITV1 for the first time and the BBC also lost viewers. BskyB is now in profit for the first time. Sky also gained subscribers from the demise of ITV digital. BskyB targeted a particular sector of the audience (men who would pay to watch sport) and it has developed a very healthy subscriber base which has now reached 6.1 million subscriber households spending an average of £350 per year. At the end of 2001, BSkyB persuaded all its digital 'refusniks' to move away from analogue by switching off the signal, thereby saving several million pounds.

Early signs are that the viewing public are also responding positively to Freeview, which replaced the collapsed ITV Digital. This joint venture between the BBC and Crown Castle on 30th October 2002 offers 30 free-to-view digital television channels, with BskyB supplying some of the content.

The formats

For the ordinary consumer, the range of digital services available is confusing, to say the least:

- Digital satellite
- Digital terrestrial
- Digital cable (which may use terrestrial or satellite material)

Service providers are in competition, but all offer a similar service to the consumer – although satellite requires a dish to receive transmissions. Digital terrestrial offers six 'multiplexes' which can carry up to 36 channels: one has been awarded to the BBC, and the remaining five are licensed by the ITC. Sky Digital dominates digital satellite TV – it could offer up to 380 channels; and NTL and Telewest share the digital cable market, where they could offer up to 400 channels. At the time of writing, digital viewers either have to subscribe to BSkyB or purchase set-top adaptors to receive the Freeview service.

In addition to this confusing information, some people report that they are put off by the perceived complexity of use. A consumer research project reported in the trade press indicated that many people were frightened of trying out interactive TV; only flying an aeroplane, riding a motorbike, or using a sewing machine was seen as more difficult.

There are early signs of a possible sea-change in attitude towards digital TV. A significant factor may be the launch of Freeview. There has been a healthy take-up of the low-cost set-top boxes providing access to the new digital terrestrial platform, and sales averaged 30,000 per week during first three months of launch.

Who is watching digital?

Forty per cent – more than one in three – of UK homes now has access to digital TV, a figure that is high compared with the rest of Europe. Although the providers are all concerned about 'churn factors' – people cancelling their subscriptions – there is now considerable evidence available about who is watching digital. Sophisticated statistics can provide a range of demographic information of value to schedulers, commissioners and advertisers alike.

A major media consultancy – Human Capital – produced a light-hearted overview of their research findings. They identified six categories of digital viewer:

1. *Schedule Sheep:*   by far the largest group. People who enjoy watching shows they've seen before. All age groups.

2. *Daytime Devotees:*   65% of this audience are housewives in their 30s and 40s who enjoy chat, lifestyle shows and old movies.

3. *Pop Tarts:*   young women, who tune in to pop, celebrity, style...

4. *Factual Fetishists:*   70% are men aged 40+ who watch endless popular history, science and natural history...

5. *Dads and Lads:*   anything to do with sport or cars... hence Granada's 'Men and Motors' channel.

6. *Primary Pets:*   children aged 5–10 who love cartoons.

What do you think? Understanding how this market works may help you move into the business elements of TV.

The business of digital

Although the BBC is in a position to launch free digital channels to cater for minority audiences, the vast majority of players in this market are in it to make money. The ITC decision to keep ITV (then

On) Digital and BSkyB apart, to ensure competition, has had long-term repercussions. The collapse of ITV Digital has cost Carlton and Granada around £100 million each and led to cutbacks in many areas of their conventional TV operation.

It's not just the platforms that have disappointed investors: countless channels, websites and interactive opportunities have come and gone. Initially the large companies expected to reap rewards from a range of retail and service facilities, for example:

- 'Commission' for selling products from jewellery to financial services and holidays
- Transaction charges which would be paid to the broadcaster for handling customer communications – perhaps with a bank.

Not only have these yet to become 'geese that lay golden eggs', there is the added irony that digital technology must, in part, be responsible for the downturn in advertising revenue – as the market fragments, the 'cake' of advertising money is cut into more and smaller pieces. Mainstream terrestrial channels have all lost viewers, and few digital channels register even 0.5% of the potential audience. It's a headache for media planners and advertising sales people alike.

A further financial consideration recently making headlines in the press is the losses caused by 'digital pirates' who provide free access to premium encrypted channels. It is thought that as many as 100,000 are in circulation.

'On demand' TV

Something else promised as part of our digital future is 'on-demand' TV. Here is a brief explanation of the most commonly used jargon:

- *Video On Demand* (VOD): stored content which can be viewed immediately on request.
- *Pay Per View* (PPV): typically an exclusive sports event, for which viewers may pay several pounds to 'attend'.
- *Near Video On Demand* (NVOD): most used for 'rolling' movie schedules which start every 15 minutes.
- *Personal Video Recorder* (PVR): an 'intelligent' machine which searches for and downloads programmes for your own taste.

Interactive TV

When this handbook was first produced, there was huge enthusiasm for the retail and commercial possibilities promised by interactivity. This has since calmed down: in fact, BSkyB closed its 'Open' channel which offered services in retail, banking, travel agencies and games after heavy losses – and other shopping channels have followed suit. However, other avenues have opened, which continue to excite the strategists. *Big Brother* was the first real interactive show, with over 22 million people voting during series 3; and *Pop Idol* attracted more votes from young people than the entire Conservative electorate in 2001... with each vote providing revenue for the producers.

Other experiments have also been encouraging. The BBC has involved viewers in interacting to good effect in recent years during both Wimbledon and the Commonwealth Games. Quiz shows increasingly offer the chance for viewers to 'participate', and BSkyB offers one show – *Fifteen to One* – which is fully interactive. 'Multistream' content is starting to happen around established programmes such as *Top of the Pops* and big sporting events, such as the World Cup... it's certainly no longer the 'technology in search of a useful application'. However, from the companies' point of view (with the qualified exception of the BBC) it's not just about adding value; it's about the opportunity to persuade viewers to part with their money... effective interactivity can add value to a programme 'brand' and increase revenue. But getting people to pay using credit cards is a big hurdle. Setting up simple ways, where a click of the mouse will link the viewer to a high-cost phone line, is likely to become more widespread – and this in turn will open doors for betting and gaming, and a range of specialist interest services. This system, already established in the on-line pornography market, is being considered for mainstream services, which will be charged through a phone bill.

Better communication with viewers is also being used in more constructive ways. Feedback can guide programme-makers, and commissioners now expect all 'pitches' from producers to have explored all the ways in which interactivity could add value to the programme idea. In future, most people will need a firm grasp of the possibilities that this technology offers for programme-makers.

How the digital technology affects television

Compression of signals allows transmission engineers to fit about five programmes or services into the space occupied by a single analogue channel (such as BBC1), and as many as ten into a satellite channel – thereby providing more programmes within the bandwidth, and creating the opportunity for the government to raise money from the sell-off of analogue space. Original estimates – of around £20 billion pounds – now seem optimistic, but it is likely to be financially well worthwhile, and there is pressure for the country to go digital early this century.

People are still very confused about the available technology, however, and many are put off by having to pay for a subscription or a set-top-box (STB). Once they have purchased and installed a STB, this will receive and decode the signals. Obviously, the possession of this type of box – essentially a computer – will be crucial to the development of the digital industry. The first 'affordable' STB went on sale in April 2002 at under £100.

The STB processes a diversity of compressed digital signals which may carry a multiplicity of TV, audio and information services. Some specialist or expensive information may need to be 'de-encrypted' before it can be viewed. Once decoded, the material can be displayed on a conventional TV.

Other technology

Technology is visible everywhere, affecting everyone's jobs in the modern industry. Advances in equipment manufacture mean that lots of people can now make and edit almost broadcast quality material. Lightweight DV cameras can go nearly anywhere without the need for a technical crew. New studios, such as 'The Lab' at the London Studios, allow for high-volume, low-budget material to be made by relatively inexperienced teams. There is the opportunity to take risks, which may work brilliantly – or not at all. Other developments – such as high-definition TV, whose very clear pictures are made up of 1125 lines (as opposed to 625 lines), and the increasing availability of widescreen 'letterbox' formats – have affected the type of programmes that are made, and allowed for screening of feature films without losing part of each frame. Increasing convergence with the web has encouraged programme-makers to build-in suitable cross-media material. Virtual studios are more popular (with producers, but often not with presenters), and virtual presenters are being tested on some channels.

Special effects are becoming ever more imaginative and sophisticated, thanks to dedicated software; and graphics, design and sets have all been affected. Although some things cost a huge amount of money, it is also possible to create exciting new ideas on a very small budget... so lateral-thinking, 'right brain' skills, combined with an aptitude for IT, are much sought-after.

On a more domestic front, after a fairly slow start DVD players were big sellers at Christmas 2001, and many people are now using them in combination with computers. But the much-vaunted PVRs (Personal Video Recorders) – which can automatically seek out, find and record your favourite TV shows (and miss out the adverts, if requested) at the touch of a button – have had disappointing sales of only about 80,000 in the UK after the first year.

The latter point underlines the fact that technology for technology's sake will only appeal to a minority of enthusiasts. Evidence from all areas of the industry shows that we welcome cheap, accessible and user-friendly technology that has a practical purpose, but we're not over-excited by 'enhancements'. A lot of households are still using ten-year-old VCRs! But help may be at hand. The ITC and Consumers' Association have backed a proposal by Easy TV partners, for the creation of a best practice guide which encourages manufacturers to produce user-friendly equipment.

Convergence – TV/IT

Many people throughout the industry feel that convergence between TV and computers is likely to become commonplace; but there is at least an equal number of sceptics who point out that we use the equipment in very different ways.

- *TV is 'lean back'*: people tend to relax to watch TV, and more often than not, wish to be entertained. The experience is often a shared one – think of *The Royle Family*.
- *PC is 'lean forward'*: concentrating on a computer screen is often a solitary activity, which excludes direct (as opposed to chatroom) contact with others – a fact which could be significant to advertisers, schedulers and producers.

People use the different media for different purposes too... for many, computers are closely linked with their work. Age also plays a part – younger people seem to be less satisfied with passive TV, and have embraced interactivity to such an extent that the government is considering using the lessons learned to try to improve their engagement in elections.

Keep up with the technology

There are a number of valuable specialist trade magazines (*see* Chapter 11, *Finding Out More*), and *Broadcast* regularly carries a 'B+' supplement which concentrates on how new equipment is being used. The Production Show – held at Olympia in London each year – is the best place for the interested public to see the newest TV technology in action. Manufacturers and facilities houses have exhibition stands, and there are many masterclasses and seminars which can be very useful – not least in finding out about potential employers and making contacts.

Employers in the television industry

The BBC

Dominating the UK broadcasting scene, the BBC employs more than 26,000 people throughout the UK, with almost 14,500 in pro-gramme-making areas. It is structured into four specialist groups:

- *Broadcasting:* World Service, TV, New Media and Technology, Radio and Music, Nations and Regions.
- *Programming:* News, Drama, Entertainment and Children's, Factual and Learning, Sport.
- *Commercial:* Worldwide Ltd, Resources Ltd, Technology Ltd.
- *Professional Services:* Public Policy, HR and International Communications, Finance, Property, Business Affairs, Market-ing and Communications, Strategy and Distribution.

Television is further subdivided as follows:

- BBC1
- BBC2
- BBC3 replacing BBC Choice – launch date February 2003

- BBC4
- Cbeebies
- CBBC
- BBC News 24
- BBC Parliament
- BBC Text
- Ceefax
- BBC2 Northern Ireland
- BBC1 Northern Ireland
- BBC Cymru at S4C
- BBC2 Wales
- BBC1 Wales
- BBC2 Scotland
- BBC1 Scotland

The BBC is the UK's largest single public service broadcaster, gaining its income from the annual licence fee and a range of commercial activities, including a joint venture with Flextech to provide a range of cable channels. Global alliances with the BBC have also created a range of BBC-branded channels, such as BBC World, BBC America and BBC Prime.

BBC Interactive (BBCi) provides 'Europe's most visited website' which draws on the BBC's programming to provide a range of news, analysis and information across an increasing diversity of subjects. Many programmes now have their own websites, and interactivity is becoming a regular feature. To find out more, *see* www.bbc.co.uk.

ITV Companies (Channel 3)

Channel 3 is made up of 15 regional licensees and GMTV, the network breakfast station. The UK is divided into 14 regions, and the different ITV companies operate under licences which were awarded after a 'sealed bid' auction. Each company pays a fee to the government every year for the right to broadcast within a specified region. The winning bids varied hugely, from a few thousand pounds to many millions, and although some have been renegotiated since the original awards, the amount paid each year inevitably affects the amount of money available for programme-making.

Thirteen of the regions have individual regional broadcasters. London has two where the 'superfranchise' is shared between Granada (LWT) and Carlton, and the licence is divided between weekdays and the weekend. In 2000 Granada plc expanded its empire, to make it the largest ITV company, by purchasing the Meridian, Anglia and HTV franchises from United News and Media. To comply with current legislation, which regulates viewing share, HTV was sold to Carlton. In October 2002, Carlton and Granada proposed a merger between the two companies. At the time of writing, the deal – which would turn ITV into a single company – has been referred to the Competition Commission.

Carlton

The 'number two' player in the ITV business, Carlton holds the ITV licences for London weekday (Carlton), the Midlands (Central), the Southwest (Westcountry) and the West and Wales (HTV). It produces around 3000 hours of programming each year, through Carlton Productions, Action Time and Planet 24. Part of the group is the leading commercial operator of outside broadcast productions in Europe. Carlton owns a hugely valuable archive of TV programmes and feature films, which sell globally. Carlton owned 50% of ITV Digital, and the company lost almost £100m through the closure. Carlton TV is part of the Carlton Communications Group, which – in addition to being free-to-air TV – also has businesses in pay-TV, interactive TV, cinema advertising and distribution, and it is one of Europe's largest media rights distributors. At the time of writing, Carlton digital cinema is due to close in March 2003. The company closed its Food Network channel at the end of 2002.

Granada

Currently owns seven major ITV licences – Granada TV (Northwest), LWT (London), Yorkshire TV (Yorkshire), Tyne Tees TV (Northeast), Meridian (South) and Anglia (Southeast). It is the largest company in the UK commercial TV sector. Recently Granada has been reorganised into two integrated businesses:

- Content (which includes TV and broadband production)
- Online and Broadcasting Enterprises.

In 2002, it produced 6500 hours of television for UK and overseas broadcasters. The company is the main programme supplier to ITV, delivering 47% of network adult programmes; 90% of all programmes attracting audiences over 10 million on ITV1 were produced by Granada. Granada has a number of overseas production interests – in the US, Australia, Germany and China. Broadband ventures include websites for Liverpool and Arsenal football clubs. Other relevant initiatives include Granada Learning. It also acts as an independent production house and has made a range of successful commissions for other channels, including *The Royle Family* for BBC1 and *Elizabeth* for C4.

Granada owned 50% of the now defunct ITV Digital and incurred huge losses, made worse by the advertising downturn. In September 2002, film production was brought in-house as part of the drama department and Granada Film ceased to be a separate company. The content-producing side of Granada was restructured into four major areas: Drama, Factual, Entertainment and Formats, and Daytime and Regional. Granada Enterprises is the commercial exploitation arm of Granada, offering advertisers a range of marketing services with which to promote their brands – including airtime sales, sponsorship, co-productions and interactive advertising.

The ITV companies are:

- Anglia Television
- Border Television
- Carlton Television
- Central Broadcasting
- Channel Television
- GMTV
- Grampian Television
- Granada Television
- HTV
- London Weekend Television (LWT)
- Meridian Broadcasting
- Scottish Television
- Tyne Tees Television
- UTV (Ulster Television)
- Westcountry Television
- Yorkshire Television

The companies work together through the ITV Network Centre to deliver a co-ordinated, nationwide network. Each company competes to make programmes for the network and also broadcasts in their own region.

Channel 4 (C4)

In November 1982, C4 was launched as a publicly supported company with a remit to provide 'information, education and entertainment' for a diverse audience. Early funding also came from the ITV companies; until recently it had to pay a proportion of annual profits to its rivals. When the 'funding formula' ended, the station had considerable scope to develop its programming. Channel 4 has combined commercial independence with a public service remit. However, its diversification into digital and interactive services, and losses incurred by a separate film production arm, coupled with the advertising downturn, pushed the company into the red for the first time in a decade.

Channel 4 was restructured in 2002; more than 200 jobs were lost and the commissioning departments were reduced from 13 to eight. The film production division was brought in-house, and sales and distribution closed. Film Four is to continue as a pay TV channel only. There was some good news with the announcement of an increase in the programming budget of £20m.

C4 now employs around 900 people and serves all of the UK, including Wales, where S4C also broadcasts under a similar remit.

Channel 4 is home to some of the UK's most innovative, challenging and distinctive programmes – from *Big Brother* to *Channel 4 News* to *Trigger Happy TV*. Channel 4 runs entertainment channel E4 and a range of educational and other interactive services. However, Channel 4 does not make any of its own programmes.

One of the strengths of the channel has always been that it commissions its programmes from hundreds of independent production companies, and so is able to choose from the best ideas that those companies can offer. Channel 4 is engaged in commissioning, financing, marketing and transmitting those programmes – and doing the hundred and one other things that are needed to get TV programmes on the air.

Information about Channel 4 can be found on the website

www.channel4.com. For information regarding career opportunities, please look at www.channel4.com/4careers.

Sianel Pedwar Cymru (S4C)

Channel 4 Wales is a public service broadcaster, which transmits
about 30 hours per week in Welsh – 10 hours of which is provided
by the BBC – as well as about 70% of C4's standard output. Welsh-
speaking independent production companies provide a range of
commissioned peak-time programmes. Funded mainly by advertising revenues, it employs a small staff of administrative and
engineering specialists.

five

Now firmly established, *five* is in the process of developing its
programming even further. The channel lost its Chief Executive,
Dawn Airey to BskyB but announced a significant increase in the
programming budget.

2002 also saw an increase in arts programming and a move away
from what has been seen sometimes as downmarket programming. Still only available to 82% of the UK population, it has
developed a reputation for clever marketing and scheduling,
innovative news reporting and the ability to target audiences of
interest to advertisers. Set up to broaden the options for
advertisers, it continued to increase its share during the recent
recession. The success of *five* has been achieved on remarkably low
budgets – less than half of that spent by either C4 or BBC2, which
both attract around 10% of the available audience. It employs
around 250 people and makes very few programmes.

Cable and satellite

The multichannel sector – which has changed the way in which
people watch TV, causing a ripple effect in every area of the
industry – is made up of platform operators (BSkyB, Freeview,
NTL) and TV companies who supply content. Around 6000 people
are employed in the sector.

BSkyB

BSkyB has succeeded in persuading almost 6 million households
to pay for their viewing, thereby changing the face of UK TV

forever. It scored another coup by 'persuading' all its subscribers to transfer to digital, resulting in substantial financial savings. Primarily a business which deals in programmes, it makes very little in-house (although a joint venture with Princess Productions has just been commissioned to fill the *Big Breakfast* slot), and generally buys-in most of its material. The appointment of Dawn Airey as Managing Director for Sky Networks has been seen as a clear commitment to increasing original production. Sport is a big 'banker' for Sky, and interactive technology is providing scope for additional revenue. Staff – there are just over 9000 employees – are mainly administrative, with increasing numbers of technical and engineering professionals. The 24-hour newsroom employs journalists on a shift basis. Customer Services operates from Scotland, employing large numbers of staff who work to retain existing and win new subscribers.

Other cable and satellite companies

There are numerous other channels now available to viewers in the UK, although many do not make programmes in this country. Some are now well established, employing 100 people or more, usually in administrative and marketing roles. Programme-making, when it occurs, is usually very low budget and uses freelancers. Details of individual companies can be obtained from the ITC, and edited lists also appear in trade directories. New companies are constantly being launched, providing specialist programming for target audiences – described as 'narrowcasting' to 'niche' markets. Examples include Artsworld (Arts), Discovery SciTrek (Science, Technology and the Paranormal), Gaming Channel (TV Betting), M4U (Indian Music), and Travel Channel (Travel and Exploration).

RSLs – Restricted Service Licences

A number of local terrestrial TV stations now operate as RSLs following the 1996 Broadcasting Act. There are two types of RSL. One covers specific events such as festivals and is issued for a term of 56 days. The other covers an establishment or a specific location for a period of four years. There have been three rounds of applications for location-based RSLs and, at the time of writing, 21 RSLs have been granted. The licences exploit spare capacity within the analogue spectrum, and broadcast to anything between 200,000 and 600,000 people in a specific geographic area.

The first RSL channel to go live was TV12, which began on the Isle of Wight in 1998. There are currently 17 companies operating in:

- Belfast
- Lanarkshire
- Leicester
- Oxford
- Londonderry/Derry
- Manchester
- Portsmouth
- Southampton
- Glasgow
- Inverness
- Norwich
- Hertford
- Twyford
- Northampton
- Isle of Wight
- Cheshire
- Cardiff

Licences are granted by the ITC for periods of four years. If there is – or is about to be – an RSL in your area, it may be a good place to gain a range of skills and experience by volunteering on a regular basis.

The independent production sector

This thriving sector 'develops, produces and exploits' intellectual property, including TV programmes, films and animated films, which is sold to media publishing and broadcasting companies, and to cable and satellite platforms. The sector emerged in line with the foundation of Channel 4 as a 'Publisher/Broadcaster' in 1982 and was fuelled by the 1992 Broadcasting Act, which compelled UK terrestrial broadcasters to commission at least 25% of their non-news/current affairs material from independent suppliers. It includes several very large and profitable companies (some of which have attracted substantial overseas investment) which negotiate rights for their formats and programmes. These are followed – in business size terms – by around 40 medium sized companies, each employing between 10 and 40 people. The vast bulk of the sector is made up of very small organisations, often 'one-man-bands' which contract additional production and technical staff on a freelance basis when the work is available.

There are approximately 1000 independents at the time of writing, the majority of which belong to the trade association PACT (the Producers Alliance for Cinema and Television – *see* also page 159). Although most of the companies specialise in a particular type of product, some are very diverse, and several produce a mix of films and TV and radio programmes. They can cover any combination of the following types of work (more information about the output of different companies can be found in the PACT directory):

- Broadcast television
- Feature films
- Short films
- Corporate video
- Commercials
- Pop 'promos'
- Animation
- Interactive content provision

A diverse range of broadcast and non-broadcast material is produced, the vast majority of which is financed and cash-flowed by a broadcaster on an agreed budget. Only occasionally will the producer take the risk of financing a programme and then selling on to the broadcaster again against a limited licence. The companies which make the programmes do not transmit them: they pitch against each other for commissions, and invest heavily in the preparation of professional proposals and supporting research materials – money which will not be recouped unless the commission is won.

Finance is an increasingly important and sensitive area for many independents. Regular features in *Broadcast, Indie Finance* and *City Watch* give an insight into the challenges – and solutions – available. The PACT journal is also full of useful information. Although the majority of successful bids will be fully funded, it is becoming more common (especially in animation and drama) for the broadcaster to promise only a percentage contribution. Some PACT members are involved, for at least part of their time, in making short or feature-length films. Read Chapter 4, *The Film Industry*, for an insight into this growing area.

Employment within the independent sector

Most new entrants into the TV industry will start their careers within this sector, and many people will continue to spend at least part of their working lives within one or more of these companies. The sector provides a pool of talent which supplies the whole industry, most of which will be freelance.

Longer term contracts or 'permanent' status jobs will be offered to individuals who can contribute consistently to the core business of the independent. Obviously this will vary with the size and complexity of the organisation, but is likely to include producers, marketeers, finance and legal/business affairs specialists and administrators. Many companies will employ one or more 'runners' to support the rest of the team, and to gain an insight into the business. People working for independents need to be commercial, well organised and 'customer focused', as they will be involved in developing, marketing and producing work to satisfy an often-demanding client. Good office and IT skills are increasingly sought-after.

Ironically, the traditional 'BBC route' from secretary to programme-maker has almost been reinvented by this sector. Working closely to provide administrative support to a producer can be an excellent training ground for TV Research and a range of production jobs.

Independents all emphasise that they work hard: there is no scope for people who can't contribute 110%, so expect to be asked to multi-task regularly. It's all about teamwork, and governed by deadlines and usually low budgets.

Some issues to consider

Although several household-name 'Super Indies' now exist, employing 200 or more people, the vast majority of independent production companies are 'SMEs' (small and medium sized employers) – and many are 'one-man bands' which call in freelance help when the work requires it. A central core of medium sized companies – employing between ten and 40 people – has grown up over the past decade, and sometimes feels 'squeezed' by the big players. Although they want to shake off the 'cottage industry' image, many are unwilling to part with their 'lifestyle business' as famously described by Sir John Harvey Jones in a BBC business programme.

Whatever the size of the business, to survive and thrive they have to win commissions. According to PACT, the industry organisation, spending by UK broadcasters on independent productions rose by 37% during the period 1996–2001. Development costs – preparing to pitch an idea to commissioners – have also risen, and many small companies spend a great deal of money, which will be lost if the business is not won, in their efforts to gain favour. Sometimes, for a major show, development money may be forthcoming – for example when the decision was taken to commission a new *Big Breakfast*. Seven independents bid for the contract; five were chosen to make pilots; and each was given £70,000 to produce them. The business was won by a partnership of BSkyB/Princess Productions.

Over the years, independent producers and organisations such as PACT have voiced concerns about broadcasters' adherence to the 25% quota, the rights taken by broadcasters, etc. There were increasing fears that the long-term economic viability of the independent production sector was being undermined by an inequitable balance between the sector and the broadcasters.

The Joint Scrutiny Committee on the draft Communications Bill raised these concerns and the Independent Television Commission was asked to carry out a review of the UK programme supply market.

At the time of writing, the Secretary of State for Culture, Media and Sport has accepted most of the findings of the review, and the following key recommendations will now be taken forward as amendments to the Communications Bill:

1. The introduction of Codes of Practice (compiled by broadcasters) governing the dealings of broadcasters with the independent production sector. These will be monitored by Ofcom and there will be penalties for non-adherence.
2. Ofcom to monitor the 25% quota of independent productions – BBC1 and BBC2 will be monitored separately.
3. Stipulations to safeguard original productions and news and current affairs programming in the event of changes at ITV and *five*.

4. New regional production targets and investment for *five*.
5. New regional investment target for Channel 4.

Investment is certainly an issue for many producers, affecting all elements of the indie sector. Some very large companies have recently had their 'independent' status reinstated following a change of rules about foreign ownership, thereby allowing them to continue to compete for the 25% independent quota at the BBC and ITV. One industry spokesperson said that 'small and medium sized indies have a stark choice – that is, to invest, diversify, or die…'. Some already join forces with the larger companies for big projects.

All of this information underlines the increasing need for professionalism, business planning, marketing and financial expertise throughout the sector. Many of the individuals who are regularly employed in the independent companies will offer these skills. There will also be opportunities for support and administrative staff. Most production staff will be employed on a freelance basis.

In many ways, the independent production sector now dominates the TV industry in the UK. Most people will be employed by these companies for the majority of their contracted time. However, even the larger independent production companies are unlikely to employ more than ten members of staff on a permanent basis. Freelance staff are employed when needed. Many new entrants into the industry will gain work experience within this sector, and some may find regular employment.

Opportunities created by low-budget TV

Most programme-makers have now accepted that – even in traditionally very expensive areas such as Drama – low, or relatively low, budget TV is now part of everyone's life. More airtime requires more content, which has to cost less, and be made faster than conventional production. Industry newcomers and experienced professionals are working flexibly together to apply new technology to produce innovative programmes, some of which have attracted the attention of mainstream executive producers, or even won awards. A huge amount can be achieved. For example, at Granada TV, two studios work regular eight-hour shifts, creating two hours of live programming every day, plus prerecorded material for a range of satellite channels. Some channels have established themselves as 'nursery slopes' for new programmes and programme-makers, and there is now a history of people developing their careers from this foundation. Some people have started to move from other areas – for example, Regionals – into these new areas to gain and use a range of new skills, which can only improve their career prospects.

It is even possible, in this more open market, to launch a new TV station: entrepreneurs who spot a gap in the market can set up a channel. This is rather similar to the dot.com world, however, and 'a gap in the market' does not always equal a business opportunity – few get it right first time. A clear proposition is essential in order to put together a credible business plan. Entrepreneurs can either sell the product to a 'retailer' – BSkyB, Freeview or NTL – or buy a satellite slot and take their chance. Some channels, especially for minority groups, have been set up with remarkably small investment.

If you are interested in the business of TV, this may be a possible route, especially once you have gained industry experience. But venture capitalists will want a great deal of factual information before they risk their money... look at the current channels (get a full list from the ITC) and think about their funding/audience and potential for future development.

Facilities houses and post-production

Technology is constantly improving, and the range of equipment now available to help producers direct and make sophisticated programmes is constantly growing. Most independent production companies have limited equipment of their own, and prefer to hire facilities and expertise for each individual project through facilities houses. The large companies – including the BBC – also use this sector, and the largest commercial facilities house is the independent BBC Resources Ltd (which is still wholly owned by the corporation).

Specialist companies have invested large amounts of money to provide equipment, studio space and highly skilled staff at a commercial rate. Some will offer a full range of studio facilities, but most concentrate on a particular area of expertise such as editing, animation, graphics or special effects. Clients decide how to 'pick and mix' within the services on offer, and will regularly use several houses in the course of a production. There is huge competition between houses, and considerable 'rate card' negotiation. 'Customer Relationship Management' is seen as increasingly important, and it is certainly an area which requires sound business and financial management. Since the first edition of this book was published, there have been several high-profile casualties in this part of the industry, where companies were forced out of business due to financial pressure.

Any advance in relevant technology puts pressure onto management (do we invest?) and technical staff (how quickly can I learn to use this?) alike. However, despite the pressures, there are considerable numbers of good – and often very well paid – jobs in this area of the industry. People with strong technical abilities and good interpersonal skills are particularly sought-after, although many people who work on the 'business' side do not come from technical backgrounds. Chapter 6, *The Facilities Sector* explains this diverse area in more detail.

Equipment manufacturers

Companies which manufacture and supply equipment for use in television studios employ specialist engineering and technical staff to work on the development and maintenance of cameras, video recorders, sound consoles, vision mixers and so on. Some staff will 'troubleshoot', visiting sites and locations to solve problems; others will work in research labs, or will be part of a team devoted to installing or upgrading equipment. Such companies often run excellent training courses, teaching people to use their equipment to its full capability. Frequently open to outsiders, these can be a very useful method of gaining expertise in state-of-the-art equipment not usually available in colleges.

Opportunities in education

Increasing numbers of colleges, universities and schools have their own TV studios. The standard of equipment varies widely, but many produce high-quality, non-broadcast material. Generally, small numbers of multi-skilled technical staff are employed; but some educational psychologists and teachers, and media theorists find work in this area. As the number of 'media' courses continues to grow, so will the requirement for people who can use and maintain TV equipment, at colleges throughout the UK.

Who works in the television industry?

People from all kinds of eductional and cultural backgrounds work within the TV industry. *Skillset* has now conducted three censuses designed to get a 'snapshot' of the diversity and size of the sector. These indicate that around 25,000 people are employed within broadcast TV, and around 4900 work within cable and satellite – a 12% decrease on the previous census. Although these sound rather large numbers, in fact the TV industry is relatively small when compared to other areas of employment. Once in, people move around, and the majority will find work through contacts. It's a business where reputation really counts – 'you're only as good as your last piece of work' is a phrase often heard. As a result, there are no 'rules' about what kind of people will get and keep the majority of jobs. Although the proportion of graduates (especially media studies graduates and postgraduates) is rising within production areas, there are at least as many very successful people who have few, or no, formal qualifications. Thus, regardless of background, individuals who will succeed tend to share a mix of 'transferable skills', including:

- Creative skills
- Communication skills
- Problem-solving abilities
- Team skills
- A flexible approach to life
- Tenacity
- The ability to sell your skills to potential employers
- An awareness of the applications of technology

Gaining a first job will require considerable effort (*see* also Chapter 10, *Getting in and Getting on*), especially as most jobs are not advertised. Career development is often unstructured, although an increasing acceptance of *Skillset* Professional Qualifications is starting to help people plan their own skills development, and improve their chances of promotion (*see* Chapter 9, *Training and Education for the Industry*).

The census indicates that there has been a significant increase in the representation of ethnic minorities in the industry. For example, in broadcast television there has been an increase from 6.3% to 7.9%. But the battle for a representative industry is not completely won. The percentage of ethnic minorities working as freelancers in the commercials sector decreased to 0% from 6.9%, as recorded in the last census. The number of disabled people employed in the industry remains at 0.8%, unchanged since the last census.

Many people entering the TV industry are young, with few financial or personal responsibilities. The uncertainty of freelance earnings, and long and often unsocial hours, may present impossible barriers for people with regular financial commitments (such as a mortgage) or the need to care for dependent children or relations – although some companies are making moves to provide more flexible working arrangements for those with caring responsibilities.

People with a passion for the industry, appropriate skills and a less conventional background may even be at an advantage in today's employment climate, as the major organisations are under pressure to employ a more representative mix of staff at every level. To date this has been most evident in the training and recruitment of women for technical jobs, and in specialist production training for under-represented ethnic minorities. Any equal-opportunity initiative in television will attract publicity in the relevant press. Such training initiatives are keen to attract well-qualified and enthusiastic applicants from a range of under-represented groups.

However, the wheels are often quite slow to turn. The majority of powerful senior people in the industry are still predominantly male, white, middle class and highly educated.

Developing your skills within the industry

Skillset exists to encourage the delivery of informed training and education provision so that the British broadcast, film, video and interactive media industry's technical, creative and economic achievements are maintained and improved. It aims to establish and maintain a full range of high-quality training pathways and qualifications in response to the needs of this creative and highly diversified industry. In 1995, a range of *Skillset* Professional Qualifications was introduced to enable individuals to develop and gain credit for competency in their chosen employment area(s). At the time of writing, more than 40 sets of industry-specific standards have been established and new areas are regularly added. These unique qualifications have been developed by respected industry practitioners and will be assessed by others who currently work in the relevant area of interest. They have been welcomed by leading figures throughout the TV, radio, film, video and interactive media world, who are convinced that this form of skills assessment – done 'on the job' – will revolutionise career pathways for both employed and freelance people. To find out more *see* Chapter 9, *Training and Education for the Industry.*

More than qualifications

Some jobs in the industry will continue to require formal qualifications or proven evidence of relevant skills, especially in technical areas like engineering. However, the consistent theme that runs through the person specifications for different jobs is the need for two things: a real interest in, and commitment to, the business; and talent! The people who gain jobs in the television industry will:

- Watch a lot of film and television
- Be critical and knowledgeable about their viewing or listening
- Notice the input of different professionals
- Have real opinions about what they like, and why.

Although there is always some space for genuine enthusiasts (in a Sports Department, for instance, you'll find people who have all the statistics of their interest area carefully documented since their schooldays), the majority of people will have a broad-based knowledge of the modern business, and will constantly absorb new information rather than remain in a small arena of interest. The 'blurring of genres' described earlier in this chapter requires people who can move comfortably between different types of programme.

People who work in the industry often 'live and breathe' it. To be surrounded by others with similar commitment and interests, in a creative atmosphere, is still one of the major benefits of working in the business. The money is often not great, the hours are very long, the work is often physically demanding – but if you love the business, it's all worthwhile. And finally, TV is a fundamentally practical business, which eats ideas. Individuals who can offer good ideas for programmes that can be easily and cheaply made are greatly in demand.

Where do people work?

Despite all the national and regional initiatives, and the 'decentralisation' of the large companies during the 1990s, the TV business is still firmly biased towards London and the South East. There are jobs throughout the UK, and every region makes positive moves to nurture a pool of local freelance talent; but, like it or not, most of the decision-making and the work takes place around London. There are some very successful independents and facilities houses around the UK, but over the past few years several high-profile outfits have closed their regional commitments. The BBC has centres of excellence throughout the country, where specialists often form a local community.

Freelancers with sought-after skills (including, in some areas, particular language skills, knowledge relevant to a local centre of excellence, or good regional contacts) may actually find that they are overloaded with the choice of work in their region. Don't migrate to London until you've checked the local opportunities.

Health & Safety

Always seen as a priority by *Skillset* when developing training and qualifications for the industry, Health & Safety is taken increasingly seriously by employers throughout all sectors. Many companies will not consider employing anyone, even for a short freelance contract, unless they can demonstrate competence. Studios, locations and even production offices can be dangerous places, and the aim of most producers and managers is to reduce risk to a minimum. Unsurprisingly, Health & Safety is fast becoming a significant career area, especially for individuals who understand the production process and can communicate with creative teams in a way that enables, rather than blocks, the process of programme-making. Specialist consultants may advise in particular genres, for example costume drama or large-scale entertainment, often earning high fees for reducing risk (and the cost of insurance premiums) through creative problem-solving.

Professional qualifications are available in this area, and *Skillset* Professional Qualifications place heavy emphasis on the need for good practice in Health & Safety. Opportunities can be of particular interest to career changers with several years' industry experience.

International perspectives

In the growing global market, the UK is still a minor player; the really big audiences come from America and the Far East. To compete in a multichannel environment, UK television companies will need to take advantage of the opportunities offered. At present, the majority of our programmes and films do not 'travel well', although there are notable exceptions: some of our popular soaps sell to more than 50 'territories' and produce continuing revenue for their makers and performers. Some dramas also sell well abroad – *Inspector Morse* is a good example, attracting more than 75 million viewers over 200 territories. The government is keen to utilise our undisputed programme- and film-making talent to increase the revenue brought to 'UK plc' through overseas sales. The Director-General of the BBC came to his job with extensive experience of the international market, a factor which must have boosted his CV, and there are specialists in the commercial companies, including the larger independents.

Co-productions – pre-sales agreements with overseas broad-casters – are becoming an almost statutory element of large-scale drama, animation or natural history programmes. Sharing the production costs (sometimes with a distributor) reduces the overheads of programme-making and guarantees international exposure, although it may dilute the editorial independence of the UK team. TV formats are also a big market – successful game-show 'formats' are sold worldwide, and produced in the different countries. Some game shows are also made with a long-term international market in mind, with very general questions, simple sets, and instructions to avoid portraying date-tied fashions. Many of these programmes are 'money-spinners', selling around the English-speaking world for a decade, or even longer.

Programme-makers are increasingly influenced by the potential for future sales, gearing the product to the international market-place. This is often a risky strategy, as different markets require different products. For example, American schedulers prefer to run series of 13 or 26 shows, whereas UK audiences are used to series of 6 or 8 episodes. Aiming (and failing) to achieve one market can be an expensive decision.

The BBC is moving strategically into international markets. For example, it has well-established links with the US Discovery

Channel, with the intention of showcasing its material to a massive audience. The BBC and ITV companies are working together in some instances, for example with Granada Media, as GB Productions. And large ITV companies have now established North American production offices; this trend is likely to continue.

MEDIA Plus, based at the Film Council in London, provides a range of support for independent TV production companies within the European Union. To attract funding of up to 500,000 euros, producers must show that 50% of production finance is already in place, and two broadcasters from at least two member states, in different language zones, must be involved. Support is also available for development costs, including the identification of industry partners, co-producers and financers, and local cast and crew members. Producers often now 'think internationally' right from the pre-production stage. Planning to shoot additional footage to appeal to different audiences – even making different endings – can increase the chances of selling to a broad international audience. The BTDA (The British TV Distributors Association – *see* their website, www.btda.org) specialises in helping producers to help boost exports, especially dramas, which often need distribution money before they can be made. There will be opportunities for sales and acquisitions professionals in this marketplace. The three main overseas markets each year (generally held in exotic locations) already attract about 10,000 buyers and sellers. Read the trade press to get the background of each event.

nations and regions

Although the bulk of the television industry is centred on London and the South East, there are genuine opportunities for individuals who want to work within their own nation or local region. The BBC makes programmes in each of its national centres, and these dedicated 'centres of excellence' are spread throughout the regions. The downside of this, from an applicant's point of view, is that genres of interest – say drama – may not be produced in their own region.

As part of its franchise agreement, every ITV company has a duty to provide quality regional broadcasting. The amount and mix of this varies quite widely, depending on individual franchise bids and agreements – for example, some companies are committed to making and broadcasting regional religious programmes. The likely move towards one ITV may well adjust the anomalies... and the growth in local RSLs (Restricted Service Licences) for TV should create a range of opportunities for work experience, with occasional paid vacancies.

Every region also has a range of local independent production and facilities companies, which pitch for work with local and national organisations. Many complain about the perceived London-bias shown by commissioners, and some TV companies have recently made a commitment to commissioning at least a percentage of their work locally. At the annual PACT Nations and Regions Conference attended by key industry figures, there was much discussion on this topic, and ideas were developed about how to maintain a sustainable regional industry. ITV has always been 'rooted' in its regions, and there is a strong history of using local suppliers – not least to satisfy franchise obligations. The BBC is currently very proactive in encouraging activity in the regions and C4 deliberately spreads its commissioning around the UK. So... watch this space, as the range of career opportunities may expand over the next few years.

Regional programming is not just about keeping a local audience happy: production costs are cheaper, and the output is often used to pilot programmes, or to offer a debut to a presenter. There are many examples of television talent and shows which started in the regions. Increasing numbers of network shows are now produced in the regions, and specialist centres – for example Daytime Shows – can provide excellent experience for people at every stage of their careers.

A regulated industry

UK commercial television is among the most regulated in the world – in stark contrast to the unregulated world of the Internet (and some cable and satellite stations). At present, commercial programme-makers have to adhere to detailed codes of practice, and the BBC has to satisfy the standards set by its Board of Governors.

Things are changing, however. The joint DTI/DCMS Communications White Paper, published in December 2000 and entitled *A New Future for Communications*, proposed a merger of the existing broadcasting regulators with those from the telecoms industry to form Ofcom, a joint body which will oversee the changing global industry. Some key industry players feel strongly that its remit should include the BBC. This is unlikely as part of the passage of this bill through Parliament, but the BBC's charter is due for renewal in 2006 and the pressure for a more consistent form of across-the-board regulation may well increase.

The Office of Communications, establishing Ofcom, received Royal Assent in March 2002. The new organisation is likely to be operating by the end of 2003 or early 2004. The new regulator will have its duties and powers fully defined when the new Communications Act comes into force, but it will bring a 'lighter touch' and pave the way for one ITV, and for increased overseas investment (even takeovers in the UK market).

Many people fear this liberalisation of cross-media ownership rates, which, in their view, could lead to domination by the Murdoch empire. And one ITV would mean that there was a monopoly within the airtime sales market: at present, ITC rulings ensure that Granada and Carlton have to compete, a factor that is important in these times of unprecedented downturn in advertising spend and budgets.

Regulation affects every aspect of the industry – it is seen as both a strength and a weakness and, at a time when there is the potential technology to transform both the production and broadcasting business, many people are anxious to know what will or will not be happening to the relevant legislation.

Industry get-togethers and awards

There are a number of industry events and award ceremonies held throughout the year. Although you are unlikely to be able to attend until you are well established in your career, they will all be reported in the media pages of the broadsheets, and in the trade magazines. Events include the Edinburgh International TV Festival (which includes TVYP – TV for Young People, which you may be able to visit, or even contribute to), the RTS Conference in Cambridge, the BAFTAS... and numerous smaller ones, all of which could help you to develop ideas and identify contacts. Articles about the major international TV Sales events – such as MIPCOM – also give a useful insight into the market.

Almost without exception, awards are worth winning. Companies and channels often benefit from a 'halo effect' after gaining an accolade, and independent producers can improve their credibility with commissioners, performers and even potential staff members. Noting who has won what can help you to identify industry trends. For example, at the time of writing, the RTS 2002 awards for Best Entertainment Programme went to *Banzai* (C4), and Best Situation Comedy and Comedy Drama to *The Office*. (There is little doubt that both shows will spawn a range of recognisable offspring.)

If you are hoping to specialise in a particular section of the TV industry, make sure that you know which programmes are currently receiving accolades, and be able to talk about them. There are also some student awards, which can act as a powerful showcase for new talent.

The future

Anyone entering the modern television industry will need to be prepared for constant change. If the recent past is any predictor of the future, we all need to be ready to respond to reorganisations, changes in the 'old order', and all the positive and negative effects caused by advances in technology. There is no doubt that the challenges of the multichannel world will continue to occupy the imagination and skills of many talented people who want, after this period of recession, to really 'get it right'. Far too much has been invested to let things drift away. We spoke to numerous people across the industry during our research for this chapter. Here are some of their predictions and observations, which should be of value to anyone hoping to establish a career in TV:

- Companies – even small independents – will be expected to be increasingly businesslike, managing finances and raising investments, often from overseas, in order to make specialist programmes. There is likely to be more foreign investment and even ownership, which may affect very big fish – even Granada or Carlton – as well as independent production companies.
- The Public Service Debate is gaining momentum, both in terms of the BBC serving all its licence payers, and the future status of Channel 4.
- Marketeers are likely to become ever more prominent, 'branding' their products for survival in the global marketplace.
- Viewers will be the subject of market research analysis, produc-

ing reams of statistics that will influence which programmes are commissioned.

- Budgets for programmes are unlikely to increase, and there will be increasing emphasis on high-volume/low-budget output.
- 'Worthy' programmes, which do not attract large audiences but may be necessary to help retain a channel's credibility (or franchise), may find themselves in 'graveyard' slots, or removed to a digital channel. This may particularly affect serious arts programmes, documentaries and religious programmes.
- Regulation may 'lighten', and the BBC may also come under the aegis of Ofcom.
- Multiculturalism will become more evident – in every aspect of the industry, including programming.
- The Internet and interactivity will become standard elements in programme-makers' lives.
- Programming and scheduling may also change, following the success of 'theme nights' which – if they work – pull in and hold an audience for a long time. Be prepared to see more 'days' along the lines of the BBC's recent NHS Day.
- Ratings are likely to become even more important, providing detailed demographic information.

And who knows what will happen to the big companies? Most people in the industry expect to see 'one ITV' within the next few years, merging many jobs to save money. The BBC is likely to become even more commercial, through the exploitation of its vast intellectual property archive, and its 'spin-offs'. The Director-General, Greg Dyke, has already influenced the atmosphere in the Corporation by delivering substantial extra money for programmes.

Channel 4 head Mark Thompson has made his own mark on the organisation in a time of decreased advertising revenue, having revised the commissioning process for independent production houses.

As for the many hundreds of individuals who are thinking of getting in and getting on in the television industry, it is a genuinely exciting time to start exploring options.

3

A Career in Radio

It is estimated that around 23,000 people work in radio – more than work in broadcast TV. Over three-quarters of all workers are on permanent contracts. A quarter of the radio industry began their careers as volunteers. The proportion of women working in the industry has more than doubled in less than 10 years. Women now make up 54% of the entire workforce. Although 28% of the industry works in London, the rest is dispersed fairly evenly throughout the UK, compared to other sectors which are more London-centric. This is largely due to the proliferation of local commercial radio stations.

Radio is a big success story in the UK, with 91% of the over-15 population listening in every day. BBC Radio comprises the national stations (Radios 1, 2, 3, 4 and 5) and its many local stations throughout England. Scotland, Wales and Northern Ireland have their own BBC radio national networks with stations peppered throughout those nations, reflecting their life and cultures. In addition, the BBC broadcasts globally via the World Service. Commercial radio is also a significant part of the industry, with stations in every part of the UK. Community, pirate, student, hospital, and even shopping-centre radio are also active sectors. Many of these stations rely heavily on unpaid volunteers for their existence.

Jobs in this industry require a multitude of skills, many of them creative and technical. Most people working in radio will be expected to operate equipment and work well in a team. Within this chapter we aim to give you an insight into this industry, and to provide some pointers which will help you to make a serious start in your research into its often under-publicised jobs.

At the time of writing there are:

- Eight UK national radio services
- More than 280 local stations
- 350–400 short-term licences awarded each year.

A regulated industry

Commercial radio in the UK is regulated by the Radio Authority. This is a statutory body which awards licences to, and oversees the performance of, independent stations. The licence-holders pay an annual fee for this privilege. Until recently, companies were committed to sticking to a detailed programming structure which they had submitted with their licence application, even if it was not attracting enough listeners. A new, 'light touch' approach from the Radio Authority allows for companies to work to a general 'format', adjusting certain details of their programming without permission from the regulator. Perhaps the best-known format in the UK is the 'GOLD' approach, which took the AM airwaves by storm in the 1980s, attracting numerous listeners with money to spend.

In an industry which is governed by market economics and advertising revenue, there is increasing pressure to loosen the controls even further. But a strong argument that regulation protects diversity has been voiced by leading industry figures. Fears that 'big players' could move in, and provide the least that they could get away with in order to minimise costs and optimise profits, have already come true in the US and Australia. At the time of writing, there are clear indications that the government is ready to radically relax media ownership rules, thereby unleashing a flurry of takeovers and mergers among the industry's main players.

An expanding career area

Radio today is big business, attracting a significant proportion of the national advertising 'spend' and communicating with an enviable percentage of the target markets. Unsurprisingly, advertisers have realised the potential of this form of communication and seek to make contact with target groups by using different stations. The ratings battle is an ongoing one, and the challenge facing individual stations is to attract as many listeners as possible away from their rivals. Until recently, that battle has been waged on a local level, but the advent of national independent stations has dented the listening figures recorded by the BBC networks. Although the BBC is not – as yet – trying to attract advertisers or sponsors, it has to prove that the service it provides is good value and worth its slice of the licence fee.

A great deal of effort has been made to improve coverage and attract new customers from currently neglected categories within the population, without alienating the traditional listeners. A number of well-publicised success stories have laid the foundation for further innovation to cater for a changing population of listeners of all ages, such as the launch of digital channels, BBC 6 Music and BBC 1xtra.

The fact that radio is becoming ever more 'businesslike' has both pros and cons for the people who work within it. The increasing importance of ratings means that the output is more 'managed' than in the past. Producers in both independent – now more commonly known as commercial – radio and the BBC focus much more on the customer (i.e. listener), which means there is less opportunity for risk-taking or innovation than previously. The obscure documentary, or the minority music show, is less likely to be broadcast on the networks. However, links with television in the BBC have encouraged a cross-fertilisation of ideas. Radio is perceived as an excellent and cheap 'test bed' for new ideas. The show *Dead Ringers*, which has transferred from Radio 4 to BBC television, is just one example of this.

At a more local level, however, the development of community radio is providing new opportunities for innovation and experimentation, and encourages access for volunteers and trainees seeking an entry point into the radio industry. The radio industry continues to provide interesting and rewarding careers, conventional and otherwise, for a broad range of talented people – although some will never be paid, in the normally accepted sense, for their efforts.

an expansion in the market
The BBC started to broadcast in digital in September 1995, with 'simulcasts' – simultaneous broadcasts on both analogue and

digital – of Radios 1, 2, 3, 4 and 5. In November 1999, the UK's first commercial, national multiplex – *Digital One* – went on air. At the time of writing, commercial radio has 80% of the population covered for digital, with the BBC at around 65% – but that's not the whole story. There are ongoing plans for further stations, both national and local. Existing broadcasters will be able to use the explosion of regional licences to 'roll out' existing local services on a national scale, and bid for new national licences.

a 'shopping mall' of choice

To date, there are 33 local multiplexes broadcasting digital radio, covering places as far apart as Inverness and Exeter, with a further ten licences timetabled for award. Each multiplex (which can carry up to ten, but more usually six or seven stations) aims to provide a 'shopping mall' for the listener, offering a mix of big 'supermarket' stations, and smaller 'boutique' stations. Choice has to be extended to persuade listeners to move from analogue stations. Improved quality of sound is not enough; people will put up with remarkably poor reception with little complaint.

The planned timetable for a further ten proposed multiplex licences are:

- South Hampshire
- Norwich
- Yorkshire (regional)
- Sussex Coast*
- Swansea
- Stoke-on-Trent
- Kent*
- Nottingham
- Reading and Basingstoke
- Plymouth

There will be scope to 'narrowcast' to niche audiences via a multiplex – providing, for instance, specialised education or business channels. It all sounds very exciting, but the ongoing challenge is to capture public imagination. 'All the sexiness of a charity shop, accompanied by the aroma of a stale anorak,' was the

*Subject to international coordination of frequencies. Source: Radio Authority website.

verdict on digital expressed in a major consultancy report. At present, it is clear that technology, rather than consumer demand, is driving the development. Falling prices, extended choice, and the public's attitude to digital TV, are all likely to help influence the development of digital radio.

The technology – analogue versus digital

Radio broadcasting is produced by very small teams – sometimes as small as one – and a knowledge of the technology is considered essential for many jobs.

'Traditional' analogue radio works like this. When a presenter speaks:

- Sound waves form in the air and spread out in all directions.
- These waves are 'picked up' by a microphone, which converts them into electrical signals.
- The signals move down an electric cable to the mixing desk where other sounds (live or recorded) are added. The mixing desk is usually operated by the presenter, unless the show is very complex – such as drama or live music.
- This complete sound moves along the cable to the transmitter.
- The transmitter converts the electrical signals into radio waves which are released into the atmosphere. These spread out in a way which reflects the power and location of the transmitter, the frequency of transmission and the shape of the land.
- A radio aerial picks up the radio waves. The electronic components convert the waves to an audio signal.
- The loudspeaker or headphones convert the signals back to sound waves.
- The sound waves are heard and 'translated' by the listener.

Digital radio – DAB, or Digital Audio Broadcasting – works in a different way. Instead of using electronic circuits to mimic sounds directly, each sound is translated into a rapid sequence of binary digits, which are converted back to analogue before they reach the radio speakers.

Digital is here to stay. The fact that at the time of writing, very few people will actually have access to a digital radio is considered fairly irrelevant by many industry figures. Time will tell when the huge investment required of the broadcasters will actually start to pay back. Most companies do not expect their digital operations to be profitable for at least five years. At present there are around 35,000 digital radio receivers available in the marketplace. The average price of around £300 is, understandably, seen as a disincentive to people buying and enjoying the undoubted benefits of digital listening. However, it is hoped that when these prices fall even further, and when sets are available in every high-street store, an average listener will not be able to resist the benefits. These include:

- Near-CD quality
- Text and picture messages displayed on the radio, such as news headlines or the name of the music being played
- A broader range of choice.

Finally, analogue transmission is prone to distortion and interference, perhaps from weather conditions, high obstacles or other equipment. Digital listeners will get a clear signal, or else nothing at all.

If you are planning to apply for jobs in radio, it will be useful to read more about the physics of broadcasting. GCSE and 'A' level textbooks often have very useful sections, which are generally understandable by non-scientists.

Radio versus television

Although the two media have much in common, one major point of difference is in the expense of broadcasting. Radio – even 'expensive' radio – is so much cheaper to produce than television that it influences all aspects of employment. Small but highly skilled teams can produce sophisticated programmes. Often, a single individual can handle a whole show; the newsroom of a small independent station will frequently be run single-handed on a shift rota with 'cross-over' periods. And, of course, recorded music can keep the show on the road for long periods without any human intervention at all. Many stations rely heavily on music programmes played out from – and by – a computer system.

Presenters' contracts may stipulate the number of days the individual is expected in studio – and the acceptable scope of pre-recorded, but apparently 'live' shows. When recording a late-night or weekend show, various options will be provided – usually involving the weather – to persuade the listener that the show is being broadcast in real time.

Because there is less money at stake, and less need for technical specialists, small radio stations are relatively 'hands-on' places which maintain good contact with their listeners. Local radio – BBC, commercial, and community – aims to respond to the demands of the surrounding community (or a targeted element of it), and the station team will be encouraged or even expected to participate in local events which may be far removed from their job description. School fêtes, supermarket openings, charity events ... if you work in local radio you should be prepared for any request!

In commercial local radio, the salaries of all staff will come from the advertising revenue. Because of this, everyone will be expected to become at least indirectly involved in selling the benefits of the station. There is little formal demarcation between jobs, although everyone will have their own responsibilities.

'Multi-skilling' – the style of working which has now spread across the broadcasting business – was originally developed in local radio. People with small budgets, lots of airtime to fill, and a talented and enthusiastic team will inevitably 'make do', each helping another to develop and apply new skills. To be successful in local radio, people need to be willing and able to turn a hand to most things.

Nationally networked radio is more formally organised, although there are vast differences between, say, Radio 4, and most independent channels. Traditionally, jobs have been more closely defined with technical and production specialists. Although this style of working is beginning to disappear in many areas, as multi-skilling is demanded, it remains true that creative, complex and comparatively well-resourced productions are still made.

Who listens to radio?

Maybe the question should be rephrased as, who *doesn't* listen to radio? The vast majority of the adult population listens regularly; many are surprisingly loyal to their favourite stations, and will often stay tuned for long periods to one station. The crucial time is the 'breakfast slot', which attracts conventional working people (who make business decisions and have access to more disposable income than those who remain in the home), 'pre-shoppers', and a large number of people who have access to the radio throughout the day. Because of this, huge investment is made in breakfast programming: high-profile presenters are employed and sometimes command high salaries. The programme planners believe – rightly, it seems – that most people will stay with the channel for the rest of their listening day. The constant battles to gain or retain these key listeners sometimes resemble the tactics of the tabloid press.

Different services target 'niche' audiences, often defined by social and demographic groupings. If you are thinking of working in radio, a very important point to note is that the majority of listeners – especially through the daytime – will not be the 'ABC1' readers of *The Guardian* and *The Independent*. The ability to communicate with a very broad cross-section of people is essential for both journalists and presenters.

The youth market is a cause of much debate. Young people tend to have a relatively high disposable income to be spent on consumer luxuries – CDs, DVDs, clothes, etc. Many commercial radio management hours are spent strategising how to win the battle for this critical group – which, they hope, will form lifetime buying habits – and thus please their advertisers. The question of whether young people will change their listening habits over time also occupies much thought and discussion.

Measuring the audience

Advertisers are increasingly keen to access detailed research into listening patterns. Because of the relative loyalty of the radio audience to a small number of stations, they see an opportunity to build a relationship with targeted listeners – for example, the 'youth market', which can be very profitable. RAJAR – Radio Joint Audience Research, which was founded and is still funded by a partnership of commercial radio operators and the BBC – is a sophisticated research system providing detailed information for media planners and buyers. Raw data is gathered from an annual sample size in excess of 160,000 people who complete detailed 'listening diaries' which provide a rich source of information for analysts. Information about age, class, sex, employment status and household tenure is regularly gathered. Additional reports on listeners' cross-media consumption can also be produced, and very detailed 'geo-demographic' statistics, which isolate particular postcodes, are increasingly commissioned by advertisers wishing to target small residential areas.

The research is issued by advertising agencies to build campaigns using radio – either alone or, increasingly, in combination with other media – to satisfy the needs of their clients, by reaching identified target markets. Programme-makers use the information to continually refine their output to satisfy the target audiences and their bosses.

The structure of the industry

The industry supports a diversity of players, and, although the number of available services continues to increase, it is clear that a relatively small number of organisations will dominate the industry for the foreseeable future. During the 1990s there was a trend for new stations to launch, do well, and then be taken over – often producing large profits for their owners but reducing the diversity of the ownership of the medium.

Everyone will be familiar with the main BBC stations – five national networks and the World Service. The BBC also broadcasts from 38 local radio stations in England, and has national networks (including specialist Welsh and Gaelic services) serving Scotland, Wales and Northern Ireland. Commercial radio has expanded steadily since the first stations were licensed in 1973. There are now more than 250 commercial stations broadcasting. Many small stations are owned and managed by larger companies. Useful information about these and the numerous smaller organisations can be found at www.radioauthority.org.uk.

Other 'cross-media' organisations, including local newspaper groups, have invested in commercial radio to maximise both their customer base and their advertising potential. They have grouped local stations together regionally to maximise the efficiencies achieved through shared resources, and are now able to offer coherent regional packages to advertisers. Others, like Reuters, have concentrated on supplying a special broadcasting service, such as news information.

Another trend is the development of a small but significant number of independent radio production companies. Operating in a similar style to the television 'indies' (some in fact work in both areas), they pitch for commissions from the BBC and commercial radio. They aim to achieve a minimum of 25% of broadcast BBC airtime – the same as their TV counterparts – and a significant showing in commercial radio. There is a degree of scepticism about equality of opportunity for the smaller, relatively 'unknown' production houses, and certainly many of the current BBC independent commissions seem to be awarded to well-known, often ex-BBC industry professionals rather than to 'new blood'.

Alongside the larger local and regional radio stations, community radio provides a popular alternative service in many parts of the country. Since 1990, more than 2000 community radio services have broadcast using temporary RSLs (restricted service licences – *see* also pp. 75–6), usually of 28-days' duration. These short-term broadcasts are often timed to coincide with local festivals or events and are largely run by volunteers. Community radio is a growing part of the radio industry, and for many aspirant radio broadcasters it provides their first real taste of making radio programmes.

In addition to the temporary nature of many community radio projects, 18 full-time community-radio licence-holders currently exist. In addition, 15 community radio groups are also going on air during 2002, for an experimental period of 12 months, as part of an 'access radio' licensing scheme.

What do people do?

Although the radio industry is as big as television, each unit employs a relatively small number of people. Even the biggest commercial stations will have fewer than 200 people on the payroll. Unsurprisingly, the BBC is far and away the largest employer. Many journalists work in radio and there are strong management, sales and administrative teams throughout the business. Jobs are distributed throughout the UK.

There is considerable overlap in job descriptions between the different sectors of the industry – a factor which helps individuals to develop careers across the sectors. However, for clarity in this chapter, we will divide the job descriptions by sector and leave it up to you to explore further.

Sought-after, basic broadcasting skills include:

- Writing for radio
- Sound mixing and balancing

- Presentation
- Editing
- Interviewing
- Production skills

Despite the differences in job titles and levels of responsibility, radio is an industry which demands universal skills, including:

- Teamworking
- Flexibility
- Practical problem-solving
- Clear communication
- Administrative ability
- Knowledge of computer software packages
- The ability to take personal responsibility
- IT/technical skills

Working in BBC network radio

The BBC publishes a considerable amount of literature about jobs in the Corporation, which should be available at your local Careers Service office (or call the *skillsformedia* free helpline on 08080 300 900).

Each BBC radio network uses a broad range of specialist and generalist staff. Individuals may work in a special-interest directorate – for example News and Current Affairs, which covers all the BBC's journalism – or in specialist departments supplying drama, classical or popular music, or feature programmes. The jobs can be organised into four main categories:

Programme producers

Producers in radio often have a broader range of responsibility than their TV counterparts. They initiate programme ideas, 'pitch' for funding and space on the schedule, and then manage the creative and technical team to produce the final broadcast product. In addition, considerable emphasis is put on being able to control budgets, and business management skills are essential. Some producers are also presenters and many do their own research. Other relevant BBC titles include Trainee, Senior Producer and Editor.

Production support

Large-scale network programmes are made by small teams of professional staff who work directly to the Producer. Such titles include Specialist Researcher or Generalist Editor, Scriptwriter and Sound Effects. A skilled production assistant with excellent secretarial and organisational skills will pull the team together.

Technical support

The BBC has invested heavily in digital radio, and production staff have been trained to handle most of the technical work which previously required specialist support. Engineers are responsible for maintenance and transmission areas.

Presenter/Reporter/Announcer/News Reader/DJ

The voices of radio will not just be reading scripts; with few exceptions they will also be filling other roles as producers, researchers or journalists. Many are freelancers who move between different elements of the media.

BBC network radio also employs a full complement of professional management and administrative staff in, for instance, finance, marketing, and personnel. Again, business and IT skills are in demand.

Working in BBC local and regional radio

Most independent stations transmit a mix of recorded music and local news and information. The BBC local radio stations offer a broader menu of features, news and documentaries of specific interest to their audience. Most new recruits will already have radio production skills, and many will be trained journalists with a good grounding in broadcasting law.

There are small management and administrative teams in BBC regional and local radio stations. Most senior managers will have production experience, but other jobs require relevant business skills. BBC radio job adverts can be found in the press and at www.bbc.co.uk/jobs.

Jobs in commercial radio

In some respects, working in commercial radio is different from working in the BBC. Commercial radio is first and foremost a business. If the station doesn't attract listeners – who in turn have to be attractive to advertisers and sponsors – the advertising airtime will not sell well, and jobs will be cut. As a result, the production, presentation, business and sales staff all work closely together. Teams are small, and supported by technology wherever possible. Much of the commercial radio airtime is filled with recorded music and so there is little demand for the research and production skills of the kind used by the BBC.

There is information about jobs in commercial radio on the website of the Commercial Radio Companies Association, at www.crca.co.uk. Job descriptions are featured on their 'Getting Into Radio' CD. There is also a 'Getting Into Commercial Radio' guide on the site as well as a free downloadable 'CRCA Work Placement Digest', aimed at helping students and new entrants with their work placement applications.

Presenters

These individuals project the chosen image of the station and are critical to its success. They need to be multi-skilled with a personality and speaking voice that are attractive to the target audience. The ability to interview in an interesting and lively manner (not easy) is essential, particularly if the programme format includes an element of 'phone-in'. In most cases presenters will operate all the studio equipment that they require for their shows.

News journalists

Many commercial stations receive the 'bones' of the up-to-date national and international news on a direct link from a news agency such as IRN or Reuters. The journalists will work as part of a small team to prepare scripts for presentation and interview people for local stories and features. Often there will only be one person on duty in the newsroom, and each journalist needs to be confident about using appropriate technology. An excellent knowledge of practical broadcasting law is essential, as a wrongly worded script can lead to expensive legal action or a Radio Authority fine, or even jeopardise the licence.

Commercial production

Advertisements are an integral part of the broadcast output of an independent station. Larger companies will have internal and free-lance staff to work with advertisers, writing scripts and employing all the production skills and effects to create a satisfactory product within an often tight budget. Again, technical ability is an asset – in a very short space of airtime, the writer needs to be able to create a memorable mini-programme which will be repeatedly played-out on air, and therefore needs to be as near-perfect as possible.

The sales team

Revenue from the sales people will keep the station afloat and the staff paid. They are key members of the team, working closely with local advertisers to promote their products. Professional training ensures that the sales men and women are skilled in the specialised business of selling airtime. As well as the consistent ability to 'close the deal', they must be able to handle the associated administration, liaising closely with finance and with traffic departments. Most will have gained experience in other sales environments before joining a radio station.

Traffic controller/airtime controller

The commercial output of a station is known as the 'traffic', and the controller is responsible for monitoring the time, duration and position of all advertisements in order to invoice the advertiser and provide factual evidence that they 'got what they paid for'. Automatically generated transmission certificates help the administration of this important job, which requires strong analytical skills to make the best possible use of commercial airtime. As many advertisers live outside the transmission area, they require documented proof that they have received value for money.

Promotions and publicity

A large commercial station is likely to have at least one person totally concerned with publicising the station, often supported by a team of regular casual staff. They work closely with the sales team to raise public awareness and sponsorship for the output of their station. Attendance at local events, running roadshows, and doing as much as possible to gain local publicity requires a good knowledge of the audience – and a personality which allows you to be comfortable doing almost anything!

Engineering and technical support

In a large station, there will be a small team of multi-skilled 'engineers' who work on a shift system, doing routine mainte-nance and being capable of troubleshooting to help with almost any problem. Good IT skills are essential, but technical ability alone will not be sufficient. Stations look for a personality that fits in well with the rest of the team.

Finance and administration

Commercial radio is above all a business, and systems will be in place to handle all necessary administration. People who work in these areas have often gained qualifications in a more conventional environment, but have enough flexibility to thrive in the commer-cial environment of independent radio. AAT (Association of Accounting Technicians) qualifications are a recognised advantage.

Management

Although a minority of managers in independent radio have moved into the field from other industries, the vast majority have gained vast relevant practical experience either as programme controllers, news editors, or – increasingly – as sales or finance managers. The actual numbers of people employed by most commercial radio stations will come as a surprise to many readers. The average is about 30 staff 'on the payroll', although the largest station employs more than 100 people and many of the small 'satellite' stations run with a very small team. Most will also use freelancers and almost every station has a few unpaid work-experience students around.

Independent radio production companies

There is now a well-established independent radio production sector, which mirrors its independent television counterpart. Small – sometimes one-person – companies will develop an idea for a one-off programme, a series or a format (perhaps for a quiz or a game show) to sell to commissioning editors. Budgets tend to be quite low. Commercial radio also commissions some independent input. Although still quite small, the sector is proving to be a source of jobs for people at the start of their careers. Most of the opportunities are likely to be on a freelance or short-contract basis, although individuals with flexible and marketable skills may be in fairly regular employment. In a similar way to the independent TV, video and film sector, a small core team (usually producer/marketeer with administrative and finance support) will pitch for a programme slot, and will hire-in the necessary talent once the agreement has been made. Very occasionally, independents will make their own product, using a regular team, and then sell it as a complete entity to an independent or BBC station. Listen at the end of broadcasts, when an independent company will be given an on-air 'credit', and follow up any that you feel you could contribute to.

The freelance sector

There are many freelancers working throughout the radio industry, especially as journalists, presenters, scriptwriters, and adapters, but also in production and technical areas. To date, the BBC and large independents have offered a significant proportion of fixed-term contracts which may range from one day to one year. If you are planning to enter the radio industry in a programme-making area, you will be well advised to develop personal marketing and business skills. In Chapter 1, *Working in the TV, Radio, Film, Video and Interactive Media Industry*, there is a good description of the qualities required to be a successful freelancer. More information can be found at www.skillsformedia.com and via the *skillsformedia/learndirect* helpline: 08080 300 900.

Community radio

The UK community radio movement started in the early 1980s as a broadcast coalition of campaigners and academics, unlicensed stations, radio workshops and community activists. The Community Media Association (until recently known as the Community Radio Association) was founded in 1983. The aims of the CMA are straightforward – to establish and maintain a 'third sector' of UK radio which will be locally owned and controlled, and not run for private commercial gain (although some stations are quite desirable small businesses). It provides advice, information, training and consultancy to its members. Membership is open to any individual or organisation who supports the code of practice.

At the time of writing there are more than 100 community radio projects throughout the UK: 18 broadcast on a full-time and permanent basis, and the others broadcast during periods when they have been awarded a temporary, usually four-week licence. Although they are not run for private gain, the majority will hope to cover some of their costs through advertising, sponsorship or local grants. Community radio is an important gateway to employment, but there are very few paid jobs in community radio itself. The short-term radio services usually depend entirely on volunteers, though some do offer short-term contracts. Full-time community radio services generally have a core of paid staff usually in administrative, sales and management roles.

Unpaid volunteers

'It's a great way to gain experience – but there's a thin line between experience and exploitation,' says one industry spokesperson. Radio stations are used to unpaid volunteers, and a quarter of those currently working in the industry started their careers this way. If you decide to offer your services for free, be sure you have a clear and realistic idea of what you want to get out of the experience. The station is getting you for free. The least it can do is offer you some quality and concrete hands-on experience (and preferably, training) in return.

Getting into the radio industry

Who works in the radio industry?

The age profile of those working in radio indicates that it is an industry of the relatively young. Very few people, even in the BBC, are over 50 years old, and many are under 30. Women are very well represented in radio, with many senior BBC jobs occupied by high-profile female producers and presenters. In commercial radio, women are in the majority in newsrooms and advertising sales teams. People from ethnic minorities are gaining a higher profile, assisted by strong initiatives from the BBC, regular ethnic language broadcasts (e.g. Radio WM), and an increase in 'niche' stations. Community radio has a number of dedicated ethnic stations which play an important role in some parts of the country.

Making yourself marketable

As in all sectors of the audio-visual industry, there's a lot of competition. Every advertisement for production vacancies attracts stacks of applications from apparently well-qualified people. How can you improve your chances of reaching the shortlist?

There are four things that recruiters will be looking for when choosing an individual to join the team.

- Skills
- Experience
- Qualifications
- Personal qualities

All of the above must be relevant to the job in question. Obviously, then, you will need to find out more about your particular area of interest. If you long to become a sports presenter, read as much as you can about the work and then think about perhaps approaching a station or programme producer whose show you admire for advice. If you've done your research and are serious in your approach, you will usually get a useful response. Professionals can be quite willing to offer constructive advice, especially if you can show that you've done some proper groundwork and research first.

Once you've found out about the reality of the job – and probably how your contact got into her or his current position – then it's time to organise a game plan.

First, ask yourself the following question – and really think about it. 'If I'm to become a reasonable candidate, what am I going to have to add to my current CV?' Let's look at the different factors in turn:

Skills

As has been made clear, most jobs need multi-skilled people with good practical ability. Doing a course which will develop your studio skills, or volunteering to 'learn on the job' of hospital, campus, or community radio, will help. Other jobs – sales, for instance – require a proven aptitude to sell a product, so experience in media sales, retailing, fund-raising or telesales is an advantage.

Experience

Nowadays, candidates without at least a short period of relevant practical experience behind them are at a disadvantage. This is where students on vocational courses are sometimes in a better position, having at least had some exposure to, and experience of, the 'real' working environment of radio. Despite this, work in student, hospital, or community radio can go along way in helping get that first job. Over a quarter of all people working in radio today started as volunteers.

Qualifications

This is a difficult one. The best advice is probably to pursue your education to a point that you think best reflects your academic abilities. Vocational postgraduate degrees and diplomas (especially in journalism) are increasingly accepted as useful additional qualifications. In addition, many universities and colleges have thriving student radio stations (*see* www.studentradio.org.uk – student membership is £15 per year at the time of writing). Student radio could give you the opportunity to gain relevant skills and experience, whatever you decide to study. NVQs/SVQs are further useful indicators to employers about a candidate's ability to do a job. A comprehensive database of courses and information on NVQs/SVQs can be found at www.skillset.org.

But there are really no rules about the best academic qualifications to go for. The obvious 'media and communications' route will not necessarily be best for everyone. Choose a subject that you enjoy – one that will stretch you intellectually, in an environment where you will meet a wide range of people – and try to couple this with the opportunity to gain the practical radio skills that will help you most. Also, because the medium of radio is essentially a practical one, relevant Edexcel, SCOTVEC or City and Guilds qualifications are welcomed – and some colleges will have good contacts in local stations.

Personal qualities

In the end, being able to do the job – any job – will not be enough. Like other sectors covered in this book, radio is largely about working well in teams. Being flexible, a good communicator, and a hard worker with much stamina are all important personal traits in doing the job well. Talk to people in the industry and question yourself about the 'fit'. Are you really going to be happy working shifts at the weekends? Are you happy to work to sometimes ludicrously short deadlines, and under tremendous pressure? Question your motives for wanting to work in this industry – if for no other reason than to prepare yourself for what's ahead!

Presenting all the relevant information

Once you have decided *what* you want to market, the next stage is to decide *how*. You will certainly need a well-presented, concise CV (*see* Chapter 10, *Getting in and Getting on*) and may need other evidence of your ability – a tape, script or CD.

Applying for jobs in radio

In common with the rest of the media, many radio jobs are never advertised at all, and people get them through contacts, direct approaches, or often just by being there. A good work placement can end in a job or a reference which may take you into another organisation.

The jobs that are advertised can be found in:

- *The Guardian* (Mondays – www.MediaGuardian.co.uk)
- *Radio Magazine* (available on subscription)
- *Broadcast* (020 7505 8000)
- *Press Gazette* (for journalists)
- *Ariel* (the BBC in-house magazine – can be found in many careers offices, or on subscription from the BBC)
- Local newspapers
- The Internet

Some job adverts may find their way into job centres or local careers services offices.

To apply effectively for jobs in radio, think about what skills and experience you can offer, rather than presenting a huge list of all the interesting things that you have done. You will need a concise, targeted CV and a letter which catches the interest of the recruiter. Many advertisements ask for supporting evidence of your ability – tapes, scripts, etc. – so make sure you always have an up-to-date selection. 'Keep it short' is the best approach – nobody will listen to a 20-minute tape, however good it is.

If you want to use your skills in an administrative or business area, apply in the same way as you would for any job, emphasising your enthusiasm for, and knowledge of, the radio industry.

Finally, recruiters will all have their own agendas and 'person specifications', so the same application (whatever the job you're applying for) will not be suitable for different parts of the industry.

Find out about the specific skills required before putting an application together.

Training and education

Pre-entry training

There are several different methods of gaining relevant pre-entry training. Surprisingly, some very good programmes also attract funding, especially from the government, the European Social Fund (www.esfnews.org.uk) and Business Link, which offers advice to small businesses in the UK (www.businesslink.org). As mentioned before, it is important to focus on the type of work you are aiming for and then attempt to get appropriate training.

Higher Education

There are numerous courses, at locations throughout the UK, which offer a mix of academic theory and practical working experience. Some are excellent, but others are of dubious worth. In Chapter 9, *Training and Education for the Industry* you will find a useful checklist of questions to ask before you commit yourself.

Remember that although you will not get an individual grant, this type of course is highly subsidised for first-time students. Choosing the wrong course can prove very expensive.

If you want to become a journalist in radio, it is more straightforward. The BJTC (Broadcast Journalism Training Council) – a consortium of employers, educators and unions – recognises a wide range of courses to ensure that they have good-quality, appropriate course content. The vast majority of students on them will be completely self-funded. Many students will spend between £4000 and £10,000 on these courses, including their living expenses, often supported by career development loans or savings from other employment. Information on loans can be found at www.lifelonglearning.co.uk.

Some courses are corporate members of the Radio Academy, an organisation for professionals working in the radio industry (www.radioacademy.org). This can be useful, especially as their student membership offers the opportunity to compete for high-profile prizes and placements. It is also possible to join the Radio Academy as an individual student member.

Otherwise, choosing a course requires considerable personal effort – and often good exam results. It's worth spending time researching something that could affect your chances of finding a job in the industry.

Training offered by CSV Media

CSV Media is the largest independent media training agency in the UK. It develops and offers nationally validated training in a wide range of production skills, which can lead to *Skillset* Professional Qualifications, NVQ/SVQ, City and Guilds or Open College Network qualifications. Most courses include useful, hands-on experience in a 'live' media environment, such as radio (or TV) studios. Although much of CSV Media's training is offered to charities, voluntary groups and people who want to 'get their message across', they also provide training for people wanting to get into – or back into – work. All courses are free to participants, paid for by the European Social Fund. Some individuals may be eligible for additional financial help while doing the course. Contact your local CSV Media group to discuss your situation if you think you may be eligible for this. The training is open to individuals from all backgrounds who are unemployed (again, check with CSV for eligibility criteria). There is a stringent application procedure to ensure that those selected are really committed to learning about radio techniques (www.csv.org.uk).

Training offered by the Community Media Association

There is a great deal of formal and on-the-job training taking place in the community radio sector. At any time, local groups may be involved in running relevant training, at low cost, for interested people. Some places may be fully subsidised and free to un-employed candidates. Significant numbers of people from ethnic minority groups take part in community radio training – one of the few areas within the radio industry which positively encourages this.

The CMA itself offers training for radio trainers and managers, as well as support services for local-community radio-training projects. The CMA can put you in touch with the nearest local-community radio project or radio training course for information about what's on offer locally (www.commedia.org.uk).

Other commercial short courses

Look at the back of the *Media Guardian* on a Monday, and you cannot fail to notice the advertisements for commercial skills courses. Some are excellent and well worth the investment, which can be considerable. Others are less useful and some are merely capitalising on people's insatiable interest in the media. Check them out before you commit yourself and beware of 'promises' of jobs following the course. Be very thorough in your research and ask searching questions of training providers. If in doubt, look for another course. Each year, many disappointed people find that such courses do not wave a magic wand over their career prospects.

Gaining relevant qualifications

Many courses throughout the country enable you to study for nationally recognised qualifications such as City and Guilds or Edexcel, or NVQs/SVQs.

The *Skillset*/BFI book *Media and Multimedia 'Short Courses'* has short courses in these areas (available online via *Skillset*'s website); and the CD-Rom produced by the Radio Academy lists a huge number of them. However, mere listing does not imply accreditation or quality; be prepared to ask questions before you commit to any training.

BBC schemes

Periodically, the BBC invites applications from specific groups of people, offering a range of schemes and training initiatives such as BBC Talent. Watch the press, or the BBC web pages for information.

The Radio Academy

Student membership of the Radio Academy can provide an invaluable mix of industry information, contacts and practical experience. The annual conference gives an opportunity for industry hopefuls to attend debates and masterclasses.

The Student Radio Association

With a membership representing more than 70 stations in the UK, the SRA provides excellent opportunities for networking and skills development. It organises three conferences each year, and various training events. Key industry figures regularly contribute to SRA events too. The Association organises radio awards; prizes include prestigious work placements. Details are on the website at www.studentradio.org.uk.

The future

The future of radio in the UK looks positive. Digital technology will increase both quality and choice; the complementary text and data services that accompany such information may soon become part of our everyday lives. As with most technological advances, general take-up is very dependent on cost, but as car manufacturers start to incorporate digital receivers into their vehicles, the overall cost to the consumer is expected to reduce.

In career terms, the radio industry's expansion can only mean good news – especially for those people with a commitment to the medium and a strong, audience-focused business sense. Short-term contracts are likely to increase, with the numbers of self-employed freelancers rising.

Finding out more

The Radio Academy's excellent CD (produced in association with the CRCA), *Getting into Radio*, is available free to applicants. Introduced by John Peel, it provides a valuable collection of advice, suggestions, hints and tips from people who work throughout the radio industry. Work areas covered are:

- Engineering
- Production
- Sales and marketing
- Journalism
- Commercial production
- Presentation

This CD-Rom can be downloaded from the Radio Academy website www.radioacademy.org (search for 'skills and studies').

Very few books are published purely on radio, but we have found the following useful:

How to get into Radio – a useful description of how an ILR station operates, with tips on getting started in radio and gaining experience abroad. It has a useful glossary and contact list. ('How To' Books, Bernie Simmons)

Radio Presentation: Theory and Practice – a guide to presentational styles and radio show formats with tips and examples. Suitable for students and those training. An associated website provides case studies, links and contacts. (Focal Press, Tim Crook)

The Technique of Radio Production – written by a former BBC producer, this is an excellent, and not too technical, overview of radio production. (Focal Press, Robert McLeish)

Careers in TV and Radio – a good general introduction to working in the broadcasting industry, with case studies and advice from practitioners. (Kogan Page, Michael Selby)

The Radio Authority Pocketbook – full of useful background information about the radio industry and containing details of all licensed stations. Available from the Radio Authority – single copies free at the time of writing. Their website www.radioauthority.co.uk has other useful information and career factsheets that you can download.

Union representation

BECTU

The Broadcasting, Entertainment, Cinematograph and Theatre Union represents individuals throughout the industry. It publishes a regular journal, *Stage, Screen and Radio*. BECTU has a range of services designed to assist people intending to build a career in the industry. Membership provides opportunities to establish contacts in the industry and to gain up-to-date information from the journal. BECTU offers graduates full membership of the union for £30 at the time of writing, for the first year after graduation. Full details and application forms are available from:

BECTU
373–377 Clapham Road, London SW9 9BT
Tel: 020 7346 0900
Website: www.bectu.org.uk

NUJ

Many journalists and news and current affairs researchers in the radio industry belong to the National Union of Journalists, and most broadcasters have agreements with the NUJ.

NUJ
Headland House, 308–312 Grays Road, London WC1X 8DP
Tel: 020 7278 7916
Website: www.nuj.org.uk
Email: info@nuj.org.uk

Useful addresses

Commercial Radio Companies Association (CRCA)
The Radiocentre, 77 Shaftesbury Avenue, London W1D 5DU
Tel: 020 7306 2603
Website: www.crca.co.uk

The Radio Academy
5 Market Place, London W1W 8AE
(*The professional membership organisation for the radio industry*)
Tel: 020 7255 2010
Website: www.radioacademy.org

The Broadcast Journalism Training Council
The Secretary, BJTC, 18 Miller's Close, Rippingale, near Bourne, Lincolnshire PE10 0TH
Tel: 01178 440025
Website: www.bjtc.org.uk

The Radio Authority
Holbrook House, 14 Great Queen Street, London WC2B 5DG
(*Licenses and regulates all independent radio services*)
Tel: 020 7430 2724
Website: www.radioauthority.org.uk

CSV Media
237 Pentonville Road, London N1 9NJ
Tel: 020 7278 6601
Website: www.csv.org.uk

Community Media Association (CMA)
The Workstation, 15 Paternoster Row, Sheffield S1 2BX
Tel: 0114 2795 219
Website: www.commedia.org.uk

BBC Recruitment
PO Box 7000, London W1A 6GJ
Tel: 0870 333 1330
Website: www.bbc.co.uk/jobs

The Radio Magazine
Crown House, 25 High Street, Rothwell, Northants NN14 6AD
Tel: 01536 418558
Website: www.theradiomagazine.co.uk

Student Radio Association
c/o: The Radio Academy, 5 Market Place, London W1W 8AE
Website: www.studentradio.org.uk

Voice of the Listener and Viewer
101 Kings Drive, Gravesend, Kent DA12 5BQ
(*A non-profit making independent society representing the citizen's voice in broadcasting*)
Tel: 01474 352835
Website: www.vlv.org.uk

4

The Film Industry

Despite the industry's very high profile, production levels have been low in recent years, generally providing work for fewer than 2500 people at any time. However, it is estimated that up to 10,000 are available to work in film production when levels demand. In addition, the facilities sectors provide some services to the film industry, and around 16,000 people work in cinemas in the exhibitions sector.

Film-making is a risky business. Pleasing the critics and pulling in the crowds remains as much of a challenge as it has always been. Success depends on astute creative and commercial judgement. And a lot of luck.

The British film industry has done well in recent years, with some high-profile successes. There are at least 1000 more screens than there were a decade ago. Cinema admissions continue to increase (although some analysts feel that the market may be close to saturation point), as more screens are opened around the country. Seven times more people go to the cinema than visit combined performances of ballet, opera, theatre and dance. Watching feature films is the number one leisure activity for many people, especially in the 18–30 age range. Couple this with widespread interest (and investment) in technology – such as DVD for home use – and the opportunities presented by the Internet and global market, and the future looks bright for popular film-makers.

Technology is changing the industry. Digital equipment can certainly increase scope, and there is a school of thought which believes that costs can be reduced at almost every stage of production – although the reduced price of stock can result in higher post-production or editing costs. Increasingly, the Internet is used to create interest in, publicise and market productions. New exhibition venues and policies are being used to bring non-mainstream films to audiences, and specialist software is in constant use during feature-film production.

Until the 1980s, film production was 'an industry apart', with its own culture, traditions and working practices. There was very little movement between TV and film, although some directors and technicians worked on commercials and also within feature films. Today, the industries are much closer. Films made for TV play a significant role in the annual production record. High-end TV (especially drama) has almost always been shot on film. The current situation encourages a sharing of skills and experience, and many people now train and work 'cross-sectorally'.

Distribution – the key to making money out of a feature film – is also going through a period of change. There is increasing contact between film-makers, sales agents and cinemas. Pre-publicity on the Internet and the growing popularity of film festivals may help more British films to cross the significant hurdle provided by the mainly US-owned distributors.

It is important to understand something of the business of film – described in some detail later in this chapter – if you hope to build a career in this area. Many new entrants into this industry have a passion for film or their specialist field, like camera or sound, but have little interest in or knowledge of the challenges presented by management or accountancy. Many senior industry figures have emphasised the need for newcomers to direct their efforts towards the 'wealth creation' aspects of the industry. 'Far too many people want to be directors and designers,' said one. 'We need really good producers and financial managers.'

When you start to talk to industry professionals, the subject of money will soon emerge. Although the industry has done well in recent years, 2001 saw a significant fall in production spending down to just over £410 million, from a record high in 2000 with little change in 2002. The average feature-film budget can work out at between three and ten million pounds, so there are marked variations: the annual *BFI Handbook* will contain current information. Most British films do not get a wide release, or do not have large enough print and advertising budgets, and therefore have very little chance of making substantial profits. However, the maxim 'Budgets for markets' was emphasised by a spokesperson at PACT: almost any film can be profitable if you understand the audience and the finances. The continuing problem that faces British film is that 'many films which earn wonderful reviews, have great casts, good scripts and fine direction simply flop'. (Frustratingly, the opposite also sometimes occurs.)

One academic consulted during the research for this chapter gave an opinion that may be valuable to anyone considering a career in this competitive business. He said:

> '...It's important to understand that there is no such thing as the "film industry"... I think of it as an anthill made up of tiny cells. You need to find out about the different cells, make a home in one of interest, and then start to develop specialist skills... There's not a lot of cross-over.'

Although this is a personal opinion, there is a strong element of truth in it. Film is a collaborative process, but teams tend to be made up of people who are already known to one another.

Within this chapter we hope to give you some ideas to help you channel your talents towards contributing to the modern, increasingly global film industry.

Government support for the UK film industry

Current government policy for the industry has come largely from a report by the Film Policy Review Group, in 1998. This group of professionals from all sectors of the industry worked together to make recommendations on how to achieve an ambitious set of objectives: *to produce, distribute and exhibit more British films to bigger and more diverse audiences.*

The outcome of this collaboration between government and the creative industries has produced a series of interlocking proposals, which should benefit both audiences *and* the economy. Underlying the proposals – some of which are described later in this chapter – are several basic assumptions.

- Government and industry must continue to work together so that each party can 'lever up' the value of the other's contribution.
- Encouraging production will not *by itself* deliver the desired outcome. The market needs to be better capitalised, with broader-based companies which are able to integrate the processes of development, production and distribution.
- The only foundation for a secure future is a talented and skilled workforce, which requires cross-industry support for high-quality, ongoing skills development at all levels.
- The film industry is global. Success in the UK depends on a free-flow of investment and talent in every aspect of the business.
- Encouraging a more lively and popular UK cinema culture will foster an informed and critically engaged audience.

Out of this work by the Review Group came the creation of the Film Council, a body created by the government to 'develop and take forwards' a comprehensive, coherent strategy for the development of film culture and a sustainable film industry. The Film Council distributes National Lottery money to the industry. Scotland, Northern Ireland, and Wales also have national funds distributed through Scottish Screen, the Northern Ireland Film and Television Commission, and Sgrîn Wales respectively. The Film Council has two key objectives:

- To develop a sustainable UK film industry
- To develop film culture in the UK by improving access to, and education about, the moving image.

It also oversees the activities of the British Film Commission and all film production activities which previously were managed by the Arts Council of England – as well as routing funding to and overseeing the activities of the British Film Institute.

The Film Council is now entering the second stage of its work for the film industry that will focus on distribution, exhibition and increased support for skills development, in partnership with *Skillset.*

The British Film Institute (BFI)
The BFI continues to play an important role in the development of the UK film industry, and works alongside the Film Council. In

particular, it contributes to the growth of 'film literacy' among the general population. Its roles are many and various, and include:

- Running the National Film Theatre and supporting specialist cinemas nationwide
- Working closely with film societies to encourage knowledge
- Running the London Film Festival (in November each year)
- Supporting film festivals throughout the UK
- Running the IMAX Cinema on London's South Bank
- Managing and conserving the nation's film and video archives
- Selling clips from, and rights to, archive materials
- Publishing *Sight and Sound* and a range of specialist film books.

a businesslike approach

Film-making is an expensive and risky business: there are no guaranteed markets. Almost every year, a big-budget film will flop at the box office, and a low-budget feature will attract huge audiences. However, risk can be reduced. Distribution of a film is key to its potential success. For a film to gain distribution, the owners have to be reassured that it is likely to attract a reasonable audience. In the US, great emphasis is placed on market research and development. Making a film for a target audience is commonplace, and every aspect of the original idea may be adjusted on the basis of research statistics. In many ways, developing a film is done in the same way as developing any other fast-moving consumer 'goods'.

To date, this approach has held little appeal for many UK film-makers (although, interestingly, a number of very successful directors have emerged from the advertising industry), and the quest for funding relies chiefly on the attraction of 'great ideas and creative teams'. The Film Council production funds are now working to improve this by requiring a more rigorous approach to the industry, and the importance of distribution, from the film-makers they support.

In order to persuade distributors to support British films, a raft of evidence needs to be gathered about potential audience appeal. These statistics will also form the basis of any marketing and publicity campaign. The Film Council has been established to support film-makers in all aspects of business development, working in partnership with Scottish Screen, the Northern Ireland Film Commission and Sgrîn.

The workforce

The UK has a great record of producing talented film professionals. The future success of the industry depends on nurturing new talent, and ensuring that the problems of skills shortages in particular work areas are tackled positively.

The production sector uses a majority of freelance staff, who with few exceptions have always been responsible for their own training and development. This has created an unbalanced labour market – overloaded in some areas (e.g. directing) and under-supplied in other, less obvious areas of film-making. The results of this imbalance can create some interesting variations on the payroll of a production, with some crafts people being able to virtually 'name their price'. It's hard to be precise about skills shortages in any area: the most recent ones reported in film include set crafts skills (e.g. scenic painting and carpentry); special effects technicians, including animatronics; and production accountants. However, this information is subject to change, and the most up-to-date information can be found through *Skillset* (www.skillset.org) which, as already mentioned, is working with the Film Council to identify and address areas of skills shortages, and to develop a strategy for dealing with them. Findings will be available during 2003.

The Film Policy Review Group identified a number of key areas for priority in training; *Skillset* has worked to fulfil those needs, and now supports the training for crafts people and production accountants for the industry. In addition, Health & Safety training and the delivery of NVQs are in place, backed by SIF – the Skills Investment Fund – whose work is detailed later in this chapter (*see* pp. 147–9). Finally, the Film Council is addressing two other key priority areas:

- Training for scriptwriters, script editors and development executives
- Training for producers/business executives/distributors.

The sum of one million pounds from the Department for Culture, Media and Sport (DCMS) each year for three years has been allocated by the Film Council to support training in both these areas.

The industry under review

The Film Council, *Skillset*, Scottish Screen, the Northern Ireland Film Commission (NIFC) and Sgrîn are currently working together to conduct research that will review current training and vocational education policy and provision in film, and will identify future needs for the industry in terms of skills, training and vocational education provision and infrastructure. This work will build on the results of the Film Policy Review and Action Group in 1998 (*see* pp. 122–3) and will be instrumental in developing the joint strategy for the next stage of support and investment in training and vocational education by the Film Council and *Skillset*.

The research element of this project will focus on collecting qualitative, as opposed to quantitative, data. However, to ensure that a thorough long-term skills strategy is developed through this work – one that can be constantly reviewed and revised – *Skillset* and the Film Council Research Statistics Unit will also be working in parallel to this project to explore suitable quantitative methodologies for surveying the film industry workforce. It is intended that this will result in a regular survey of employment trends and training and vocational education needs, enabling the film industry to have a skills strategy that is responsive to changing demands and priorities.

Making a feature film

The original idea for a feature film may come from a writer, director or producer. After initial discussions, a short outline will be produced in the hope of attracting positive attention from possible investors. In the US, most of the money that goes into film production will come – directly or indirectly – from distributors, thereby improving the long-term chances of exhibition to a paying audience. As detailed later in this chapter, the UK experience is much more variable. If the idea attracts enough attention, the process of film-making will start... but it may also stop at almost any time. It's not a business for the fainthearted or those without good problem-solving skills!

A treatment will then be produced, which is a fairly complex document (usually 5–25 pages long) containing a detailed story-line, ideas about cast members and locations, and an indication of the proposed 'look' of the film. The 'core team' – e.g. Production

Designer, Producer, Director, Director of Photography – would be described in this document, along with information about financial management input.

If potential investors are interested, they may agree to put up 'seedcorn' money to develop a package of information about the proposed project. This is likely to contain further details of:

- The Director and Producer (including their CVs)
- Stars and leading actors
- Proposed special effects
- Genre/relationship with other films
- Themes/storyline
- Soundtrack/music
- Target audience, and – crucially – outline budgets and timescales.

Sometimes a film 'packager' will put together all these ingredients and then, at an early stage, appoint a highly skilled 'line producer' to manage every aspect of the process.

At this stage, money may be secured for development of the script. This may involve several drafts and several writers. Research and information will influence the Script Editor, who will attempt to ensure that the storytelling will be attractive to a defined target audience.

Further finance may be agreed – from a variety of sources, including public funding and financiers from outside the UK. Public subsidies, usually in the form of grants through the Film Council, Scottish Screen, the Northern Ireland Film Commission, or Sgrîn Wales, may be applied for and awarded. Other, private investors – including members of the public and co-producers – provide financial support for many productions. City institutions will often produce glossy brochures which will be sent to potential investors inviting contributions. Occasionally, an entire film may be supported by private investment.

Any film which raises finance through a bank, co-production deals, or public funding will require a completion bond (a legal agreement, detailing what the Producer has agreed to deliver, with dates and budgets) with tough penalties for overspend or overrun. It is rare for principal photography to start before the bond is in place.

Outside the US studio system (where as few as one in 20 projects will be converted from the development stage), development of the initial script has been a neglected area for many film-makers. However, there is increasing support and funding now available to encourage a concentration of effort on this critical area. The Film Council's Development Fund has £5 million a year for three years to allocate to the development of scripts.

Most investment comes with strings attached; very few sources of finance will give their money for nothing. Film-makers may agree to give up potentially lucrative rights at this stage, and banks may insist on 'structured' loans, which organise payback at high interest rates. Such measures reduce the chance of profitability, even if the film is a box office success.

Once the production budget and schedule are written and agreed, the film-making can start in earnest. The Producer and Director work together to build a 'wish list' of actors, technicians and support staff. The 'top team' is hired; other members of the cast and crew are approached to ensure availability, and may be hired before the budget is fully financed. This stage is called, 'pre-production' ('prep'). Negotiations take place to agree payment and contractual terms for cast and crew members. Freelancers, who will comprise 98% of the workers on a film in production, are formally hired. Locations are selected and fees are negotiated: sets are designed and built, costumes designed and made, bought or borrowed, and props are agreed. All of this provides a great deal of work for the Line Producer and his or her team, and requires specialist input from lawyers and other experts. Time and effort spent at this stage increases the chances of a smooth-running production which sticks to schedule and budget, and which provides communication routes to ensure that the financiers are properly informed of progress.

Production, in the accepted sense, can now begin. The film unit is assembled and filming begins, according to the daily non-linear schedules. The day's work is processed overnight, and rushes are viewed: on a good day these rushes may eventually provide five minutes of the finished film, but it's usually considerably less. All members of the team need to work well together, or the schedule will be disrupted and the budget will slip. The main publicity process starts at this time, too. Still photographs are taken, press releases produced, and journalists invited to report on the production in order to whet the appetite of the target audience. During this period, there is a tremendous amount of organisational and administrative work. Daily reports on progress (for shooting) and weekly expenditure reports will be produced for the funders and the Producer.

Post-production usually starts when the bulk of the photography has been completed, although increasingly, this is happening sooner or simultaneously on bigger productions. Editing of sound and vision takes place, and a 'working print' is assembled which will include special effects. This is screened to industry contacts (especially distributors, if the film has not yet gained an agreement in this critical area). Feedback is taken very seriously at this stage. Music – which may be specially composed – is put against the rough-cut working print, and the 'fine cut' edit begins. The soundtrack – including dubbing and effects – will be added once the picture is 'locked'.

Once the fine cut starts to emerge, a marketing strategy is developed to publicise the film, and the relevant people or organisations contacted. When the fine cut is approved, the first press and 'focus group' screenings will take place; there is still scope for final changes following critical feedback. The finished film is then submitted to the censor for classification. If there is no pre-agreed distribution, the Producer will initiate active 'selling' of the film, trying to persuade a distribution company to accept the finished product. If the film does have pre-agreed distribution and merchandising, the advertising and marketing campaign will be launched. Depending on budgets this may include a diversity of 'above- and below-the-line' projects and events (*see* pp. 142–3).

Once distribution is agreed, prints of the finished film will be made (at considerable expense) in response to the breadth of agreed distribution. Some films will not gain cinema release, but will immediately be put on to video for the rental market. Many low-budget films designed primarily for the art-house circuits may have only 6–10 prints, compared with the hundreds produced for blockbusters.

The film will be released to cinemas after press previews. Some UK films will gain first release in the US. The finished film may be entered in international film festivals, and may gain an overseas release. Video/DVD copies are made and distributed for sale and rental. Longer term, the producers and/or rights owners will negotiate for satellite, cable, TV, video and DVD sales. Unsurprisingly, the entire process may take years, and cost a great deal of money. The vast majority of independently financed films will have a 'completion guarantee' or bond with tough penalties for overspend or overrun.

The finances

Production accountants are very important members of a film-making team, working closely with the Producer or Line Producer. It is their responsibility to ensure that all financial aspects are managed professionally. Money rules many aspects of film-making: if there is low or no investment, the film is unlikely to get made at all – although there are some examples of very successful films being made on very small budgets. Young film-makers will usually fund their own shorts, taking them around or showcasing them in festivals or on the Internet – hoping to inspire enough confidence to persuade financial backers to give them a chance on a feature film.

Sadly, many UK films never get distribution, forever denying their producers and backers the chance to benefit from box office sales. Even the lucky ones that do get a general showing may find that, due to tight pre-distribution deals, very little of the profit goes to the film-makers.

Understanding the money side of film is key to success in this industry. First films may be made to very tight budgets, but subsequent projects (sometimes supported by US money) have often got into problems. A classic film industry book which charts the downfall of Goldcrest Films – *My Indecision is Final* – documents the all-too-familiar problems of financial mismanagement. In the US, most studios are very closely aligned with a distributor, who will provide funding from the pre-production research and development stages, knowing that they should at least get back their investment through large takings at cinema box-offices. (It doesn't always go to plan, however.) In the UK, a series of government and industry initiatives, including the setting up of the Film Council, is starting to help develop the future business to work in a more similar way to the US model. There is little doubt that future, public funding of projects is likely to be on the basis of thorough market research and an increased emphasis on high-quality development. Public support may also help to ensure that home-grown films are professionally marketed, and that the rights are exploited in a way that will benefit the UK.

New technology also has the potential to reduce costs dramatically. Digital movie cameras, computer editing and special effects which minimise the need for expensive locations or large casts are now increasingly being used.

a taxing problem

Accountants and tax specialists explore all options to reduce the tax bill on feature films, and play an increasingly important part in the production team. Decisions about where and when to make a film (for example, Ireland has offered substantial tax breaks for several years, attracting productions from all over the world), who to employ, and who to consider as co-producers, can make a huge difference to the viability of a film. Specialists can advise producers to help them make the best decisions.

Selling on

Film packages are also made 'with an eye on the small screen', in the knowledge that they are likely to be shown on a diversity of television channels. Negotiating the long-term rights, and agreeing the financial arrangements for continuing exploitation of a feature film, is becoming even more important as the number of channels grows. Similarly, long-term revenue may come in from video/DVD sales and rentals, and associated merchandise. The lifespan of such merchandise is usually quite short, and deals have to be arranged quickly if the owners of the rights are to make maximum profit.

Making a film – the movement of money

UK film production budgets are almost always substantially lower than those of the big studios in the US (although there are also a lot of very low-budget US independent films). However, UK film budgets are still increasingly likely to run into millions of pounds. Getting the money together, and then managing it properly in order to make a profit, requires both commitment and expertise.

Before the production, the initial funding or investment may come from a variety of sources.

- *Distributors* – these may 'buy' the film before it is made, thus covering all production costs in return for the right to show the finished product – although this is more common in the US.

- *A diversity of investors* – City institutions, banks, companies, broadcasters and individual people may all provide money. Often, there is a rich mixture of investors. This form of investment generally requires some kind of payback, ranging from an Executive Producer credit to the ownership of potentially lucrative rights.
- *Loans and co-productions* – film-makers may benefit from favourable loan terms (perhaps organised through the MEDIA Plus programme – *see* pp. 88 and 135), or increase the money available for production by joining forces with another nationality. This can be a complex process but it can be worth it and productions can benefit.

With the source(s) of funding arranged, the budgets will need to be finalised and agreed. The detail of each budget will obviously vary, but the finances of most films will usually look something like this:

Production costs	60%
(Cast and crew, sets, locations, equipment, costumes, etc.)	
Key personnel costs	15%
(Stars, Director, Writer, Director of Photography, Producer)	
Overheads	12%
(Production company costs, studio rental, etc.)	
Other artists	5%
(Extras, musicians, etc.)	
Legal, financial and other professional costs	4%
Other general expenses	4%

Expenditure is divided into two categories: 'above-the-line' (ABC) – for example fees for key personnel; and 'below-the-line' (BC) – changeable items such as film stock, equipment hire, hotel and travel expenses. All costs are agreed prior to shooting and the budget is 'locked' with the expectation of reported variances against both ABC and BC.

Films that have not arranged distribution prior to production will inevitably try to cut down on these costs. UK films are very seldom 'star vehicles', for instance, and corners are often cut in other areas to save money. Although this may in some cases produce memorable positive effects, it may also be generally counterproductive, when matched against the preferences of the bulk of the cinema-going public.

Once the film is complete, a new tranche of money is required to fund the marketing and advertising campaign. Attracting the broad potential audience can eat up a lot of money, and many films sink into obscurity because their public profile has not been sufficiently established due to an insufficient print and advertising budget.

Sometimes it's all worthwhile

If all the hard work has the desired effect, it is possible to make a lot of money from feature films. Sources of revenue include:

- Cinema box office sales
- Video/DVD sales
- Video/DVD rentals
- Licensing and merchandising
- UK terrestrial TV
- Pay-TV channels
- International sales

Producers and financial investors may have arranged profit shares, which pay back over a period of many years. Although it can take a long time for a film to reach 'break-even', there is a revenue threshold beyond which it can become very profitable.

Getting the money together

A major factor behind the current growth in domestic feature-film production is the injection of new finance, now managed and distributed through the new Film Council and the relevant national organisations – Scottish Screen, Sgrîn, and the Northern Ireland Film and Television Commission. The Film Council has £27 million in National Lottery funds available each year, broken down as follows:

- The Film Development Fund: £5 million a year, to 'support the development of a stream of high-quality, innovative and commercially attractive screenplays'.
- The Premiere Fund: £10 million a year, to 'facilitate the production of popular mainstream British films'.

- The New Cinema Fund: £5 million a year, to 'back radical and innovative film-makers, most especially new talent, and to explore new electronic production technologies'.

The Film Council is also responsible for three Lottery-funded film franchise companies. (These were set up by the Arts Council of England in 1996–7 to provide three commercial film-franchises modelled on the lines of Hollywood 'mini-studios'. The aim was to finance a range of UK films, rather than just individual projects, with the intention of building centres of excellence and knowledge. Traditionally, the British film industry had been characterised by production companies being established for one film and then disbanded.) Three franchise-winners were announced at the 1997 Cannes Film Festival, each of which holds its franchise for six years:

- DNA Pictures (£29 million)
- Pathé Pictures (£33 million)
- The Film Consortium (£33.5 million)

It is expected that the franchises will produce 90 or more British qualifying films during their six-year 'tenure'.

The annual BFI handbook lists all the National Lottery awards as a proportion of the total budget. Reading this can give considerable insight into the type of film that is likely to attract National Lottery funding.

Funding for short and low-budget films

There is a surprising amount of money around to support film-makers at the start of their careers. Most aspiring film-makers will get advice about local initiatives and funding possibilities through their Regional Screen Agencies. In London, responsibility is divided between the London Film and Video Development Agency (LFVDA) and the London Production Fund. Other sources include:

- The broadcasters
- www.filmcouncil.org.uk/shorts
- British Council (help with festivals, etc.)
- Local initiatives, e.g. The Glasgow Film Fund
- Local Authority Arts Departments

There is also a diversity of European sources of finance – especially for co-productions and films which will offer work and training in areas requiring urban regeneration. MEDIA Plus supports projects associated with training, development and distribution. CARTOON provides a range of assistance for animated film in Europe – *see* also page 167.

Applying for public funding

Funding in the regions and nations
Through its Regional Investment Fund (RIFE), the Film Council invests £6 million into regional film activities. RIFE funds are available across the English regions, through its nine Regional Partnerships; while the aforementioned Scottish Screen, Sgrîn in Wales, and the Northern Ireland Film and Television Commission administer public funds in those nations.

The aim of these partnerships is 'to provide a variety of resources aimed at developing public access to and education about film'. The funds available will include:

- Production funding
- Exhibition development funding
- Education projects funding
- Archive development funds
- Training and development funds
- Funds for audience development

Guidelines for applying
We spoke to the London Film and Video Development Agency, and asked their advice about how to apply for public funding. The agency records approximately 600 applications each year from people looking for financial assistance with development, production and completion of film. Only about 3% are selected for funding. To improve your chances of getting on this, or similar, shortlists, here are some hints:

- Potential backers will look for reassurance, and a track record of 'delivering'.
- Applications have to be professional: 'There is a big difference

between telling a story and writing a treatment.' Make sure you provide what is asked for.

- Read the notes – and follow the instructions on the application form. Many people ignore this critical aspect. Remember that the work has to be 'do-able' within time and budget.
- Team applications can work best, with members balancing each other's strengths and weaknesses.
- Find out what 'drives' different funders. For example, the National Lottery likes to hear about creativity and audience appeal; the European Regional Development Fund needs information about the economic sustainability of your project and the contribution it will make to your region. Don't use the same words and phrases on each application.
- Always bear in mind that the chance of raising money for a film correlates with how well and how concisely you can tell the story.

Before you apply for funding, *get advice* – and understand the level of competition. Early funding is often easier to access in areas outside London. Remember that wanting to make a film is not enough – think about the audience.

Getting development money

As has been mentioned earlier in this chapter, development funding is available. But if you are planning to apply for development funding, be realistic about your proposed product: 'budgets for markets' is a good maxim. Even a very modest film can produce a healthy profit if money has not been spent on unnecessary extras. A development budget may include:

- Office overheads
- Expenses (travel, etc.)
- Research (researcher fees, archive and library expenses, interviewee expenses)
- Pilot costs (hire of equipment, stock, crew, edit)
- Fees for scriptwriters and script editors (finding good writers is not easy; to increase your chances of funding, it is wise to concentrate on this critical area)

Other sources of finance

If you really want to make your film, and feel that it could be a commercial or critical success, do not be deterred if you are unable to gain funding from public sources. Independent, or 'indie', films tend to fall into four general budget categories – though of course, many films cost amounts that fall between them:

- Microbudget – under £5000
- Small – between £5000 and £10,000
- Medium – between £80,000 and £100,000
- Funded – between £2 million and £4 million

'Obvious' sources of money include: bank loans; venture capital investment; splitting costs with other productions; gaining investment from distributors (very unlikely); and pre-sales (this used to be very unlikely, but the Internet is changing things). Less obvious sources include: credit management to gain time between production and payment dates (friends with large credit limits); and borrowing from friends and family (increasingly common) to make a trailer that can be marketed to attract investors.

If you are looking at any of these options, remember that for everyone that makes a fortune in film, there are many who lose their entire investment – and sometimes, even their property.

Other funding initiatives

NESTA – the National Endowment for Science, Technology and the Arts – is another government initiative which aims to encourage entrepreneurship and support talented individuals. It will be particularly interested in helping to turn ideas into 'bankable, employment-generating businesses', which may be of particular interest to young production companies. The Film Council is also working with NESTA to 'nurture individual creativity in film'.

NESTA
Fishmongers Chambers, 110 Upper Thames Street,
London ECAR 3TW
Tel: 020 7645 9500
Website: www.nesta.org.uk

And of course, public funding isn't the only way. City institutions (and some of their wealthy clients) are now more inclined to get involved in supporting film production in the UK, thanks to a favourable tax write-off regime. Producers who understand how to communicate with the City will be at an increasing advantage.

Other sources of funding

- The broadcasters (especially the BBC and Channel 4, which both have a public service remit)
- Local Authority arts sections
- Commercial sponsors
- Charitable foundations and trusts

Applying for funding – a summary

Although some sources of funding will have specific political agendas (which you will need to understand), the majority are faced with hard decisions about which projects to support and which to reject. To improve your chances, it is essential that you know – *before* you start to complete an application form – what the organisation is looking for. This information is usually freely available in published literature, but talking to people closely associated with the specific organisation will be invaluable in helping you to get the emphasis right. Many applicants fall at the first hurdle because they make a poor, unresearched application.

Your aim is to reassure the potential funders that you won't let them down, and hopefully, that your work will contribute to their own credibility and success – as well as pleasing their funders and supporters. Here are some tips from one of the awarding bodies:

- Complete every section of the form, providing information in an easy-to-read format.
- Follow the rules. If you are asked for a maximum of 100 words about your project, *do not* write 120 – you will be penalised.
- Get the figures right. Too many applicants give general budget outlines which cannot be justified. Others forget about VAT, etc.
- Only provide information that is relevant to the application.
- Have a clear vision of your audience, researched if possible.
- Keep supporting materials (showreel, storyboards, scripts, etc.) to a manageable minimum.
- Never submit precious original materials.

Also, more generally:

- Provide evidence to reassure the funders that your project is achievable within the budget and schedule.
- Many funders are looking for a diversity of cultural and artistic voices – something out of the mainstream, but practical and achievable.
- Film-making is a collaborative process, so team applications are often more successful than individual ones. Many new directors would benefit from linking with an experienced producer.

Film Council applications can be downloaded from their website, www.filmcouncil.org.uk. Their other contact details can be found on page 293.

The creative challenge

Some film-makers have achieved success without any early funding. 'Microbudget' films are now commonplace; technological developments can be used to cut costs (for instance, by using digital video cameras). Financial support for completion, marketing and distribution may then come from a variety of sources. *The Guerilla Film Makers' Handbook* (*see* page 154) provides some useful ideas and case histories.

Distribution is the key

It doesn't matter how 'good' a film is: if it doesn't get distributed either theatrically or on TV, then the bulk of the potential audience will never get to see it. Many producers and directors have watched their film doing really well on the 'art-house' circuit without it ever moving towards profitability.

Marketing is essential, if the potential audience is to be made aware of a film's existence. 'Positioning' a film – attracting specific audiences – requires considerable skill, especially since communicating effectively with 18–25 year olds is very different from communicating with, say, 35 year olds. The same film may be 'packaged' differently for a range of potential audiences to attract the maximum number of viewers. For example, compare the content of adverts for the same film in *The Guardian* and *The Sun* to identify differences in the 'message'.

Big-budget films allow for a 'build-up' to create interest before a film is released – sometimes months in advance. Most British films do not have this luxury, though, due to a lack of dedicated budgets and access to experienced film marketeers. Word-of-mouth recommendation is essential to build an audience for lower budget productions: a combination of good reviews, confirmatory word-of-mouth feedback (the two do not always go together), and a nomination or award can take the place of a substantial marketing budget.

Access to the Internet has created new opportunities for filmmakers to publicise their work, bypassing the traditional routes favoured by the Hollywood studios. *The Blair Witch Project* led the way by producing huge box-office profits, following pre-release publicity on a quirky website. Undoubtedly, web technology has opened doors for many new films, although quality-control aspects may deter the less motivated browser from fully exploiting this medium.

Launch times occupy a great deal of thought. Some British films are now released in the US before being shown to the home market: this can be a risky strategy, but the potential size of the US audience, combined with the power of the media, can help to build a film's reputation before it is released in the UK and in Europe.

Box-office takings provide the most visible source of revenue. To see a large number of people part with their own money to view your film is immensely satisfying – but it's not easy money. The first week is crucial for most films. Takings will then start to tail off, and attracting a substantial audience for more than two or three weeks is unusual (unless of course the film wins, or is nominated for, a high-profile award).

When a film is in development and production, it is essentially a 'prototype' which can be altered relatively easily. Once made, it is a product which has to be sold to the widest range of potential purchasers. Effective distribution is the key to this. If the film already has agreed distribution, and the distributors are satisfied that the filmmakers have achieved their brief, the distribution process will begin.

The distribution process

- The film 'goes on to the books' of a distributor.
- A decision is taken about the number of 'prints' for release.
- The timing of release is agreed, together with the geographic distribution.

- Trailers are made, publicity materials developed, and advertising booked.
- Local and national promotional events and partnerships are arranged.
- The prints are delivered to the right place, at the right time.

For each distribution project, a range of skilled individuals will contribute their expertise as follows:

- 'Selling' the film to cinemas – persuading the management to give the film an early showing
- Ordering the optimum number of (expensive) prints, and then physically producing high-quality prints for distribution – a process known as print production.

When a distributor agrees to take on a film, a budget will be agreed that reflects the expected profitability of the film. This is not always easy to predict, with many different factors coming into play:

- US box-office takings (if relevant)
- Relevant income from cinemas in the UK
- Audience research findings
- Appeal of some or all of the cast
- Appeal of the crew (especially the Director)
- Level of certification
- Timing of the release
- Number of prints available (usually between 60 and 300), and the distributor's experience

All of the above are likely to affect profitability. Broadly speaking, to make a profit, the film has to bring in at least two-and-a-half times the production cost.

Some of the above factors are especially critical, and are expanded on below.

Audience research – this is becoming increasingly important. Before a film is released nationally, the distributors are likely to 'test the product' with different audiences. In addition to preview screenings there are often sophisticated focus groups. Reviews are also taken into consideration, but may be ignored if the market research is positive. Negative feedback may affect the breadth of distribution, or even result in the film being released directly on to video without a cinema showing.

Cast and crew – some stars will 'guarantee' an audience, whatever the film. In the US particularly, a 'star name' may replace an inspirationally cast actor because the distributors are unwilling to risk the outcome of their investment. There have been cases of British films being given additional financial support from the US, on the condition that the main character be played by a high-profile actor. Similarly, some directors will bring a solid – if fairly predictable – audience with them, especially if they remain within a successful genre.

Classification – the distributor submits the 'finished' film for classification (i.e. what level of certificate it will get for viewing, such as PG or 15) and pays for it to be assessed. The outcome (too high? too low?) can limit the potential audience and will certainly influence the marketing and advertising strategy.

Timing of release – for some films this is very obvious (e.g. children's films are generally released during school holidays), but others require more careful calculation to assess the competition at that time, or the potential for good weather ...

The importance of pre-publicity

However many factors may affect the outcome, one thing at least is certain: pre-publicity is critical to the success of most films. Big productions will have a dedicated 'P+A' (Print and Advertising) budget, which for large-scale films is usually about 40% of the estimated box-office income. This sort of money is very difficult to raise for films without a 'known' cast or crew. Many exhibitors (cinemas) book and schedule films months in advance – usually before the film is complete. They rely on a 'publicity machine' to raise audience interest. This is achieved by applying a variety of marketing techniques.

- Above-the-line – real money is spent on advertising in a range of media, and also on promotional materials, posters and cinema 'trailers'.

- Below-the-line – the publicists try to raise audience interest through interviews, press, editorial, promotional activities, etc.

above-the-line

The key to effective advertising and publicity is deciding who the target audience is. Placing attractive adverts in appropriate media takes considerable expertise, with research statistics and consumer reports 'crunched' to improve targeting. The Internet is also an important tool used in communicating with the target audience, and local independent radio provides a valuable vehicle for mainstream films.

Posters – surprisingly, these are still seen as a primary communication medium. Displayed inside and outside cinemas, and often on billboards and in various public places, they are very effective in attracting regular cinema-goers. (A dedicated website for the latest release, always plainly visible on each poster, ensures that the Internet is used to its full potential in the marketing strategy.) Design and text are both very important in pulling in the mass audience. Some films which start on the 'art house' circuit and later move to the mainstream – usually by winning a prestigious award – often have to revise their poster design substantially so as not to alienate those mainstream sections of the population.

Trailers – like them or loathe them, trailers do work. Short 'tasters' of between 45 and 60 seconds may be produced to whet an audience's appetite months before a film is released. The tasters may be followed by a 2–3 minute trailer some six weeks before the film is due to be screened. An art form in themselves, they are carefully made to provide appeal to the widest possible range of potential viewers.

Below-the-line

Free publicity – this is sought from a variety of sources. Readers tend to believe editorial content more than advertising copy. Press kits will be sent to journalists; some will be electronic, moving-image versions. 'Star interviews' and appearances will be negotiated to try and raise the film's profile with the target audience. Some films may be given high-profile 'premieres'. Positive 'word-of-mouth' publicity can be encouraged, for example through offers of free screenings printed in the relevant listings magazines.

Merchandising – this is also increasing in importance, but getting it right is not easy. Deciding on suitable (and profitable) linked products requires lots of research and often complex negotiations with manufacturers. Timing is crucial, as are other factors such as distribution, packaging and stock control.

Exhibiting a film

Multiplexes and multiscreen cinemas

The point of contact between a new feature film and its audience is almost always the cinema. Investment in the development of out-of-town multiplexes, and the refurbishment of city-centre venues has encouraged increasing numbers of people to visit, and to pay to watch a film. More screens should mean more opportunities for British shorts and feature films to gain exhibition – but it's not a straightforward equation. The large multiplexes are usually located close to other leisure facilities and their aim is to provide a broad-based entertainment, especially for families who will visit in groups and spend money on a range of facilities. Specialist films may be incorporated into the screening schedule at times when the bulk audience may not be so available – such as late at night. This will usually reduce the potential audience and thus the box-office takings. However, some cinema complexes are now proactively building a reputation for showing films that would normally be confined to the art-house circuit, and it is hoped that this trend will continue.

To attract a more specialist, often older audience, the cinemas are having first to market themselves, and then to deliver a good experience to encourage future visits. Cinema or venue management requires strong organisational and motivational skills to ensure that every visit is enjoyable.

'Indie' and art-house cinemas

These venues – which are not owned by the major distributors – offer a very different programme of films, usually to a relatively loyal but smaller audience. The cinemas may be supported by public subsidy, or owned by interested individuals. This allows for a much freer programming policy, which can in turn provide opportunities for many British film-makers. Features or even shorts that do well on this circuit may gain further exhibition in the mainstream. Independent cinemas often offer 'added value' by having a membership, or providing additional experiences in the form of cafés, bookshops and masterclasses. Some are very successful, but few make a substantial profit.

Regardless of venue, film bookers schedule the films into the calendar (although in the case of smaller 'indies', the manager may do this as part of his or her general job description). Persuaded to screen a film by the distributor or producer, they will decide on the best time of day and year to attract a profitable audience. This requires considerable judgement, and a real knowledge of the local population.

Young people spend the most money in cinemas: 16–23 year olds have been identified as being particularly 'profitable', buying 'add-ons' such as popcorn and soft drinks from cinema concessions. The older, more educated (and theoretically more affluent) section of the population will often only buy tickets.

What happens to the money, once taken, depends on the agreed deal. On average, owners of cinemas keep approximately 60% of the box-office takings.

What are the jobs?

Watch the credits at the end of a feature film, and you'll get an idea of the size of crew required by a major production. Many of the jobs are only found in film, or in high-budget TV drama. Some are obvious, and everyone is familiar with them – but there are many, many positions that most new entrants into the industry are unaware of. Aiming for a less publicised job, especially in an area of skills shortage, can sometimes hugely improve your chances of regular, well-paid freelance employment.

Below is a selection of job titles, to get you thinking. On a feature film, there are often more than 100 different jobs; on a £2 million or £3 million film there may be as many as 150 people employed. This number will rise to more than 500 for a major 'James Bond' type of production. Many of these jobs are described in Chapter 1, *Working in the TV, Radio, Film, Video and Interactive Media Industry*. Very specialist areas of employment can be researched in books about the film industry, or by talking to industry practitioners. A full list of *Skillset's* job profiles which list in detail jobs in film (and all other sectors of the audio-visual industries) can be viewed at www.skillset.org.

Rigger	Scaffolder
Stagehand	Location Manager
Make-up Designer	Prosthetics Designer
Production Accountant	Publicity Assistant
Props Master/Mistress	Special Effects Trainee/Assistant
Wardrobe Assistant	Production Buyer
Script Supervisor	Scenic Artist
Sound Assistant	Director of Photography
Line Producer	Librarian
Publicity Assistant	Special Effects Supervisor
Props Woman/Man	Standby Props
Set Dresser	Model Maker
Rostrum Camera	Sound Technician

Rates of pay vary hugely, reflecting supply and demand.

Working in commercials

Commercials are really 'mini feature films'. Lasting anything from 10 seconds to two-and-a-half minutes, they tell a story with a beginning, middle and end, using a variety of techniques to get a specific message across. Often made with proportionately high budgets, they have a reputation for using specialist techniques and effects, and can provide a valuable training ground for would-be feature-film-makers.

However, it's important to remember that the 'production story' of a commercial is different from that of a film. The initial 'driver' comes from a client (marketing) need, rather than the idea of a writer or director. The client selects an advertising agency which is responsible for coming up with ideas and outline scripts for presentation. A huge amount of time is spent on research and development to maximise the chance of success in targeting and influencing a defined audience, before the project moves into production.

At this stage, a production crew is hired to bring the agreed storyboards to life. Getting experience with such a team has proved invaluable to many aspiring directors, but it is far from easy. Because a great deal of money is involved (above-the-line in terms of budget, and below-the-line in terms of the continuing client relationship), great care is taken to select a production team that will 'deliver' in a client-focused way. As a result, many agencies tend to have longstanding 'favourite' freelancers who are used regularly. Establishing credibility with, and being useful to one of these regular contributors is essential for anyone hoping to gain relevant work experience in this area.

Investing in British film talent – the Skills Investment Fund

The Skills Investment Fund (SIF) was launched in October 1999 to be part of the coherent policy for training in the UK film industry, and to ensure that a professional pool of film-making talent is available to the industry – both the home-grown productions and the often larger-budget international productions that are wholly or partly made in the UK.

The SIF is made up of contributions from all productions due for theatrical release that are based in the UK or in receipt of UK public funding. Productions based in the UK are asked to, and those with public funding are required to, contribute 0.5% of the total production budget up to a maximum of £39,500. The SIF is managed by *Skillset* on behalf of the industry and monitored by DCMS. Key partners in this work include the industry union BECTU, the independent producers association PACT and the Motion Picture Association (MPA). The SIF also has the support of some key industry organisations that have agreed to ensure that the SIF contribution is a line in the budgets for all the films in which they invest.

The money raised through the SIF is then re-invested into training provision and assessment. It is currently charged with addressing the industry-identified priorities (listed below), alongside £1m per year that is allocated to the Film Council by the Department for Culture, Media and Sport to address the training of scriptwriters and development personnel and to equip producers, directors and business executives with appropriate skills training. *Current SIF achievements include*:

new entrants in craft, technical and production grades
The SIF has invested over £500,000 into established new-entrant training provision – schemes like FT2 and the new-entrants

training course at Scottish Screen. These schemes offer structured entry into the industry over a period of 18 months or two years, comprising placements on production and short courses.

Health & Safety

Skillset's Freelance Training Fund and the Skills Investment Fund have joined together to launch a competitive bursary scheme to subsidise the cost of Health & Safety training for freelancers. This support for the industry through Health & Safety bursaries is essential to help reduce the risks inherent in film-making. Additionally, insurance premiums can be high unless the team is well qualified in this area.

Developing skills of production accountants

This area was highlighted as a priority for the industry because of the shortage of suitably experienced or qualified production accountants who can 'cross the divide' between the financiers and the creative team and provide the right figures at the right time – both for home-grown films, and for large-budget films that are wholly or partly made in the UK.

There have been significant developments in this area, and *Skillset* has worked predominantly with the Production Guild of Great Britain to address this priority. Firstly, to ensure a widening of access into the grade by the establishment of the Assistant Production Accountant Training Scheme. In parallel, the Production Guild has also launched subsidised short courses in payroll, accounting, cost reporting, legal and financial compliance, personnel and media business management for freelance accountants and assistants.

Qualifying the industry

Skillset Professional Qualifications can provide a real indication of a person's skills and competence – which is vital for people working in this industry who need to put together 'instant teams'. Funding to enable new entrants to gain their *Skillset* Professional Qualification is an intrinsic part of all the structured schemes supported.

In addition, funds have also been allocated to enable free registration and assessment for 350 freelance lighting electricians, supervisors and grips in partnership with ASPEC (Association of

Studio and Production Equipment Companies); for Riggers in association with CITB (Construction Industry Training Board); and for Editors through the FT2 assessment centre.

Film Council Training Fund

The Film Council has allocated £1 million a year to support training. The main aim of the Training Fund is to work with partners to maintain and develop the skills base of the film industry.

In its first three years of operation the Fund will support training in two key areas:

- Script writers and development executives
- Business executives, primarily producers and distributors.

The fund will focus particularly on training in project development, marketing, business and entrepreneurial skills, and raising the level of awareness of the international marketplace. It also runs a bursary scheme, which offers bursaries of up to £500 to support individuals on short courses – mostly in the areas of scriptwriting, editing, and producing – taking place outside the UK.

For information on these or other specific schemes you have heard of, please contact the Training Fund Administrator on 020 7861 7894 or check the Film Council website, www.filmcouncil.org.uk.

Education for film-makers

If you are aiming to become a director, producer or writer, then you are probably considering investing in a film school course. Do your research: there are hundreds of courses around, of very variable quality and cost. According to one industry advisor, the market is 'flooded' with people from general media studies courses. Postgraduate-level film courses are generally better respected, building on skills and knowledge gained from an academic or art degree. However, some of these courses are *very* expensive. Refer to the checklist in Chapter 9, *Training and Education for the Industry* (*see* pp. 219–21) to get an idea of the questions to ask before committing yourself to a specific course. You can also call the *skillsformedia* free helpline on 08080 300 900, and speak to a specialist media careers advisor.

Establishing yourself in the film industry

Here are some 'insider tips' to help you establish yourself in the film industry.

Make yourself indispensable

Film is a very small world. People move jobs through contacts, and gaining a positive reputation is essential if you hope to build a career in this industry. The first jobs – however humble – are critical. Many senior people started as runners, and established their reputation as professionals from very early on. One production executive advised, 'Make yourself totally indispensable.' Ensure that people will notice if you're not there for a day. This means doing much more than the minimum, anticipating and solving problems before anyone else notices that they have occurred. Check that the kitchen is always immaculate, that the photocopier never runs out, and that difficult people find you helpful; this can be of far more use to your career development potential than any number of postgraduate qualifications.

Be flexible – and reliable

Placing yourself in a good position to take advantage of career opportunities is essential, and can present serious difficulties for people who cannot be very flexible. You may be asked to travel away from home, even abroad at short notice, and most contracts are for long six-day weeks – this will prevent you from taking on regular commitments, even at weekends. People with family responsibilities or health restrictions often find that the demands are very high. Even maintaining a long-term relationship can be difficult. Filming days start very early, so one of the first career decisions is about how good you are at getting up!

Work experience

Chapter 9 includes some useful pointers for getting work experience. The best advice is to research any placement as thoroughly as if you were going on a training course. Be sure that you're going to get what you want out of it.

An element of maturity

Many people feel that new entrants need quite a lot of 'life skills' and experience if they are to survive some aspects of the film industry. Although good teamwork is essential, not everyone will be interested in nurturing and supporting an inexperienced individual. 'You will get shouted at, and you have to be able to weather it and not shout back,' said one producer. Expectations of reliability, capability and general 'worldly wisdom' are also quite high.

Here is some advice from another source. There are three rules in this business:

1. Never risk your own money on a feature film.
2. Choose the people with whom you work with care.
3. Never forget the importance of luck in this business.

Managing your film

There are a number of useful workshops – usually lasting one day – held at locations throughout the country. Often heavily subsidised, they can offer a range of practical insights into the 'dos and don'ts' of successful film-making.

Here is an example programme:

- *The Business of Film* – sources of finance, business plans, cash-flows.
- *Production Insurance* – understanding this complex and potentially expensive area.
- *Arranging Locations* – making arrangements, help and advice from the British Film Commission and their network of offices throughout the UK.
- *Legal Issues* – how they affect production, finance, distribution and long-term rights.
- *Short Film Distribution and Exhibition* – UK and global.

The appropriate National or Regional Screen Agency will have details about similar events in your area.

An example of career progression in the film industry

Many short film-makers have dismal careers fraught with uncertainty and lack of finance – but some do climb towards the summit of a very broad-based pyramid. Everyone agrees that there are far too many short film-makers, but everyone also knows that a minority will succeed both in critical and financial terms. Here is an example of a lucky (and talented) one.

> The film is well received and 'opens the door' for additional regional funding, perhaps from European regeneration subsidies. Another short film is made, again with friends
>
> ↓
>
> Decides (reluctantly) to move to London and apply for a mix of funds (e.g. London Production Fund, National Lottery – some teams are awarded up to £60,000 for a 10–15 minute film). This time the Director links with an experienced Producer
>
> ↓
>
> The film attracts a broadcast funder (e.g. Film Four Lab) which commissions a short (10–11 minute) film with quite a large (£80,000+) budget. (This is often used as a 'test bed' to observe how a producer and director manage the project, before risking a feature film budget. Any team that wins such funding has a proven record of managing schedules and finances)
>
> ↓
>
> All works well, and a feature film commission of more than £1,000,000 is forthcoming

And that, for many people, is sadly the end of the story. However difficult it is to get this far – and the drop-out along the progression route is massive – it is still *much* easier to get funding for the first feature film than the second... unless the first is a real box-office success.

The majority of aspiring film-makers will drop out

Every year, thousands of people – some of whom have invested heavily in the hope of a film-making career – will decide to take their skills and creativity into a more predictable arena. For many, the big question is how long they can manage without a regular income. Individuals or teams that never get any public funding, despite numerous applications, usually drop out – as do others who have had one or more injections of public funding, but have never made the leap into features. Although many young film-makers fund their own first films, several industry practitioners have said that continuing to provide private funding (if that is even a possibility) is not a good idea. Within the minds of many, gaining public or commercial funding gives a director or producer a 'stamp of credibility'.

Festivals

There are more than 1000 film festivals each year: a list of these can be found at www.screendaily.com. There is a film festival almost every week, somewhere in the world; most will have a theme, but some will be very general. Festivals can be great showcases for short films. Talent scouts, buyers and programmers for other festivals attend a diversity of events and certainly do not just concentrate on the larger, high-profile markets.

Find out as much as you can about any festival which appears attractive. Although their ostensible aim is always to celebrate the art of film-making, increasingly there are commercial 'sub-agendas'... local businesses, restaurants and hotels may be the real drivers (and beneficiaries) of an event. Each year, the Cannes Film Festival – at the top of the profitability tree – generates more than £50 million for the town and its neighbours.

Finding out more

Useful film books

A wonderful source of books about the film industry is:

The Cinema Bookshop
13/14 Great Russell Street, London WC1B 3NH
Tel: 020 7637 0206

The following is a selection of relevant and useful books on film. Many of these books are available in the BFI library, or in colleges that offer film courses. If you wish to buy a specific title, most booksellers will order on your behalf. The Internet is a valuable source of information on new and second-hand books.

Getting into Films and Television
www.getintofilm.com
Robert Angell: How to Books Ltd. ISBN 1857037715

Directory of International Film and Video Festivals
British Council
www.britishcouncil.org
(*Useful film category index. The British Council supports approximately 50 festivals each year.*)

Film Festival Guide
Adam Langer: Chicago Review Press Inc.
ISBN 1556524153
(*Worldwide guide – how to submit, etc.*)

First Facts
First Film Foundation
www.firstfilm.co.uk

Making a Winning Short
Henry Holt & Co. Inc. NY: Edmond Levy ISBN 0-8050-2680-0
(*How to write, direct, edit and produce a short film*)

The Complete Film Production Handbook
Eve Light Honthaner: Focal Press ISBN 0-240-80236-5
(*American and computer disk. Lots of forms, contracts, deal memos etc. Fantastic checklists*)

The Guerrilla Film Makers Handbook, also on CD-rom
Chris Jones and Genevieve Jolliffe: Cassell
ISBN 0826447139
www.livingspirit.com

The Guerrilla Film Makers Movie Blueprint
(a diary of the UK film-making process – coming soon)

Arts Funding Guide
Anne-Marie Doulton
(*Directory of social change: fundraising, contacts*)

The Art of the Deal
Dorothy Viljoen: PACT
www.pact.co.uk
(*Latest edition covers the Internet, new media, and digital channels*)

Directory of International Film and Video Festivals
British Council
(*Biennial*)

The Film Marketing Handbook
John Durie: BFI/British Media School

The Production Handbook
Diane Freeman: PACT

Production Management for Film and Video
Richard Gates: Focal Press

Useful film directories
Film and Television Yearbook
British Film Institute, 21 Stephen St, London W1P 1PL
Tel: 020 7255 1444

Kays – Video, Film and Television Yearbook
Kays Publishing Co., Pinewood Studios, Pinewood Road, Iver
Heath, Bucks SLO ONH
Tel: 020 8749 1214 or 01753 651171

Kemps International Film, TV and Video Yearbook
Reed Information Services Ltd, Windsor Court, East Grinstead
House, East Grinstead, West Sussex RH19 1XA
Tel: 01342 326972

The Knowledge
Riverbank House, Angel Lane, Tonbridge, Kent TN9 1SN
Tel: 01732 362666

Screen International Film & TV Directory
Emap Media Information, 33–39 Bowling Green Lane,
London EC1 ODA
Tel: 020 7837 1212

Variety International Film Guide
Variety, 34–35 Newman Street, London WIP 3PD
Tel: 020 7637 3663
(*Note*: Directories tend to be very expensive, and are available in
specialist reference libraries.)

Useful film magazines and journals
American Cinematographer www.theasc.com
American Film Magazine www.afi.com
British Cinematographer (01753 650101)
BFM-Black Filmmaker www.blackfilmmakermagazine.com
Broadcast www.emap.com
Cahiers du Cinema (Paris)
Cineaction! (Toronto)
Cineaste www.cineaste.com
Cinefex www.cinefex.com
Creation www.creationmag.com
DVD Monthly (01392 434477) www.ukonline.net/dvd
Empire www.empire.online.co.uk
Film Comment (USA) www.filmlinc.com
Film Quarterly (USA) www.ucpress.edu
Films in Review (USA)
The Hollywood Reporter www.holiwoodreporter.com
Independent Film & Video Monthly www.aivf.org
Journal of Popular Film and Television (USA) www.heldref.org
Jump Cut www.ejumpcut.org
Moving Pictures Magazine www.filmfestivals.com
PACT Magazine www.pact.co.uk
PCR, Production and Casting Report www.pcrnewsletter.com
Magazine Positif (France) www.jmplace.com
Premiere (USA) www.premiere.com
Screen Digest www.screendigest.com
Screen International www.emap.com
Sight and Sound (BFI) (www.bfi.org.uk)

The Spotlight (casting directory) www.spotlightcd.com
Stage, Screen and Radio BECTU.org.uk
Starburst (www.visimag.com) – sci-fi movies
Total Film www.totalfilmco.uk
Variety (newspaper) (UK) www.variety.com
Velvet Light Trap (Wisconsin, USA) (www.utexas.edu)
Wide Angle (USA quarterly) www.press.jhu.edu/press/journals

Your Regional Screen Agency should have information about titles available locally.

Many local organisations also produce useful newsletters (your RSA will have details) and some specialist professional organisations produce regular updates, for example *Media Law*, or *Accountancy Age*.

Useful film websites

www.screendaily.com – website of Screen International
www.imdb.com – the Internet Movie Database
www.shootingpeople.org – network for UK indies. A Q&A facility can provide advice from film professionals
www.explodingcinema.org – exploding cinema site... a coalition of film-makers with advice on getting low/no budget films made and shown
www.britfilmcom.co.uk – the British Film Commission site. Technical, location and facilities advice
www.cinemagine.com – working film-makers pass on knowledge and tips, and recommend books, etc.
www.brightlightsfilm.com (USA – black orientated film reviews)
www.frameworkonline.com (Journal of Cinema & Media – focus on International Cinema)

Specialist film industry organisations

There are numerous organisations associated with the industry. These are some of the national players. For local contacts, speak to people at your Regional Screen Agency.

The Production Guild (of Great Britain)

Lynne Hames, Pinewood Studios, Iver Heath, Bucks SL0 0NH
Tel: 01753 651767
Website: www.productionguild.com

The British Film Institute
21 Stephen Street, London W1T 1LN
Tel: 020 7255 1444
Website: www.bfi.org.uk

The Cine Guilds of Great Britain
72 Pembroke Road, London W8 6NX
Tel/Fax: 020 7602 8319
Website: www.cineguildgb@btinternet.com

British Academy of Film & Television Arts (BAFTA)
195 Piccadilly, London W1J 9LN
Tel: 020 7734 0022
Website: www.bafta.org

Film Council
10 Little Portland Street, London W1W 7JG
Tel: 020 7861 7861
Website: www.filmcouncil.org.uk

First Film Foundation
9 Bourlet Close, London W1W 7BP
Tel: 020 7580 2111
Website: www.firstfilm.co.uk
(*A charity which exists to help new British writers/producers and directors based in the UK and Ireland to make their first film. Offers impartial, practical advice and several programmes for training and development, detailed elsewhere*)

New Producers Alliance
9 Bourlet Close, London W1W 7BP
Tel: 020 7580 2480
Website: www.npa.org.uk
(*A membership organisation for independent new directors, producers and scriptwriters which produces a useful directory of members and relevant suppliers – e.g. specialist lawyers, equipment hire, film guarantors, insurance brokers. It also offers training*)

PACT
45 Mortimer Street, London W1W 8HJ
Tel: 020 7331 6000
Website: www.pact.co.uk
249 West George Street, Glasgow G2 4QE
Tel: 0141 222 4880
(*The Producers Alliance for Cinema and Television represents independent television, feature film, animation and interactive media production companies*)

London Film & Video Development Agency
114 Whitfield Street, London W1T 5EF
Tel: 020 7383 7755
Website: www.lfvda.demon.co.uk

NESTA
Fishmongers Chambers, 110 Upper Thames Street,
London EC4R 3TW
Tel: 020 7645 9538
Website: www.nesta.org.uk

The Northern Ireland Film and Television Commission
3rd Floor, Alfred House, 21 Alfred Street, Belfast BT2 8ED
Tel: 02890 232444
Website: www.nifc.co.uk

Sgrîn – Media Agency for Wales
The Bank, 10 Mount Stuart Square, Cardiff Bay, Cardiff CF10 5EE
Tel: 02920 333300
Website: www.sgrin.co.uk (in Welsh & English)

Scottish Screen
2nd Floor, 249 West George Street, Glasgow G2 4QE
Tel: 0141 302 1700
Website: www.scottishscreen.com

The London Film Commission Database carries a huge amount of information to help producers planning to make a film in Greater London. Details of crew, facilities, local services and locations are all available. If you have appropriate skills to be considered as a runner, or a more experienced crew member, contact them for an application form. Once accepted, the LFC will send your CV to potential employers when requested for certain crew. The forms are available on the website www.london-film.co.uk. The service is impartial and free of charge. Tel: 020 7387 8787 for details.

Note: At the time of writing, the London Film Commission is about to become part of the new Regional Agency of London – Film London. Other regional and national screen commissions also operate in the same way. Contact your local Regional or National Screen Agency for details.

Watch this space

- The British Film Institute is planning a re-vamped National Film Theatre, which will include extended screen facilities, exhibition space, a library, a café and a bar.
- There are a number of employment registers, which charge the individual for being listed, and then approach employers to market their skills. Be very careful before you commit yourself to this sort of financial 'investment' in your future.

The Animation Sector

Animation is a small but growing sector, employing around 2000 people – half of them on a freelance basis. Unlike some other sectors, animation has a number of distinct and highly successful centres of excellence outside of London. This means that high-quality, sector-specific training and education is also available in these areas.

We're all familiar with animation, and increasing numbers of people are considering making a career in this internationally respected, multi-million-pound sector. Courses proliferate – and yet the industry still reports a shortage of 'good' candidates who can move comfortably from an academic environment into the working world. Within this chapter, we hope to provide a general introduction to the demands and requirements of this exciting sector.

Animation – whether produced by the traditional drawn (or 'cel') method, with models, or through sophisticated computer systems – is a very costly, labour-intensive business. In today's world of budgets and accountants, persuading anyone to invest very large sums of money takes enormous effort. A half-hour of TV animation may cost well in excess of £500,000 – animation series will cost between £5000 and £10,000 per minute at least – and a programme will take between nine months and two years to make. Compare this with the spend on most network TV (even top quality drama), and you may begin to understand that the skills required by the industry are a mixture of creative talent and sound business acumen.

However, animation can have many advantages over more commonplace TV and film productions. From pre-school to prime-time mainstream, the popularity of the genre with viewers is increasing. Animation 'travels well' and can be marketed globally. It has a long shelf-life, dating far less quickly than its competitors. In fact, some animation features (think of *The Snowman*, *Wallace & Gromit* and *Chicken Run*) become almost instant 'classics' which can be repeated to an appreciative audience over and over again. New audiences can be attracted from a new generation. If an animation production company can 'get it right', the long-term results can be outstanding. But there is enormous risk.

Technological developments, combined with the increasing need of broadcasters to 'fill space' in this multichannel age, have encouraged a new breed of animators to challenge some of the old ways. A new wave of 'adult' animation, which may be as dependent on clever scripting or music as on visual characterisation, has reduced costs – but has also exposed a lack of good writers. After years of only using films of standard length, commissioning editors and schedulers in broadcast companies are starting to be more flexible in their approach to investment (including co-production), and are including short (usually 6–10 minute) features within their schedules. The reason for this is that animation can be very popular, and the ratings attracted can more than justify such decisions. All the big companies employ commissioning editors who specialise in the genre. If only production costs could be reduced, we would certainly see more animation on our screens. Flash animation software, however, is now significantly cheaper and an increasingly used method of digitally drawn animation, which is allowing productions to be commissioned to broadcast standard with lower budgets. Also, more recently, one of the big employers of people leaving college with animation skills, is the computer games industry.

A broad-based genre

The UK industry leads the way in creative and artistic talent in this sector and yet, currently, less than 5% of animation on our television screens originated in the UK. In addition, key players are often headhunted to work abroad, or tempted away by the favourable tax systems in some other countries. For financial reasons, production is sometimes contracted out to other countries, particularly the Far East, Spain, Eastern Europe and, more recently, India.

The industry produces a diversity of animated products, including:

- Commercials
- Music promotion videos
- Children's programmes (usually divided into pre-school and 5–12 years)
- Feature films
- Adult comedy
- Adult series
- Adult drama
- Games
- Multimedia

The mix of genius and technology to be found in the UK has gelled to establish a commercially successful industry whose overseas sales are net contributors to the national economy. The government is keen to encourage further development.

Different types of animation

Animation can be divided into several distinct areas. From childhood days, most of us have a general idea about traditional, handdrawn *'cel' animation*, with every movement and facial expression painstakingly drawn and then transferred onto clear cellulose for filming or digital finishing. Between 12 and 25 drawings will be consumed every second, and as many as 20,000 drawings may be required for a half-hour episode. However, as the genre (and its audience) develops, cel animation is responding with a diversity of new approaches. The 'squash and stretch' of some well-loved cartoon characters has been joined by simple line-drawn characters, or beautiful pastel drawings. There are also techniques such as painting on glass. It is an area which embraces innovation.

Another approach is the *clay animation* made famous by Aardman's *Wallace and Gromit*, and 3D model animation such as that from Cosgrove Hall and HIT entertainment. Again, painstaking attention to detail is required, together with lots of people-power, to make the characters 'come to life'. In order to produce realistic expressions, the animator must be able to 'get inside' the character, using a mirror to study his or her own expressions, and rehearsing movements, just as an actor would. We heard of one person who spent several days minutely moving whiskers as their contribution to lifelike facial expressions ...

Computer animation, or CGI, is taking on a high profile at present, with increasingly sophisticated software demonstrated at every industry event. Again, it can be very expensive and time-consuming – the feature film *Antz* used 400 state-of-the-art computers – but computers are, as yet, not as good as humans at producing believable facial expressions. The challenges are enormous. Think, for instance, about a smile... as the mouth turns up, all the facial muscles are affected, and especially those around the eyes – a huge amount of detail needs to go into each frame to achieve a realistic result.

But techniques are developing very fast, allowing for effects (such as very large crowd scenes) that would not have been possible a short while ago. 'Motion sequencers' allow a series of static characters to be 'blended' from – say – a walk to a run, or to cope with obstacles on a computer screen. There are huge opportunities in this area for individuals with a mix of creativity and computer skills. This digital technology is also used in live action feature films like *Titanic* and *Gladiator*, enabling the film-makers to reproduce scenes and animate them. Another example of animation and this technology in action was the BBC production *Walking with Dinosaurs*.

Many new productions are now taking advantage of opportunities to mix cel or model animation with computer-generated additions and combining all forms of animation with live action.

What are the jobs?

A surprising number of people are employed, in a diversity of capacities, within the modern animation industry. Far from the solitary existence of 'one man and a drawing-board' that many people may expect, there is an increasing emphasis on teamwork and multi-tasking. As production lead-times decrease, and budgets have to be managed, it is cost-effective if people can move between several projects at any one time. There are still plenty of people who do work almost alone – traditional animation often requires long hours of concentration, which are difficult to find in a busy studio. Graduates often find the transition from college to a commercial environment very difficult.

Recruiters in this sector often comment on the limited knowledge exhibited by many applicants about the diversity of work available within many animation companies. Some jobs are hugely oversubscribed, and others are very difficult to fill. When you are reading up on the subject, or talking to practitioners at industry events or during a period of work experience, ask about the range of work available.

The following are some job titles found in this sector, a selection of which (underlined) are detailed within the *Skillset* job profiles in Chapter 1 (*see* pp. 11–43):

Animation Director	Key Animator
<u>Animator</u>	Layout Artist
<u>Animation Assistant</u>	Model Maker
Background Painter	Special Effects Animator
Compositor	Storyboard Artist
In-Betweener	3D Renderer

A comprehensive description of all jobs in animation can be found in the *Skillset* job profiles at <u>www.skillset.org</u> (*see* under 'Careers').

The business of animation

The show is just beginning... the industry is tremendously positive about the potential for the genre. International ventures are becoming commonplace – often to take advantage of tax benefits or funding from, say, the European Union. In addition to the obvious money for production, and the potential for long-term earnings (one advantage of animation is that there are no 'star' expenses or repeat fees, except perhaps for voice-overs) in a multi-channel environment, animation has a range of 'added value' activities. For example:

International Sales – animation 'travels well', and can lend itself to dubbing into different languages.

Licensing and Marketing – characters can become sought-after 'brands' and used to sell a vast array of directly or indirectly related products such as toys, clothes and books which produce money for the animation company through licensing agreements. In some instances, the production may be driven by the marketeers; it is not unknown for a successful series to evolve from a commercially inspired base.

Videos and DVDs – the children's market, in particular, lends itself to video reproduction. Sales, rental or archive material (sometimes specially modified for video) can produce huge revenues.

Compilations – the material can be 'reworked' and used in a different way, producing additional income.

Finance is crucial

Due to a shortage of funding, money is an issue which dominates the industry – unless you are commissioned by an agency to make a commercial or corporate production that works on a bidding system. Some very successful producers are also qualified accountants. It's very rare to gain full funding from one source, and a 'jigsaw' of investors generally has to be built before a production can go ahead. Short (and therefore relatively cheap) films are difficult to sell, although the Internet has provided a welcome new market for short and experimental animated pieces. Half-hour films sell well, but are very expensive to make. And the 13- or 26-week series favoured by many overseas buyers can be prohibitively expensive. Anyone who can solve this problem will be fêted by the industry!

Disney has dominated the feature-film end of the market for many years, but is now facing competition. Other major studios including Universal, Fox, Warner Bros and Dreamworks are increasingly interested in the potential of animation. Aardman (of *Wallace and Gromit* fame) produced their first full-length feature – *Chicken Run* – in 2000. An Academy Award for animated features was introduced in 2002 – Dreamworks won the first ever Oscar in this category for *Shrek* – and with these incentives other studios are joining the market. With budgets of at least £40 million, the marketplace is unlikely to become crowded for some time, but it is worth pointing out that box-office returns for films such as *Toy Story* and *Shrek* more than compensate for the initial investment!

However, it wouldn't be fair to say that there isn't money around – and it is always worth finding out about funding available through the National Lottery for animated feature films. There is also increased interest from European producers to make these kinds of productions.

European support
CARTOON: the European Association of Animated Film
Boulevard Lambermont 418, 1030 Brussels, Belgium
Provides financial assistance for development, studio grouping and training, and also 'seedcorn' money for a number of young animators to help produce pilot videos.

The marketplace
Animation festivals are held throughout the year, at locations around the world. They provide an international showcase for films, and a wonderful opportunity for industry recognition, publicity and 'networking'. Details of both are published in the trade press, and also in the *Animation UK* Directory (a BECTU publication). *See* also http://www.awn.com on the Internet: The Animation World Network.

Centres of excellence
Looking through a variety of industry directories, you will notice that animation companies are distributed throughout the UK. However, distinct 'clusters' appear around six established centres of excellence:

* London
* Bristol
* Manchester
* Cardiff
* Edinburgh
* Glasgow

According to the old phrase, 'Nothing succeeds like success,' new companies have moved into these areas to build on the established expertise available. These 'cluster' groups consist of a variety of animation companies as well as set builders, prop makers and scenic artists to support them. Training and education courses have also developed in these areas.

Getting the business

Most of the money spent on animation in the UK is associated with the advertising industry. Huge budgets may be allocated for a 30-second commercial. Inevitably, there is serious competition for commissions, and art directors are constantly approached by animators wishing to publicise their work. The Internet is used increasingly as an accessible showcase for the work of different companies and individuals. Pitching for a broadcast slot is, in many ways, even more difficult. Not only does the animator have to attract the Commissioning Editor; he or she also has to understand the business context of expected ratings, budgets and so on. Professional teams work together to present a coherent argument to the decision-makers.

And, as mentioned before, it's rare to get 100% funding for a project. A pitch to commissioners may result in a promise which will only materialise once the film is made. Getting the business requires sophisticated marketing, negotiation and decision-making skills. It's easier to attract commissions in some areas than others. The UK leads the world in the production of pre-school storytelling and design, and its reputation will continue to attract investors; other areas are growing steadily. There are currently more than 300 companies in the UK producing a tremendous variety of work, including:

- Films
- Series
- Games
- Shorts
- Commercials
- Titles
- 'Idents'
- CD-Roms (especially for educational purposes)
- Pop promos
- Corporate production
- The Internet

Making an animated film

Broadcast regularly produces special supplements featuring industry areas. An animation special contained several articles, including one on the making of an animated series which has been successfully shown on BBC TV. Here is a brief overview of the stages described which involved using a mix of traditional cel and computer techniques.

- Original story idea, based around a central character, sold to BBC Worldwide and an international distribution company which provided production finance.
- Script developed (this is a process that can take a great deal of time – the script will be re-worked many times over before and during the production).
- Animators developed the characters and backgrounds to fit the 'feel' of the production. (This is, inevitably, a slow process, involving much consultation.)
- Actors chosen for the voice of each character.
- Animators produced work in line with storyboards/time plans.
- Soundtrack recorded in 'sound dead' booth.
- Detailed design check on drawings for international target markets (there are specialists who advise on this).
- Continuing research to ensure that background looked OK.
- *Storyreel or Animatic* – where panels of the storyboards are scanned into a computer to give a 'rough cut' of the show.
- After a number of adjustments, the detailed animation built to produce moving colour footage with voices.
- 'Final' draft viewed, frame by frame.
- List of retakes made, to be shot and dropped in later.
- Final film edited to required length.
- Sound mixed.
- Final post-production.

No wonder it costs so much! A large team of people worked on this. It's a challenge to produce a continuous style 'as if one hand had drawn everything'.

Training and education

College courses

There are numerous relevant courses running throughout the UK
– although some leading industry figures have strong feelings
about the quality of many of them. If you are considering investing
time and money in a course, be sure to ask tough questions, and
find out about its reputation with the sort of employers you may
wish to attract. The questions listed in Chapter 9, *Training and
Education for the Industry* are useful guidelines. Courses are
detailed in the BFI Publication, *Media Courses UK*. And you can
also call the *skillsformedia/learndirect* helpline on 08080 300 900
for information.

Many full-time courses have very general titles, such as:

- BA (Hons) Animation
- BTEC HND in Media and Animation
- Animation

However, these will all differ in content. By contrast, some may
appear very specific but actually have a very similar content to the
above:

- Illustration with Animation
- Graphic Arts (Animation)
- Animation and Multimedia

Read the prospectus, visit, talk to current students and *ask
questions before you decide*. 2D and Model Animation usually
require a long (three- or four-year) course heavily based on life
drawing and observation. Relevant computer-based animation
training is increasingly dependent on 'industry standard'
technology, as well as on tutors who understand about the
business and not just the computers. It is becoming increasingly
popular for animators to 'learn the techniques' during a full-length
art or film-school course, and then top up these skills with an
industry-based course – usually self-funded. Postgraduate
Animation courses are also available across the UK.

Short courses

The *Skillset*/BFI handbook, *Media and Multimedia* lists an array of course titles, aimed at both the newcomer and the more experienced. These courses all vary in price. Some may be free to the local unwaged; others may costs hundreds of pounds. A few may attract subsidies for freelancers from the *Skillset* Investment Funds.

The same advice applies: find out if the course will deliver what you need. Sometimes it is a better investment to take out a career development loan for a highly regarded course, than only to go for the one that you can afford yourself.

Training

Training – on or off the job – is at the top of the agenda for many industry specialists. Recruiting and developing people who can apply a mix of craft, technical, interpersonal and, increasingly, business skills is a difficult task. As a result, some of the UK's leading companies have become directly involved in the provision of relevant, practical training.

The Bristol Animation Course is a good example of this. Run by the University of the West of England, the course is supported by a group of industry specialists who teach on the course and also provide supervised work experience. The aim is to develop 'talented but raw' animators, who have 'some experience and a lot of motivation', into highly employable people. Students work an eight-hour day, five days a week for 11 weeks (which comes as a major shock to most art or film school graduates!) and quickly learn about the demands of the modern industry. The impetus for the course came from recruiters who – despite being inundated with CVs – were despairing of finding people who could actually do the job!

Another project, which has evolved for similar reasons, is the London Animation Studio (LAS) based at the Central St Martin's College of Art and Design in London. This concentrates on drawn and computer animation, and aims to develop industry standard skills which should make individuals more marketable. It also offers postgraduate studies in Animation (*see* www.london animationstudio.tv). The studio is open to a diversity of people, including those already working in the industry.

During the Bristol course, students are assessed on a variety of attributes, including:

- Observation/characterisation
- Movement/animation
- Staging/editing/storyboarding
- Sculpting and drawing
- Computer skills
- Attitude to work

... as well as their ability to turn up on time every morning! Other courses will use similar, industry-relevant criteria to assess students. Cosgrove Hall actually provides in-house training to 'grow their own' breed of talent.

Employers are keen to support training that develops a range of skills needed by the industry. *Skillset* Professional Qualifications have been designed to incorporate these (*see* also pp. 251–8), and a number of assessment centres have been established – including FT2, which offers assessment for freelancers. Sought-after (but perhaps not terribly obvious) attributes include:

- The ability to communicate ideas clearly
- Persuasiveness
- Patience
- Attention to detail
- Lateral thinking
- The ability to work under pressure
- Numeracy/financial ability
- Fundraising/talking to investors

Areas of particular skills shortage have been identified for scriptwriters, producers, storyboarders and layout artists, production accountants, production managers, editors and scriptwriters.

As the industry grows, the need for high-quality training increases, not least to keep freelancers up-to-date with the requirements of employers. The Government has recently identified animation as a sector in need of further investment, and new short courses are being designed so that the industry can continue to expand its contribution to the UK economy and reputation. The industry has recently convened an Animation Forum with *Skillset* that will be looking at all the issues affecting skills development for this sector – including the reinstatement of a new entrants training scheme following the closure of the British Animation Training Scheme.

Finding out more

The Animation UK Directory – published annually by Venture Publishing, in association with BECTU – is an invaluable source of reference containing information about:

- Specialist production companies, including special effects, multimedia, games designers, etc.
- People who work in all areas of the industry, with names and contact details
- Relevant service providers, including equipment hire and sales, specialist consultants and agents
- European production companies
- All sorts of other useful information – such as training providers, industry support organisations, sources of funding, distributors, festivals, markets and awards.

Animation UK also publishes an industry magazine called *Imagine*. Published quarterly, it has all the latest news from the animation sector. Visit their website: http://www.animationuk.com.

The benefits of work experience

Getting 'behind the scenes' at an animation company will provide invaluable experience for anyone considering a career in this area. Think about any useful skills that you can offer, and read the section in Chapter 10, *Getting in and Getting on in the TV, Radio, Film, Video and Interactive Media Industry*.

Places to visit

The Animation Art Gallery
13–14 Great Castle Street, London W1

The National Museum of Photography, Film and TV
Pictureville, Bradford BD1 1NQ
Tel: 01274 202030

Animation festivals

There are several annual UK animation festivals, including Animated Encounters (www.animated-encounters.org.uk) and Animated Exeter. The Bradford Animation Festival is held in

November at the National Museum of Photography, Film and Television – *see* www.baf.org.uk. These are well worth visiting to see new work, attend seminars and workshops, and learn about what's happening in the business.

Things to watch

BFI Collections hire out examples from their extensive animation collection to schools, colleges, film societies and community groups. It's an excellent way to get a 'feel' for the breadth of the industry. Some material has been put on to video for hire or purchase.

Further reading

The Animator's Survival Kit, Richard Williams (Faber & Faber)
Creating 3D Animation – the Aaardmath Book of Film-making, Peter Lord and Brian Sibley (Harry N Adams)
Mouse or Superhero, the UK Animation Production Sector (PACT)
The Animator (monthly US magazine)
Televisual
Creative Review
Imagine (quarterly)

Things to remember

- Try to prepare yourself for the 'culture shock' of leaving college and becoming a freelancer. You will need to be very disciplined and hardworking to start your career.
- Utilise as many contacts as you have in the industry.
- Prepare your CV, and when you send it to companies make sure you send it to the right person. It may also help to design your letter so that it stands out from the crowd and shows that you have made an effort.
- Make sure that throughout college and school you compile a show reel so that you have some proof of what you can do. Keep this up to date and make sure that the box or cover of the VHS or disc is designed (rather than blank cardboard) and includes your contact details.
- Finally, continue to work on your own projects when you leave college. Starting to find work shouldn't spell the end of your creative life, and may give you the edge at interviews as you can talk about your own projects and ideas.

6

The Facilities Sector

Overall, the facilities sector, including post-production, employs fewer than 10,000 people and has seen a decrease in recent years. Women make up around a quarter of this workforce, which tends to comprise employees rather than freelancers. Most facilities companies are based around the London area, with some centred in the English regions. Scotland, Wales, and Northern Ireland are served by companies based in those nations, and facilitating the industry there.

What is the facilities sector?

The facilities sector supplies specialised technical equipment and services to every sector of the audio-visual industries: broad-casters, independents making programmes for broadcasters, feature films, commercials, pop promos, the corporate sector and sometimes for other organisations as well: major conferences, government departments. Almost every production will use at least one facilities company; often many for various types of work.

Facilities companies own and maintain high-value kit – cameras, cranes, lighting equipment, special effects kit, studios, and other items, much of it leading-edge technology. They supply it on demand – and at a price – to production companies as and when they need it. This set-up gives producers the flexibility to achieve their desired style for each production by using the most appropriate technical equipment – without having to own all the kit themselves.

How does it work?

Facilities companies are clustered near the major centres of production. Well over half the sector is located in and around west and northwest London, many on industrial estates which can provide the relatively cheap space needed for equipment storage. While there are a handful of facilities companies with 100 or more employed staff, most are small, with fewer than 50 employees – and some are tiny, with fewer than 10. Many of the freelancers working in this sector got their start through a facilities company.

Some companies are family owned and run; others grew out of the technical knowledge and skill of the founder (who may or may not still be involved). Many current companies are reincarnations of earlier versions, possibly due to the retirement of the founder or financial difficulties.

This is a relationship industry. Facilities companies have regular clients and there are many long-standing links to certain production or broadcast companies, or specific programmes. Competitive tendering exists in principle, and does happen, but it is less prevalent than in many other industries. It is also a niche industry: companies try to differentiate themselves from others by providing very specialised, often very expensive equipment or by understanding the specific requirements of a particular type of customer.

What is it like to work for a facilities house?

Facilities companies provide a key route into lucrative freelance work for technicians across the industry. This is the main goal of most newcomers, after a period within a company to learn the ropes. Most companies share this perception as 'the normal pattern of work'. Typically, new people join in a training capacity (though they may be called runners or drivers) and spend about two years learning the job, with or without a formal external training component. This is followed by another couple of years during which the 'trained up' person forms part of the company's core team.

Most employees choose to leave at this stage, some four years or so post-recruitment, to go freelance for the significantly higher earnings available. Some companies make it absolutely clear, on recruitment, that there will be no employment at the end of the training period; everyone is expected to go freelance. Others would like to keep hold of at least some of their departing freelance people but cannot afford to pay freelance rates. At least one larger company has introduced a deliberate policy to shift the balance from mainly freelance to mainly employed technicians, following legal advice on liability. They are gradually achieving their goal by offering a range of inducements not available to freelancers: holiday pay, training, and advantageous insurance schemes.

However, most companies accept the prevailing pattern of a steady stream of new blood coming through, and see positive advantages in having known, trained people out in the market with company links. The frequent throughput of staff also increases the opportunities for new entrants. Both sides are likely to expect to have a continuing relationship of some sort: 'first call' perhaps, or some form of guaranteed work.

What are the jobs?

Jobs in facilities companies fall within a fairly narrow range. All companies will have at least some core staff involved in kit maintenance. This is typically the basic technical job and requires aptitude, time and perseverance to become expert. The actual kit to be maintained varies with the company: e.g. film or video cameras, lighting equipment, cranes.

The next step up is generally kit preparation: ensuring that the required equipment is set up to meet client needs (for example, the right lenses, or the correct settings, or cabling). This requires a thorough knowledge of all the equipment and the ability to troubleshoot when clients run into problems.

Kit maintenance and preparation staff may include qualified electricians, camera engineers, video engineers, optics specialists, crane builders and engineers, and others specific to the particular equipment. Most companies will have one or more trainees in the workshop or preparation area, learning the job. These jobs can provide a solid, thorough grounding in the industry. Familiarity with the kit can be a passport to further work.

Companies involved in 'wet hire' will send their own people out with the kit – either directly employed staff or closely linked free-lancers. The 'out with the kit' people are those who are fully trained and probably doing a final couple of years with the company before going freelance. Lighting companies almost always use their own crews, for insurance and Health & Safety reasons. On a big production there would be one or two 'sparks', perhaps a lighting technician /supervisor or two, a Best Boy and, at the top, the Gaffer – who manages the job and the team. All will be qualified electricians.

Camera hire is more often 'dry hire', with the production client providing their own crew, usually from the freelance pool.

Where the company provides editing suites, on-line or off-line, they may have a few in-house editors but also provide dry hire for clients to bring in their own people.

All of the above jobs (and others) in the facilities sector *may* grow out of the basic entry level of trainee/driver/runner. Once new entrants show that they have the aptitude and personal qualities to stay the course, the sector is flexible enough for the individual to find and exploit opportunities.

Management and administrative jobs include sales and marketing, booking and accounts, and differ from other sectors mainly in the nature of the products and services being administered.

The way in

There are various routes into jobs with facilities companies – but no formal channel or standard practice. Family connections remain a common starting point for new blood, but many top-rank technicians got their start without such links. Above all, you must love the industry and be enthusiastic about working within it. Get to know which facilities companies exist – locally or more widely – and what they do. Speculative, imaginative applications, persistently submitted to as many companies as possible, are likely to give the highest success rate.

All companies expect 'a reasonable standard' of general education, without clearly defining what they mean. Some companies take school leavers with no vocational qualifications; others recruit college leavers with basic City and Guilds; several companies recruit graduates for runner positions. Sometimes experienced freelancers apply, seeking better hours and a more stable life.

There is no shortage of applicants. Most companies reported more people applying than are needed – perhaps because there are limited alternative routes into the technical side of the industry these days.

What are they looking for?

Technical interest and aptitude are essential, though these qualities may be identified in various ways. Very few companies insist on particular qualifications at the recruitment stage: they are more likely to be interested in what you do with your spare time. Stripping-down bikes, rebuilding engines, or an extensive interest in cameras or electronics would all be positive factors in your favour – and the more evidence you can give, the better. Companies are looking for people with a curiosity about how things work and a practical bent for keeping things working. While not necessarily an academic skill, the ability to spot a fault, identify the technical problem and solve it is a key attribute in this sector.

But this is a high-tech industry with a difference. Personal skills and attributes are equally as important as technical knowledge and experience. All employees and freelancers must have the ability to relate to clients; to be reliable and always turn up on time in the right place; and to be knowledgeable and quick on the job. The ability 'to fit in' as part of the team is crucial.

As small employers, facilities companies do not generally put candidates through a formal assessment process. They 'test for attitude' by starting new people off at the bottom – often as drivers or runners – to introduce them to the unsociable hours and tiring nature of the business, and to the type of work and people involved. Survive six months on the bottom rung and show willing and skill, and there may be an opportunity to move up a tier.

Companies often say that they need people with three sets of skills: knowing the equipment inside and out; good skills in using it; and client liaison skills. Their problem is getting all three together. If you've got the right combination of these attributes, you are likely to do well in the facilities sector.

Is training available?

All facilities companies train their kit maintenance and 'client facing' staff. 'Trainees' are recruited regularly, by most companies; sometimes called drivers or runners, and rarely employed in supernumerary roles, these are almost always recruited as core staff. Several companies – mainly but not entirely the larger ones – have systematic training programmes in-house, with planned stages, assessments and certification. Company training programmes, whether structured or entirely on the job, are geared very much towards learning the kit and understanding it thoroughly. Equipment is highly complex and the range can be huge; company staff must be familiar with it all in order to advise clients.

This can be a dangerous industry. There is heavy equipment about, a lot of electrical kit, and it's a fast-moving environment. Health & Safety is always a major concern within all companies. All have a strong company policy; most have company-specific manuals. Training is regular and thorough: you must be 'safety aware' at all times.

Strong emphasis is placed on the need for all workers, including freelancers, to identify with the company, acting as ambassadors. This requires a mix of ability, loyalty and personality – and companies use different ways of developing and maintaining this 'brand identification'. Good induction programmes and lots of ongoing opportunities to stay in touch with the company, its business and future prospects are just some examples.

In some sub-sectors – lighting hire companies in particular – appropriate qualifications are essential, though sponsored training to obtain them is often on offer. Lighting hire companies are more likely to use day release to colleges, as formal qualifications are required for insurance purposes. They would typically recruit school-leavers and sponsor on day release (for City and Guilds 256 or IE Regulations 16th Edition), with the trainees doing four days in the maintenance workshop and receiving in-house, usually informal, training on company-specific kit.

Grips comprise a specialist, almost separate subgroup of the sector. Grips are responsible for positioning the cameras and moving them about. While this is relatively straightforward in a studio, on location it can be one of the most challenging – and potentially dangerous – jobs. A few facilities houses employ grips, but most are freelance. As with other skills in this sector, there is no standard route into the occupation – but as grips work largely on their own, there is no on-the-job framework for new entrants to obtain training. Discussions are currently underway to design and provide clearer entry routes and robust training specifications for this occupational group.

What are the long-term prospects for the sector?

The facilities sector in the UK is under pressure. In recent years, there has been a steady reduction in budget size, which means that productions have less money to spend. This in turn leads to a big squeeze on profits. Productions are often moving abroad, to newly open markets whose technicians are learning quickly and working in capital-intensive departments, with new equipment.

However, the UK audio-visual industries have a track record of bouncing back, rising to the need. The facilities sector is unlikely to disappear in the foreseeable future and could provide just the right opportunity for someone with the right set of skills.

Finding out more

The British Film Commission provides information on filming in the UK, and they have a list of UK studios on their website at www.bfc.co.uk (Industry Directory – Studios).

Industry directories like *The Knowledge* and *The Production Guide* list all types of facilities companies; larger libraries may have copies (www.theknowledgeonline.com).

Industry magazines

Broadcast
Stage Screen and Radio (www.bectu.org)
Televisual

Web directory

www.mandy.com – choose 'Services'. Here you can search world-wide for facilities from A–Z, covering equipment hire, editing, studios, vehicle supply and everything in between.

7

Corporate Film, Video and Interactive Media – the 'non-Broadcast' Sector

> The UK corporate/business-to-business sector turned over around £2.7 billion in 2002 (more than is spent on all European film production) and is one of the fastest-growing business sectors in the economy. Dominated by small and medium sized employers (SMEs) which employ around 20–25 people, it has an estimated total workforce of about 3500 (adapted from the *Skillset* Workforce Development Plan 2000).

Would you like to be associated with high-quality – and often high-budget – programmes that will be viewed on numerous occasions by a discerning audience? It sounds like utopia for many aspiring documentary or drama programme-makers – and in the world of broadcast TV, it's increasingly rare. By contrast, professionals in corporate production know that their work is made to be shown over and over again. 'Getting it right' – not least because the cracks will be obvious – can be both satisfying and financially rewarding. So why is this fast-growing sector – which is a significant contributor to the UK economy – almost unknown to many people at the start of their media careers? The answer is probably multi-layered, but is likely to include the following factors:

- The sector is made up of many small and medium sized organisations, which tend not to advertise to the general public
- The audience for any one production is likely to be quite small
- There are few 'household names' in the corporate sector.

Despite the above, this dynamic and internationally admired sector has much to offer talented, business-aware individuals from a diversity of backgrounds. The production budgets are often remarkably high – it is not unknown for a 10-minute corporate film to have a budget of between £80,000 and £100,000, when many satellite programme-makers or short film-makers will be working on a fraction of that amount – and high-quality actors, presenters and production staff are employed on a multiplicity of projects.

Satisfying the target audience

Almost all programme-making nowadays is closely related to a business need. In the corporate sector this is particularly true. Persuading a client that your team can deliver a particular message or service – and then being judged on the outcome – provides an intellectual and creative challenge to programme-makers and their colleagues. To succeed, everyone concerned must understand the needs of their client, and also their target audience. Storytelling has to be excellent – especially as the brief may be to actually have a measurable effect on the way in which people think or behave. It can be infinitely tougher than producing a piece of broadcast material which will only be judged in terms of overall ratings.

Working in partnership with commissioners

Corporate production teams aim to build positive – often long-term – relationships with the people who commission them. They become almost independent members of the employing organisation for the period of production. And because the effectiveness of their work will be quantified, the relationship should continue after completion of the production. Professionals on both sides of the partnership emphasise that the way to ensure that this relationship is as effective as possible is to be organised from the start. This involves:

1. Agreeing a clear brief which defines the aims and objectives of the project, how it will be used, the intended audience, quality and budget guidelines, time for completion, etc. – basically leaving no doubt about the intended business requirement.
2. Producing a detailed proposal, including a budget breakdown. This should be a well-defined outline of their solution to the business requirement.
3. Discussing ideas – both in terms of creative input and of maximising the business benefits. The product should be a team effort and one that satisfies all parties – including the audience.
4. Establishing and maintaining trust. There should be no surprises... especially in terms of deadlines or additional costs. Regular communication is essential.
5. Evaluating the effectiveness of the product... the next commission is likely to depend of the success of this one.

Unsurprisingly, corporate production companies look for multi-skilled individuals who can move seamlessly from business considerations to creative ideas.

Essential research

When planning a production, corporate programme-makers have to analyse which techniques work and which ones don't. Sophisticated research is used to influence content. It's not a sector for 'hunches' (although there's plenty of scope for creativity); when you are aiming to deliver something very specific, you have to feel confident that it will work. For example, one major food manufacturing company conducted an extensive survey into UK consumer attitudes to cooking, and life in general. A huge amount of data was collected, at a cost of £100,000. To get maximum value from this investment, a video was produced to turn the dry data into a powerful tool that the whole organisation could understand and use with a diversity of 'customers'. Quite a task... but thorough research provided a platform for ideas that were likely to achieve the desired outcome.

An unusually successful industry

Research information from *Skillset* and the IVCA (the trade association representing the corporate sector) indicates that the corporate sector is made up of around 2500 companies located throughout the UK. With an annual turnover of around £2.7 billion (that's more than the spend on all European film production), and new business ideas and opportunities emerging in line with technological developments, the future of the corporate sector looks positive. Corporate video remains at the heart of the industry, with a turnover of around £550 million a year. Very well-established in the UK, it expects to continue to grow steadily – by around 5% each year.

Growth has been observed in some of the newer ventures into this sector. For example:

	Current turnover	**Predicted growth**
Video Conferencing	£110 million	5%
Business TV	£50 million	Steady
Live Events	£600 million	5%

However, the brave new(ish) world of the Internet and interactive multimedia is expected to provide the most significant long-term growth opportunities.

Who are the commissioners?

Corporate production companies bid for each commission, usually against tough competition. Preliminary research and planning, and professional presentation are essential if a company is to be taken seriously. Before a contract is signed, a huge amount of work – preparing schedules, budgets, storylines and casting proposals – will need to be completed. Impressing a commissioner is not an easy task, especially as they tend to have a thorough knowledge of the target audience. A range of senior people throughout both public and private sectors have budgets which can be spent on a corporate production.

For example:

Position in organisation	Aims/objectives
Marketing Directors	Product information for sales team, or for customers
Directors of Training/ Human Resources	Training, motivational communications, provision of information
Public Relation Specialists	To raise or improve the image of a product or service without going above 'the line' into advertising
Internal Communications Managers (internal communications is a growing market, especially in global organisations, where it is important that staff throughout the company receive information simultaneously)	Staff communications, contact with senior executives

Most major European companies use visual communications to increase their business effectiveness. They may commission work for a range of target audiences, including:

- Shareholders
- Current employees
- Trainees/new starters
- Potential staff
- Current or potential stakeholders
- The local community

Building long-term relationships

Some of the most successful corporate organisations can expect at least half of their work to come through repeat business, since a satisfied customer is very likely to want to continue a positive and productive relationship. People who work in this sector need to understand – even if they don't absolutely agree with – the views, expectations and needs of a client throughout any project. For many companies, the 'best' sort of client is one who knows what he or she wants to achieve, and trusts the production team to deliver it… but of course, it's often not quite like that. The ability to communicate effectively with the commissioners is an essential attribute; tact, diplomacy, flexibility and highly developed problem-solving abilities are other important skills.

A range of opportunities

Corporate video

'Linear video', which conveys a message or tells a story, remains the core business of the industry – although other areas such as Internet communications and live events are increasingly important. Linear video is used when a particularly targeted audience is identified for:

- Training
- Employee Communications
- Public Relations
- Sales and Marketing

Video is used for a variety of obvious and less obvious purposes.

- It's great for telling stories – being edited to produce a single, clear and consistent message using a variety of techniques.
- In group situations, video can be a valuable catalyst to discussion and brainstorming. Watching is a shared experience.
- Practically, it's very simple and cheap to use. The cassettes are easy to transport, and VHS players are available almost everywhere.
- As part of an overall communications strategy, videos can produce both quantitative and qualitative results.

Live events

Developing and project-managing a live event requires a diversity of organisational, interpersonal, creative and analytical skills. It also demands a steady belief – based on experience – that it will be 'all right on the night'.

Corporate communications firms can be involved in events ranging from small meetings to major public extravaganzas. 'Bringing people together effectively' is not always easy but, when done well, it's a powerful tool. Examples of large events could include international sales conferences, or product launches and relaunches. The contributors to such events are as diverse as the events themselves. A major commission might involve:

- Theatre
- Business TV
- Interactive media
- Graphic and set designers
- Entertainment
- Print
- Video
- Environmental design
- Team or individual activities

In the IT age, the role of live communication has increased significantly with the decentralisation of many organisations. A well-planned event can motivate and unite staff, educate people, develop teamwork, enhance or revitalise a corporate brand image, boost sales... or reward employees. A mix of media is regularly used.

Strong teamwork, creative problem-solving, and the ability to remain calm at all times have built up the reputations of specialist event management organisations. Generalist firms also event-manage, especially when extending their services to existing clients.

Business TV via satellite

An increasingly important business tool, these private TV networks are delivered from one fixed site to multiple sites. Specially commissioned programmes are encrypted for security, and then decoded at their destination. One of the fastest growing areas of corporate communication, this takes information straight into the business environment. Destinations all over the world can be reached simultaneously, linking together everyone who should be involved. Such communication need not be just one-way: by using the telephone or interactive keypads, the audience can give instant feedback – providing direct contact with, say, senior management.

Business TV via video cassette

Some businesses – for example in the retail sector – want to communicate on a regular basis with their employees or franchisees, but prefer a more flexible (and cheaper) approach. One company produces a monthly 20-minute video, and sends it out to 1500 shops in 42 different countries. Non-English-speaking countries receive specially dubbed or subtitled versions. Other companies do things on a more modest scale! This is a popular and accessible form of communication, which can be viewed at times to suit (for example, employees can take the tape home) and can link with printed materials or, for example, new products.

The Internet

Well established now as a global business communications tool, the Internet offers considerable scope for corporate communications professionals. New markets open every day, creating huge opportunities for new media developers who can 'cut through the technology' and communicate effectively with commissioners, and e-commerce is foremost in the minds of many people throughout the industry. The web is also used for a range of 'business to business' communications which can contribute to the success of an organisation, including:

- Interactivity between customers and employees
- Communication with identified target audiences
- Market research – 'focus groups on the net'
- Cost-effective global communications

There are genuine opportunities to contribute significantly to this expanding area, which involves a diversity of media.

Interactive media, CD-ROM and DVD

By definition, interactive media involves people. It is very useful as a corporate communications tool, allowing for easy exchange of views. When mixed with pictures, voices, music and all the other qualities of TV and audio-visual production, and supported by the storage capacity of CD-ROM and DVD, the possibilities for effective use seem endless. To corporate production companies (and their clients) the benefits include:

- *Creating a memorable experience:* people remember much more if they participate and engage.
- *Immediacy:* web-based content can be updated whenever required.
- *Flexibility:* interactive media can be tailored for target audiences.
- *Integration of new and traditional media:* video can be delivered on the Internet, CD-ROM and DVD.

- *Creativity:* by using multiskilled teams, new ideas emerge.
- *Capacity:* a DVD disk can hold up to 27 times more than a standard CD-ROM, including more than two hours of full-motion visuals and sound.
- *Globalisation:* DVDs can hold up to eight different language tracks and 32 subtitle channels – great for multi-territory and multi-language projects.

Conveniently, the output can be shown on a PC or laptop screen, or on a TV set with a DVD player.

Other opportunities

Other organisations in the corporate sector provide specialised services, as follows.

Equipment hire – providing a diversity of equipment, much of it very high-tech, for live events, presentations and programme-making. Equipment may be hired 'dry' (equipment only) or 'wet' (with technicians).

Archive libraries – specialist libraries maintain still and moving images, music and soundtrack effects which are used by production companies, event managers and so on.

Facilities houses – some facilities houses work solely or primarily for the corporate sector, building an excellent relationship with business clients and providing high-quality equipment and accommodation (*see* also Chapter 6, *The Facilities Sector*, for more details).

The corporate production process

Whatever method of communication is selected by the client, the overall process is very similar:

- *Stage 1* – agree the business requirement
- *Stage 2* – work as a partnership to produce a product which satisfies both client and production team
- *Stage 3* – test and evaluate the effectiveness of the product

Some corporate 'products' – for example training videos – may have an effective shelf-life of many years.

a diverse business

The IVCA (International Visual Communication Association) award-categories give a valuable insight into the type of corporate communications that are commissioned, and the sort of clients who are commissioning them. Each year, a diversity of organisations are nominated for awards, giving a valuable insight into the range of clients available to corporate production companies. The 2002 winners give an indication of their diversity:

IVCA Award Winners 2002	
Category	**Commissioning Client**
Motivational Training	RSNETT
Practical Training	HSBC
Health & Safety	National Blood Service
Charity & Public Welfare	The Alzheimer's Society
Education	British Heart Foundation
Recruitment	Central Office of Information
Sales and Product Services	Tesco Stores
Corporate Image	The Media Edge
Public Relations	Kingfisher
Internal Communications	Guiness UDV
Regular Communications	Norwich Union Insurance
Business to Consumer Promotion	Crisis
Business to Consumer Information	BBC Open University
Live Events and Public Display	bmi british midland
External Live Events	Guinness UDV
Internal Multimedia	Young & Rubicon
External Multimedia	Campbell Distillers
Interactive Multimedia Publishing	BBC Multimedia
Websites	Comic Relief

The Biz-nets

In addition to the awards described above, the IVCA has introduced a range of new interactive business awards called the 'Biz-Nets' – judged on the quality of content, how well it is delivered, and how well it is targeted to the chosen audience.

Categories include:

- Learning Websites
- Public Information
- Business to Consumer (transactional)
- Business to Consumer (non-transactional)
- Business to Business
- Innovation
- Business Media

What jobs do people do?

The corporate sector employs a range of talented, multi-skilled individuals in a diversity of areas – for example:

Aerial Filming	Foreign Language Services
Animation	Graphics
Art Direction	Internet/Intranet Design
Business Development	Lighting Camera
Business Event Production	Marketing and Sales
Camera Operator	Multimedia Specialists
Casting	Presenters
Communication Consultants	Producers
Composers	Production Assistants
Computer Graphics	Research
Copyright Consultants	Scripting
Design	Sound Dubbing
Duplication	Standards Conversion
Editing	Voice-over Artists
Equipment Hire	Writers
Floor Managers	

For more information on individual job descriptions and job profiles, refer to Chapter 1, *Working in the TV, Radio, Film, Video and Interactive Media Industry*. Production teams are usually very small, consisting of a director, a cameraperson and one or two others. Several producers mentioned that it is becoming increasingly common – especially on location – to involve one or more of the client's own staff, as runners or administrative assistants.

In addition, people with good organisational, administrative and project management or sales abilities work throughout the sector. A minority are in regular, full-time employment (although corporate production companies often provide considerably more reliable employment than most independent production companies), and others run their own specialist companies or work as freelancers. Companies often actively prefer to use a predominately freelance team for specific projects, for a variety of reasons.

- It's usually cheaper to use a freelancer for a finite period than to provide full-time employment.
- Because freelancers work with different people, they are often an excellent source of ideas.
- Experienced freelancers offer a wide portfolio of skills, knowledge and contacts.
- They are often at the forefront of new media.

Freelancers, who will almost always get their first corporate work through contracts, have the opportunity to build long-term and productive relationships with the people who employ them – and if they remain highly motivated, to continue to provide a quality service. It's a very competitive business, and future contracts depend on reputation. For some, it's a very lucrative and enjoyable mode of work.

Entry routes for freelancers

About 50% of the people who work in the corporate sector are freelance. The last *Skillset* Freelance Survey (2001 – the next one will be carried out later in 2003) identified their original pathway into this sector by asking: 'How did you get your first freelance work?' Here are the results:

Direct approach	33%
Through an advertisement	26%
Friend, relation	22%

Employer contact	12%
Word-of-mouth	11%
Careers Service	4%
Trainer HE/FE	4%
Agency/Diary Service	3%
Trade Union	2%

So, if you plan to work in this sector, build up your database of friends and acquaintances, and be prepared to take the initiative.

The same *Skillset* research also asked about the level of qualifications offered by freelancers in this sector:

Undergraduate degree in other subjects	33%
Undergraduate degree in Media	28%
Relevant technical qualification	26%
Postgraduate degree/diploma in Media	14%
Postgraduate degree/diploma in other subjects	14%
NVQ	13%
Other technical qualification	11%
Modern apprenticeship	1%

Where do people work?

Look through the IVCA Directory (*see* Chapter 11, *Finding Out More*) and it's obvious that most corporate sector companies are based in and around London. However, there *are* several – some very successful – in other locations throughout the UK, and there is good 'home-grown' representation in Scotland, Wales and Northern Ireland.

Getting In

Sought-after skills

The following are considered to be sought-after skills and attributes within this sector:

* The ability to be customer-focused and audience aware
* A capable personality
* An interest in business, current affairs, and world issues
* Good self-management and organisational skills

- IT literacy
- The ability to communicate with a very wide range of people – including those quite different from yourself
- The ability to work within, and sometimes manage, budgets
- The ability to structure thoughts and ideas, and defend them
- The ability to see things from another person's point of view
- Knowing when to stop and ask
- The ability to motivate others
- Commonsense
- The ability to become an instant member of a team

approaching potential employers

CVs and letters targeted to individual companies should include examples of what you do, and your relevant work experience. Provide an example: one good example of your work is often more powerful than a mixed showreel. Check if the person you are to meet would prefer to receive this before, or on the day of your meeting. Above all, be businesslike and organised.

Professional representation

The IVCA (International Visual Communication Association) is the professional membership body for the corporate sector. It provides a range of member services and also:

- Campaigns on behalf of the industry
- Co-ordinates relevant research and business intelligence
- Provides a forum for debate, networking and contacts.

At present the IVCA is developing links with a selected forum of universities and colleges to ensure that relevant information is built into the curriculum. Check if you are currently studying, or planning to study, a relevant course.

Summing up

There are genuine opportunities for bright, creative and well-organised people in this under-publicised area. Many individuals will choose to specialise in the corporate sector, thus developing satisfying and often well-paid careers, and becoming involved in innovative and often long-lived products – in the process building up profitable relationships with commissioning clients.

The Interactive Media Sector

The interactive media sector is made up of a loose association of around 3000 companies, which employ around 50,000 people – 20,000 in the area of games development. Most people work in small or medium sized companies (SMEs) which employ 20 people or fewer on a regular basis. Although negative publicity about the collapse of some high-profile dot.coms had affected confidence in the sector at the time of writing, many professionals working in this exciting area remain enthusiastic about the prospects for talented individuals who want to develop creative or commercial careers.

Interactive media products come in an ever-increasing range of formats, with one thing in common – they all provide the opportunity for their audience (the user) to play a positive role in the content of their media experience. 'Old' media producers make programmes, films or music that are completed and effectively unchangeable by the time they are communicated; whereas interactive media products involve the user in a different way, allowing him or her to make selections or decisions that change the content of the production. Digital technology enables every stage of the process – from initial programming to the computers, consoles, mobile devices and software products which support the individual experience.

The following diagram illustrates some of the outcomes of convergence caused by the coming together of three previously distinct industries:

- Information technology
- Traditional media, including TV, film and radio
- Telecommunications

Website production depends on convergence, and the opportunities it creates have changed the face of TV, film and radio production forever. New programmes or films are often commissioned with accompanying interactive activities (for example, online games) which can add value – and hopefully, revenue – to a production.

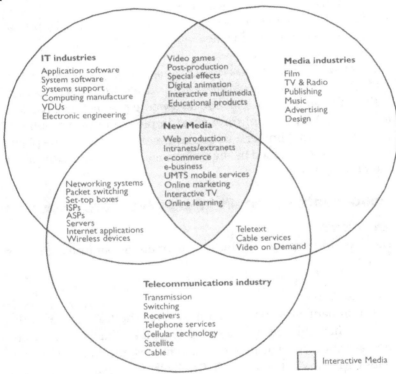

IT industries

Application software
System software
Systems support
Computing manufacture
VDUs
Electronic engineering

Networking systems
Packet switching
Set-top boxes
ISPs
ASPs
Servers
Internet applications
Wireless devices

Video games
Post-production
Special effects
Digital animation
Interactive multimedia
Educational products

New Media

Web production
Intranets/extranets
e-commerce
e-business
UMTS mobile services
Online marketing
Interactive TV
Online learning

Teletext
Cable services
Video on Demand

Media industries

Film
TV & Radio
Publishing
Music
Advertising
Design

Telecommunications industry

Transmission
Switching
Receivers
Telephone services
Cellular technology
Satellite
Cable

Interactive Media

The interactive media sector is still relatively young and, as yet, many aspects are a little hazy. The industry is still evolving, and in career terms this particularly affects job titles and job descriptions. Two jobs with the same title may be very different in different organisations, and some people at the very start of their careers may be given job titles – such as producer – which can easily be misinterpreted. Never be afraid to ask questions, and don't make any assumptions!

Similarly, the phrases 'interactive media' and 'new media' are often used interchangeably, although there is a distinction between the two:

- New media utilises the convergence between IT, telecoms and the media to create products which reflect the input of each sector in – for example – websites.
- Interactive media, however, does not need an online or telecoms component for the audience to interact.

Interactive media encompasses a diversity of activities and sectors and offers a huge range of interactivity levels, from the personalisation of content for an individual viewer (e.g. selecting a particular court at Wimbledon) through a simple menu of navigational options to a 'total immersion' games experience, where the player is likely to be consumed by the experience as he or she determines their own pathway.

Components of the UK interactive media industry

New media
There are three main distribution channels, or platforms, for new media.

The Internet
The dominant new media platform, over the last ten years the Internet has enjoyed a faster rise in uptake than any previous media technology. For new media activities, the most important platform is the World Wide Web. Originally intended for academics and scientists, the web proved wildly popular with computer enthusiasts and has gone on to become one of the world's principal media channels – and a key method of communication for almost every organisation and business. It is estimated that there are currently almost 10 million unique websites in the world, and sites can be as varied as human society itself. However, an organisation's website will normally be intended to provide some

or all of the following: news and information, advertising and marketing, e-commerce, online learning, entertainment, and community activities. In addition, there are many sites (such as search engines and portals) which serve to provide links to and information about other websites.

Accompanying the rise of the Internet, there has been an explosion of new media agencies – companies whose activities focus on designing, building, managing and providing consultancy on websites for their clients. In addition to websites, much new media activity centres around intranets (essentially, websites intended for internal use by an organisation) and email, with companies keen to exploit the latter's potential for marketing purposes. Many new media agencies have expanded their expertise beyond the Internet, and now aim to provide similar services for emerging wireless and interactive TV platforms.

The 'dot.com' boom of the late 1990s and its subsequent crash has left many Internet-related businesses in a state of some disarray, and this has had an impact on the vitality of the UK's new media industry. The end of 2001 saw some of the most high-profile new media design companies facing up to redundancies and even closure. The long-term future of the industry is, however, more promising – more than 40% of the UK is now regularly using the Internet, and this is steadily rising into a genuine mass audience; while the (albeit painfully slow) roll-out of broadband Internet access should result in new creative and commercial opportunities for new media professionals.

Interactive TV
The growing number of digital TV subscribers in the UK has created a mass market for interactive media content and services, which is still only beginning to be explored. More than 40% of households have access to digital TV.

Wireless platforms
The new generation of mobile phones and other handheld devices has opened up a market for wirelessly transmitted interactive content. Constraints in screen size and transmission rate have meant that this has been mainly confined to limited services (text-based news, travel information, etc.), but there are genuine

creative opportunities emerging for interactive content which can be highly personalised and localised. Already games and even adult content have been developed specifically for the more advanced mobile devices.

Multimedia formats

The interactive media industry first came to prominence with multimedia CD-ROM publishing in the mid-1990s, and although largely superseded by the growth of the Internet, there is still a market for interactive CDs – particularly in the areas of training and education. The last few years have seen the rapid uptake of DVD (Digital Versatile Disk) players, and there is an increasing demand for high-quality interactive entertainment, usually based around film and music releases. Kiosks and digital installations (for instance in exhibitions, museums or retail outlets) are another source for this kind of work, although here the emphasis is more on providing information and education.

Video games

The games industry is the largest and most established of all the interactive media sectors, and could easily warrant a chapter to itself. Games production predates the web and other interactive media activities. The first computer games were created in the 1960s, and as early as the 1970s there was a recognised games industry, with video arcades and home entertainment consoles introducing the public to such 'classic' games as Space Invaders, Pac Man and Asteroids.

With the growth of home computing in the 1980s, the UK computer games industry enjoyed a period of expansion and creative innovation. Throughout the country, games companies sprang up, often consisting of just one or two talented enthusiasts working from their homes. The limited processing power of PCs at that time meant that it was relatively easy for one person, or two or three people working in small teams on low budgets, to produce games that were considered state-of-the-art, and the industry was renowned for its creative mavericks – talented individuals responsible for almost every aspect of a game's production, from originating the concept through to its visual design, gameplay, music and programming.

As PCs became more powerful, with faster processing speeds and enhanced capacities for sound and graphics, so the complexity and ambition of games increased. These advancements in game design were further encouraged with the advent in the early 1990s of a new generation of games consoles manufactured by Sega, Nintendo and later Sony. Throughout the decade, continual improvements in hardware greatly expanded the creative possibilities open to games producers, particularly the introduction of 3-D graphics in the mid-1990s.

More recently, probably the most important development in the industry has been the impact of the Internet, and the emergence of online multi-player gaming. PC users can now access the Internet and play against one another, or even collaborate in team games. Many of the most popular titles now have an online component, allowing players to test themselves not just against the computer or their friends, but against fellow players all around the world.

Today, gaming – whether based around the console, PC or Internet – is a hugely popular pastime and an enormous global industry. Traditionally considered the preserve of teenage boys, the market for games is broadening: in the US, some 30% of gamers are over 36 years old, while the proportion of female gamers is rising slowly.

The era of the games maverick is over. Games production today has strong similarities with the film industry, with 18-month production schedules or longer, and budgets often in excess of £2 million. Games are now produced by much larger teams, composed of specialist programmers, artists, games designers, project managers, scriptwriters, audio engineers and music composers. Further similarities with the film industry lie in the importance of generating game franchises that allow for constant sequels and updates. More directly, games ally themselves with Hollywood films and other entertainment properties (such as sports stars) through the use of multi-million pound licences that are attached to games to enhance their commercial appeal. Although most new entrants into this sector of the industry have completed 'relevant' training, at the time of writing the preferred qualification was a degree in mathematics.

Like the film and music industries, games has an established structure, with studios and production houses developing 'third party' games on behalf of publishers, in addition to the in-house development studios owned by many publishers. Independent studios receive a fee for their work and a share of royalties, while the publishers own the rights and will market and distribute the games – taking the bulk of the revenues, but also the commercial risk. In the case of the successful Tomb Raider games series, for instance, the publisher is Eidos (named as the UK's most successful company in any industry in 1999) while the games are developed by the Derbyshire-based studio, Core Design.

A feature of the UK games industry is that (unlike almost every other sector of the media) it is not dominated by London. Although most of the major games publishers are based in central London, the studios tend to be far more widely dispersed around the UK. Important centres for games production can be found in places such as Manchester/Liverpool, Surrey, Warwickshire, Sheffield and Dundee.

For those who are interested in learning more about the industry, a number of books have been published on the history of video games, which explore further the commercial, creative and technological drivers of the industry. Particularly recommended are Stephen Poole's *Trigger Happy* (Arcade Publishing, ISBN 1559705396) and David Sheff's *Game Over* (Game Press, ISBN 0966961706).

Influencing all media communications

As a result of convergence, it is increasingly difficult to distinguish between new media and the traditional media industries. It is possible to create entire feature films using digital technology, and computerised post-production is becoming a commonplace part of the creative process. As mentioned earlier, many films and animations are now produced in parallel with websites, video games and DVDs; while the emergence of media conglomerates, most famously AOL Time Warner, has created a new era in media communications, in which content and platform owners are able to produce and distribute content across a wide range of delivery channels.

In the UK, the major broadcasters and traditional media businesses are extensively involved in interactive media activities, principally the BBC, which is thought to be the largest publisher of online content in Europe. Many TV programmes, films, magazines and music acts now have accompanying websites, providing a more in-depth and involved experience for audiences. The Big Brother website and SMS mobile messages, for instance, have become key elements of the overall show – moving it far beyond the confines of simply a TV programme.

The implications of these developments for production, creativity, commerce, skills requirements, business models, intellectual property rights, advertisers, audiences, regulators and policy-makers are both enormous and difficult to define, and far beyond the scope of this or any other single publication. However, what seems certain is that there will be increasing value placed on 'multi-skillers' – those who are comfortable with both traditional and interactive media, who can quickly acquire the necessary knowledge and competencies to move effortlessly between media. In particular, there is a real need for people with high-level analytical skills who can communicate effectively with traditional programme- and film-makers.

Employment

Who are the employers?

With such a wide variety of activities, ranging from the technical implementation of e-commerce systems through to the composition of video-games soundtracks, interactive media employers are widespread. Expect the unexpected, but below is a sample of some of the types of companies who employ interactive media professionals:

Broadcasters
Charities
Companies with in-house interactive media departments
DVD and CD-ROM authoring companies
E-learning suppliers
Educational institutions
Games publishers
Games studios
Information providers, e.g. government
Interactive design agencies
ISPs and web hosting services

IT services
Marketing and advertising agencies
Professional services companies providing research and
   consultancy
Publishers
Retailers
Software development
Systems integration
Wireless service providers

The freelance option

As with other media industries, much interactive work takes place on a project-by-project basis, and there are good opportunities for freelancers and contract workers. This is particularly the case for those with specialised technical skills, who are often contracted at premium rates to perform particular tasks over short periods of time, rather than over the course of a whole project. However, the need to share knowledge and ideas between members means that many positions are of a more permanent nature, with companies keen for the knowledge and expertise learned from one project to be taken forward into the next.

Learning resources and opportunities for freelancers in the UK's new media industry can be found at the Freelancers Network (www.freelancers.net).

Recruitment consultants

In common with the advertising and IT industries, one of the best methods of finding work in interactive media (whether freelance or permanent positions) is through specialist recruitment consultants. This was particularly true at the height of the dot.com boom in the late 1990s, when companies were struggling to recruit staff with the skills they required, and were far more willing to pay expensive recruitment fees. A good recruitment company will do much more than simply bring positions to your notice – it will provide advice and detailed industry knowledge, helping you to pursue an appropriate career path and best present yourself to potential employers.

Recruiters throughout the sector mentioned consultants whom they had found useful, and these are listed below:

new media
Major Players (www.majorplayers.co.uk)
MediaCentrix (www.mediacentrix.com)
Media Types (www.media-types.co.uk)
Prospect (www.prospectmsl.com)
Recruit Media (www.recruitmedia.co.uk)
Work Thing (www.workthing.com)

Games and new media
Aardvark Swift (www.aswift.com)
Datascope (www.datascope.co.uk)
OPM (www.opmjobs.com)

In many cases, their websites provide useful information, tips and articles on skills, employment trends and finding work. (However, inclusion in this handbook does not imply that *Skillset* recommends these consultancies.)

Work experience
Work experience can be an excellent way of improving your employment prospects. Some courses, particularly those offered by universities and colleges, have links with employers; while most interactive media companies, even the very small ones, are happy to offer placements to well-organised and reliable people with an enthusiasm for the industry. In the games industry, for example, it is common for companies to use young interns to help on their testing procedures. Many companies are interested in reasonably lengthy placements, perhaps as an ongoing part of a training course, and it's not unusual for such placements to gradually lead into full-time employment with the company.

It should be noted, however, that certain roles are more suitable for work experience than others. While many production skills can be learnt on the job, with interns quickly becoming valued members of the team, for the more technical disciplines – such as database programming – companies are more likely to hire those with proven expertise or qualifications, rather than hoping to train up inexperienced staff.

Starting your own business

As personal computers have become more powerful, and equipment less expensive to buy, it has been increasingly common for people to set up a company themselves, with many starting out by working at home with friends or relatives. However, while activities such as web design can still be undertaken in this manner, the scale and complexity of other forms of production (such as games), and the increasing demands for professionalism from clients, mean that it is not generally the most effective way of entering the industry. Going it alone is an exciting and profitable option for many individuals. The best advice is usually to gain skills, experience and contacts in an established part of the industry before embarking on an independent career.

Working practices

In common with TV and film, interactive media production is very much a team activity, and to succeed you must be able to work with a diversity of people, communicating clearly and understanding one another's demands. There are often tensions and a lack of understanding between the creative and technical members of a project, and it is important that you can maintain a good humour and respect each other's different skills and responsibilities, while at the same time demonstrating the drive and attention to detail to see projects through to completion on time, and within budget. People who can communicate effectively with both creative production and technical specialists are highly sought-after, and many become senior managers.

Despite the close relationship between the industry and telecommunications, 'teleworking' is not yet widespread, and few people have the luxury of working from home. This is an industry where teamwork, knowledge-sharing and brainstorming are crucial elements of any project, and employees are expected to participate fully in these activities. Partly as a result of this, interactive media industries can present problems for those with family commitments, or who are unwilling to work unsocial hours. The games industry is notorious for its demands on the workforce's time beyond normal 9–5 hours – it is by no means unheard-of for games developers to sleep in cots at the workplace, and to work round the clock as a deadline approaches. Many believe, incidentally, that this is the principal reason why games production in the UK is almost completely dominated by young men.

Skills, training and qualifications

In such a fast-moving industry, with a continuous churn of companies, technologies, delivery platforms, software packages and working practices, equipping yourself with up-to-date knowledge and skills is a never-ending challenge. For long-term success in the interactive media industries, it is not so much a case of learning the right tools, but rather becoming adept in the skill of learning. This means acquiring the technical principles, confidence and skills to quickly adapt to new software packages and business developments, and being able to take advantage of new creative and commercial opportunities as and when they arrive. Ideally, therefore, learning and training should be a continuous process – something that goes hand-in-hand with your career, rather than interrupting it; and you should take every opportunity, at your workplace and beyond, to increase your knowledge and skills-base. One employer said that members of his team would expect to master a new piece of software 'about every two weeks'.

Qualifications

Although most senior people tend to be educated to at least degree level, there are large numbers of people with more vocational qualifications working in both technical and creative positions, such as programming and graphic design. In these areas, employers often tend to be less concerned with formal qualifications than with relevant experience, portfolios and knowledge of specific software tools.

Many of the most successful interactive media professionals are qualified in the broad-based disciplines that draw on both creative and analytical approaches, and the industry contains creative and technical directors from a diverse range of backgrounds, such as philosophy, architecture, art and design, artificial intelligence, computer science, psychology and music. Specialist postgraduate training in interactive media, following a more general degree, seems to be a good approach if you are ambitious and aiming for a senior position. This has proved a popular option for many experienced TV and film professionals attracted by the opportunities – and money – associated with interactive media.

Roles and responsibilities

Most interactive media projects require a wide range of skills and expertise, ranging from specialised technical roles to the highly creative. As a new and rapidly changing sector, job titles in interactive media are notoriously misleading: 'web manager', for instance, could describe a technical, administrative or editorial role. Below is a sample list of job titles, but you should try to find out exactly what skills are required when applying for a position.

- Project Manager/Producer (overall responsibility for managing a project)
- Creative Director (oversees creative aspects of project)
- Technical Director (oversees technical aspects)
- Designer/Graphic Designer (responsible for the visual appearance)
- Programmer/Developer
- Scripter/Coder (supports the programmer on less technical duties, such as writing HTML to present the content)
- Web Manager/Master (responsible for the running of a website)
- Content Co-ordinator (brings various content elements – graphics, text, video, etc. – together for presentation)
- Editor/Copywriter/Author
- Information Architect (works on the structure of an interactive media product, and how the end-user experiences and navigates through it)
- Video Editor
- Video Compressor (prepares video in an appropriate format for delivery)
- Music Composer
- Animator

In addition to the production roles, many interactive media companies have a large range of more conventional business roles, similar to those found in advertising and other industries. These include: account management; market research; business strategy and consultancy (especially around e-business); business development; sales, marketing and advertising; public relations, recruitment, and Human Resources; IT services; legal services (particularly in the areas of intellectual property and contract law); finance and general administration.

In some cases, there is easy movement between production and business roles, and going into the production side can be a good way of getting into business, and vice-versa. For instance, in smaller new media agencies, the same individual will often be responsible for account and project management, while many interactive media producers go on to more senior management and business strategy roles.

Self-learning

Even those established in the industry can feel 'left behind', and there is a real impetus for individuals to be continually learning new skills – whether this be specific software packages or expertise in more general creative, technical and managerial activities. The Internet is the obvious starting point for much self-learning, particularly with regards to software and technical issues, and there are many introductory articles, Frequently Asked Questions (FAQs), tutorials and reference works to be found online. Even more useful are the online developers' communities, based around websites or email lists, where you can tap into the knowledge of thousands of industry professionals around the world. Popular examples include Slashdot (http://slashdot.org) and webmonkey (http://hotwired.lycos.com/webmonkey). Provided that you observe the appropriate 'netiquette', it can be easy to find those who are happy to share their knowledge and expertise.

In addition, there are numerous manuals and training guides for all the software packages that you would expect to encounter, as well as good general introductions to interactive media production. These publications can be quite expensive, so you should try to get a good recommendation before you buy one – again the Internet should provide some answers, and it is always worth checking the readers' reviews at www.amazon.co.uk.

Training providers

There are hundreds of courses available throughout the UK, many of which attract some level of public funding. Choosing one that will add to your skill set can be a daunting task. Given the rapidly changing, multi-disciplined nature of interactive media, you should be wary of investing too much time and money into learning a single software package. There is still little in the way of standard industry practice, with many companies favouring different tools and working practices. A broad-based approach to training is more sensible, in which you learn the principles of production, and familiarise yourself with a range of software packages, so that you are in a position to quickly learn the specifics of a number of packages as required. Talk to other people who have attended a course that you are considering before committing to it, and look for courses that draw on the experience of individuals who have worked as practitioners in the field that interests you.

In Chapter 9 there is a useful checklist of questions to ask (*see* pp. 219–21), and information to research, to help you make an informed choice. If you are looking at a short course, the *Skillset*/BFI guide *Media and Multimedia Short Courses* is an invaluable source of information. Updated three times a year, it is published by the BFI in association with *Skillset*, while its companion volume *Media Courses UK* – also published by the BFI – provides comprehensive information and contact details for Further Education and Higher Education courses, with descriptions written by the training providers. *skillsformedia* advisors can provide specialist advice about different types of training for careers in this sector and sources of funding. Call 08080 300 900.

Comprehensive listings of courses may also be accessed from the *Skillset*/BFI database, through the *Skillset* website: www.skillset.org. Broadly speaking, it's good advice to look for courses that have established links with the industry activities in which you are interested: be sure to ask about external examiners, visiting lecturers and work placements.

Many of the industry bodies and networking groups organise training and development sessions for members. *Skillset* supports a national network of training providers. These national and regional training partners are detailed in Chapter 9, *Training and Education for the Industry*. Details about these training providers, which can give information about local course provision, are also available on the *Skillset* website www.skillset.org.

For more localised information, the Learning and Skills Councils and the Businesslink Service may have preferred training suppliers. Training offered by these suppliers is often subsidised, and there may even be several free places on each course. Check the Yellow Pages for addresses.

Industry organisations

The British Interactive Media association (BIMa)

The trade association representing the UK's interactive media industries was established in 1985, and its role has grown and changed over the years. Its aim is 'to exchange information and advice on the technology, application and business of new media, and to promote the use of interactive technology to business and the public'. BIMA runs events and networking opportunities, but is probably best-known for its annual awards, which celebrate the industry's most creative and effective work. BIMA is a membership organisation, and both individuals and organisations with an interest in interactive media can apply to join.
Tel: 01277 658107 (www.bima.co.uk)

new Media Knowledge (nMK)

Owned by the University of Westminster, NMK is a not-for-profit body working to analyse, support and promote the UK's digital media industries through a programme of events, one-day courses, seminars, international trade missions, publications and research projects. The website is a valuable information resource, and the regular events in London offer good opportunities to network and get to know the industry. There is no membership policy, but a fortnightly email newsletter goes out to some 7000 digital media professionals, keeping them informed of NMK's activities.
Tel: 020 8357 7349 (www.nmk.co.uk)

TIGa

The Independent Games Developers Trade Association was founded in 2001 and provides support, lobbying, networking opportunities and events for those companies involved principally in the production (rather than the publishing or selling) of games.
Tel: 07003 999 989 (www.tiga.org.uk)

In addition, some of the established organisations representing the film and broadcasting industries now also provide support and training for interactive media professionals. It is therefore worth getting in touch with bodies such as BECTU, BAFTA, IVCA, PACT and *Skillset*. (You will find information and contact details for these and many other industry bodies in Chapter 11.)

networking groups and associations

Often more useful, in terms of making contacts and finding employment opportunities, are the many new media networking groups which have proliferated in the UK in recent years. These tend to be based around socialising and group discussion, rather than formal membership, and individuals can normally register online in order to participate in online discussions or attend events, many of which are free and offer drinks and refreshments. A number of networks are listed below, varying in terms of their local or national remits, and the extent to which they are serious industry forums or largely opportunities to socialise.

Boobnight – rather raucous social events for new media professionals. (www.boobnight.co.uk)

Bristol Interactive Cluster – membership association for interactive TV and broadband content production companies based in the South West of England. (www.cluster.org)

Broadband Bananas – networking events for those working in the converging media industries. (www.broadbandbananas.com)

Chinwag – email list and online forum for new media marketing professionals. (www.chinwag.co.uk)

Clerkenwell Social – networking events for new media professionals in London. (http://groups.yahoo.com/group/clerkenwell)

Cybersalon – looking at the social, cultural and creative implications of digital media. (www.cybersalon.org)

e-Women Networking – events for women working in ICT and new media. (www.e-women.org)

New Media Scotland – agency supporting creative activities shaped by digital technologies. (www.mediascot.org)

New Media Group Wales – networking and support for the Welsh new media industry. (www.sgrin.co.uk)

Niima – the Northern Ireland Interactive Multimedia Association. (www.niima.org.uk)

North West Vision – screen and media agency for the North West. (www.northwestvision.co.uk)

WAP Wednesday – discussions on developments in mobile media and business. (www.wapwednesday.com)

Wired Sussex – the focal point for Brighton's new media cluster, Wired Sussex runs an active and highly regarded programme for interactive media professionals. There are now similar organisations based on the Wired Sussex model in Oxford, Berkshire and Surrey. (www.wiredsussex.com)

Industry press

Newspapers

The broadsheet national newspapers all follow the interactive media industry, usually from a business or technology perspective. The most comprehensive coverage can be found in *The Guardian*'s Media supplement every Monday, which includes a distinct new media section featuring industry news, commentary and job vacancies. Given the converging nature of the media industries, it is also sensible to keep abreast of reports in the traditional media pages, as well as the business, technology and computing sections of the national press. *Guardian Online* on Thursdays, *The Daily Telegraph*'s 'Wired' (Wednesdays) and the *Financial Times*' 'Creative Business' (Tuesdays) are all recommended.

Magazines

Accompanying the rapid growth of interactive media, a number of industry magazines have sprung up in the last few years. The dot.com crash and advertising downturn brought many of these to an end, but there are still a number of high-quality weekly and monthly magazines which will give you a feel for what's going on, the major players and future trends. Again, it is also useful to keep an eye on those magazines covering the marketing, design, computing and broadcast industries. Below are some of the better-known industry titles.

new media

Creation Magazine (www.creationmag.com)
Create Online (www.createonline.co.uk/publication/CT/)
Creative Review (www.mad.co.uk)
New Media Age (www.nma.co.uk)
Revolution (www.revolutionmagazine.com)

Games

Develop (www.developmag.com)
MCV (www.mcvuk.com)
Edge (www.edge-online.com)

Training and Education for the Industry

If you are one of the many thousands of people who wish to get into – or get on in – the industry, then relevant and affordable training and education will be a top priority. This chapter will give you an idea of the range of courses available. Some are full-time, primarily academic and with lots of exams; others are very practical, taught and assessed by industry professionals. There is no single approach to training and education for the industry. Opportunities are available for talented and committed people from the full spectrum of educational and cultural backgrounds and almost anyone has a reasonable chance of finding a first job, provided that they offer a relevant and attractive package of skills, experience and enthusiasm. Choosing and investing in the right course *for you* will be an important element in your early career planning. But the future competitiveness of this fast-changing industry depends on developing skilled and talented people with the ability to keep on learning, so this chapter also provides information on sources of help to maintain your skills.

Developing your skills

Deciding about training and education is a difficult task. Higher Education will not necessarily get you into the industry, but it may help you get on; and in this career area, like any other, you should feel comfortable with the level of educational attainment that you achieve. This really means staying in the system until you have evidence to show off your academic abilities. Doing a degree won't necessarily improve your chances of getting a job, but it will give you three or four years in which to develop your thoughts and improve your analytical and critical skills. These may be essential at a later stage in your career. And, despite the financial problems that many students face, the majority are not sorry to have decided to study as long as they are happy with the quality of their course. Meeting a wide range of people and developing new ideas are just two of the benefits that they mentioned. Many entrants into the industry are graduates – a growing proportion with Media Studies degrees.

Entry-level jobs often require a combination of practical and personal skills, and it is important to look at ways of developing both if you are serious about gaining work anywhere in the industry. There are many opportunities (at widely differing levels of cost) to gain useful skills, some of which are signposted within this chapter. Bear in mind that the essential criterion for usefulness is *practicality*. Studying for a specialised theoretical qualification – however interesting it may be – may not improve your employment prospects. The acquisition of an apparently less prestigious vocational qualification, coupled with genuine practical experience, might open the door to a junior entry-level job – but again, there are no guarantees. Some companies offer 'Modern Apprenticeships' for young people who have not attended Higher Education – check with your local Learning and Skills Council (LSC) by ringing the general enquiries helpline 0870 900 6800, or via the website www.lsc.gov.uk. Alternatively, ring *skillsformedia*'s free helpline on 08080 300 900.

Changes in the industry have also accentuated the need for everyone involved in the 'creative' aspects of work to be conversant with the available technology, especially as many of the jobs are now 'multi-skilled' – requiring individuals to cross traditional job areas and often work in teams, supporting each other. Some types of work which traditionally have involved groups of people – for example, local news gathering – are often now the responsibility of one person, who will light and record images and also record sound.

It is useful for anyone thinking of a technical career to gain a solid foundation in maths and physics. Gaining at least a GCSE/standard grade qualification will be helpful. It is generally accepted that women tend to give up these subjects relatively quickly, reducing their career options as a result. Almost all jobs in broadcast, film and video now require some computer literacy, so that familiarity with the keyboard and reasonable word-processing skills will be essential for most entry-level jobs.

General National Vocational Qualifications (GNVQs), or Vocational 'A' Levels, are now well established in schools and colleges. They offer a mix of projects and practical experience, and encourage students to take a good deal of personal responsibility for learning – and so may be more attractive to many parts of the industry than other, more academic qualifications. In some areas (for example art, design and construction) this is certainly true. In other recruitment areas, recruiters have yet to be absolutely convinced, saying that they will always choose the 'best' candidate regardless of educational background. Similarly, some university media courses seem to be biased against applicants who offer Media GNVQs. Check the stated entry requirements, and talk to admissions tutors about the reality of the situation *before* you make choices between GNVQs (Vocational) and 'A' levels.

Finding out about courses

The *skillsformedia/learndirect* helpline 08080 300 900 is a partnership between *Skillset* and BECTU's media careers service, *skillsformedia*, and the government's national learning advice line, *learndirect*. Specialist advisors can provide details of media and other courses throughout the UK – including online learning – as well as available funding. Online advice is available at www.skillsformedia.com. Two other invaluable sources of information are:

- *Media Courses UK* – a comprehensive guide, providing useful information and contact details on the FE, HE and short-course providers drawn from the *Skillset*/BFI database. Descriptions are written by the course leaders. Published by the BFI and edited by Lavinia Orton.
- *Media and Multimedia Short Courses* – a detailed guide to short courses available (at vastly differing costs) to people at all stages of involvement with the industry. Details include fees, entry requirements and target audience. Updated three times a year, published by the BFI in association with *Skillset*, and compiled by Lavinia Orton.

The Skillset/*BFI course database*

Comprehensive listings of courses can be accessed through the *Skillset* and BFI websites. Bear in mind that inclusion in the database does not mean that the individual course carries a *Skillset* or a BFI seal of approval. Ask for the prospectus and/or publicity material, and do some research before deciding which is the most suitable for you.

Choosing an appropriate course

There are so many courses around that it is easy to be swamped by information, and assume that they must all be, broadly speaking, of equal value. While there are indeed many high-quality and interesting courses available, choosing one that will meet your needs – academic, social and practical – will require considerable time and effort. Before you start, ask yourself this key question: '*Why do I want to do this?*' If the answer is that you want to do a course to develop particular skills and improve your chances of getting relevant work, be prepared to do a lot of research. If however you plan to do something that interests you, but is likely to improve your career prospects only in general terms, you may have an easier (but still not easy!) task.

Higher Education in the UK is big business. Colleges vie with each other to compete for students, each of whom carries a significant amount of government funding. It is not unknown for the marketing people to get slightly carried away in their publicity material. Don't believe everything that is written until you've checked it out for yourself. Because there is a demand for media and film courses, their numbers continue to grow – despite the lack of real job opportunities within the industry.

If you do wish to work in this industry, try to choose a course which offers good practical skills and has a track record of getting graduates into relevant employment. At present there is no 'consumer guide' to the relative merits of courses, although *Skillset* is working towards an accreditation scheme in consultation with HE and the industry. Even the most highly regarded courses can be badly affected by the loss of a key figure, or the inability to renew equipment, or over-expansion of student numbers. The best advice is to check out every course of interest to ensure that it meets your needs. This could require tenacity, as the information may not be readily available. The best courses are the ones that take an interest in their students or trainees, and they should be able to give you enough information on which to base your decision. Be warned that gaining a place on some of the most successful courses can at times seem as daunting as that very first job. But *don't lose heart* – keep trying!

Check the facts

To make sure that you choose the right course for you, check the facts. Treat the exercise as a research project – set up a file, and ask the same questions of each potentially interesting course or training scheme in order to help you make an informed decision.

Gather together information about any relevant factor, and obviously about the costs. The industry-based, new-entrants schemes pay their trainees, but most training will cost you money. Courses with practical projects may also involve additional expense, for such things as film, tape, hire of outside facilities, and actors. Many students raise sponsorship to help with this, but the cost always needs to be considered. Shorter courses are available from a wide range of providers. Some are heavily subsidised by local authorities, Regional Screen Agencies and European funding; others are run commercially. Be sure that you can afford a course before you start – and remember that high cost is not always synonymous with high quality.

Ask the questions

Prospectus/publicity

Where appropriate, read the prospectus or any publicity carefully. Ask what validation or accreditation a course currently has. A look at the reading list will give you an insight into course content. Ask the tutors about what has happened to previous students or trainees. Try to visit the centre while a course is taking place. Talk to current students, and, if possible, people who have graduated from the course and are now working in the industry.

Equipment

Look at the equipment that is used. Will it meet your needs? Does the centre own it, or hire it in? How much 'hands on' contact will you actually get? What level of expertise can you reasonably expect upon completion of the course? How does this match up to the skills required within the industry? For technical jobs it is increasingly important that colleges can offer 'industry standard' software.

Trainers/lecturers

Find out about the trainers or lecturers. What experience do they have within the industry? Are they permanently attached to the course, or will they disappear if a contract comes up? Do they have proven teaching skills? Some courses indicate 'big names' as 'visiting tutors' or 'course directors' – establish what this really means. And what is the ratio of students to tutors? How much personal tuition can you expect? Some of the best-respected courses employ part-time lecturers who continue as industry practitioners, thereby ensuring up-to-date knowledge and contacts.

Placements

Some of the most useful, longer courses include compulsory industry-based work placements. Ask about the established industry contacts, where previous students have gained experience, and who has organised these placements. (Don't be put off if you have to organise your own work experience – this can be excellent training for a freelance career.) Where there are non-compulsory placements, ask about the proportion of students who found placements and also about the nature and length of these periods of experience. The independent producers' organisation PACT has produced a voluntary code of practice that gives a guide to what you should expect from a work experience placement.

Budgets

An attractive feature of some courses is the opportunity to make a video or audio tape, a film or a 'showreel' of work to add to your CV when you start the job hunt. Ask about the funding for student/trainee productions – would you be expected to pay anything in addition to your course fee? And is there a 'ceiling' on the amount that students are allowed to spend on their end-of-course project?

Entry qualifications

How stringent are the entry qualifications for the course? Is there a diversity policy? Are they selecting people on the basis of qualifications and skills, or on the ability to pay? The colleagues you meet on a course could be very useful future contacts within the industry, if they have the same level of commitment and skills as you do.

Skillset *Professional Qualifications (NVQs/SVQs)*
Skillset Professional Qualifications and agreed industry standards have influenced the design and content of many courses. Ask if the practical elements of the course are based on the relevant standards.

accreditation of courses
A few courses have been accredited by industry bodies, which will supply details upon request. Again, these cannot be taken as absolute guarantees of quality, and some excellent courses have not applied for this type of recognition. The accrediting organisations are: BKSTS – The Moving Image Society; and the Broadcasting Journalism Training Council.

Skillset is currently working on the development of a quality approval system for training and education, to support the needs of the audio-visual industries. This will include frameworks for apprenticeships and a 'kitemark' for regional training providers, as well as an approval system for industry-based new entrants' programmes. In the longer term *Skillset* aims to introduce an accreditation policy for Higher Education. *Skillset* is also working with industry to bring about the development of Further Education Centres of Vocational Excellence (CoVEs) that will be linked into relevant local industry networks.

Training within the industry
The audio-visual industries are more and more reliant on self-employed freelancers, and this trend is likely to continue. This freelance workforce is expected to have increasingly high levels of skill and versatility, which calls for training. Unfortunately, the flexible working practices demanded of freelancers also make it difficult for them to plan their own training, even if they are willing to fund it themselves. Any freelancer will tell you that whenever they block out days for training, someone is bound to offer them work on the same dates. Uncertainty about where the next job is coming from makes it tempting to accept the paid work, rather than do the training.

The most recent *Skillset* survey of industry freelancers (*Skillset* Freelance Survey, 2001 – the next survey will be carried out later in 2003) reflects the problem (*see* also pp. 193–4):

- 69% of freelancers reported that they have training needs
- More than 50% of freelancers indicated that there was a lack of suitable training
- 60% said that the high cost of training was a major obstacle, with 37% citing loss of potential earnings as a barrier
- Only 15% of freelancers had received training funded by employers in the past year.

Since its launch in January 1993, *Skillset* has made considerable progress in improving the quality and availability of relevant training. One of its chief roles is to ensure quality standards and training to meet the needs of this creative and changing industry, in order to maintain and enhance its reputation for quality skills.

Skillset does this by co-ordinating the work of a range of individuals and organisations (employers, trade associations, unions, industry bodies, and education providers), as well as the Government and its public agencies, to put together an in-depth picture of current and future training provision for the industry throughout the nations and regions. By finding out what skills issues exist, *Skillset* can ensure that long-term strategies are put in place to address them. The freelance survey quoted above is just one example of the type of research *Skillset* carries out. Its findings can be used to assist training providers to plan relevant training and ensures that investment is targeted to areas where there is genuine need. *Skillset* administers the *Skillset* Investment Funds on behalf of the industry. An Investment Committee comprising leading industry figures and employers manages these funds. The *Skillset* Investment Funds have two main funding streams:

- The Freelance Training Fund
- The Skills Investment Fund

The Freelance Training Fund (FTF)

This fund provides a pool of money to subsidise essential, high-quality training for freelancers. The major industry employers – BBC, Channel Four, ITV, and the Independent Production Training

Fund (IPTF) administered by PACT – contribute just under £1 million per year to this fund.

The Skills Investment Fund (SIF)

This fund is made up of voluntary contributions of 0.5% of production spend from UK film productions up to a ceiling of £39,500. This could represent contributions of over £1 million per year to invest in the national training strategy for film. The SIF is described in more detail in Chapter 4.

Skillset also manages large amounts of European funding and funding from other public sources, such as DfES, as well as the Millennium Awards, a three-year scheme to develop the media skills of 120 people from ethnic minority communities throughout the UK, with BBC support and a grant from the Millennium Commission.

Modern Apprenticeships have been successfully trialled throughout the industry, and not just in the larger organisations. Speak to your careers advisor, or ask at the local Learning and Skills Council to find out if any are operating in your area.

Entry-level, industry-based training schemes

Several well-established, industry-led schemes operate to provide the independent broadcast and film production sector with a pool of well-trained, freelance technical and production people. Designed and operated as co-operative ventures between employers, unions and trainers, they provide some of the best methods of developing employable skills. Participants combine formal training with industry-based work placements. Educational qualifications are not necessary to get on to these schemes. They all operate positive Equal Opportunities policies, and their ex-trainees come from widely differing backgrounds. They are looking for individuals with a proven commitment to their chosen area of work, and the personal skills to enable them to work as a successful freelancer. Participants are paid during the period of their training.

FT2 – Film and Television Freelance Training

FT2 is the only UK-wide provider of training for people seeking to establish a career in the construction, technical and production grades of the film and TV industry. Funded and managed by the industry, through *Skillset's* Investment Funds, the European Social Fund (ESF) and C4, it provides the following – with the intention of training and developing talented individuals for the freelance labour market:

- New Entrant Technical Training Programme
- Set Crafts Apprenticeship Training Scheme
- Independent Companies Researcher Training Scheme
- Freelance *Skillset* Professional Qualification Assessment Service Centre

New entrants into the Technical Training Programme are attached to a variety of productions over a two-year period and paid a monthly allowance. Practical experience is supplemented by specially commissioned intensive short courses. After an initial grounding in a wide range of pre-production, production and post-production areas, trainees choose to concentrate during the second year on a specialist area – for example, camera, sound, make-up or props. Set Crafts is a two-year apprenticeship in set painting, carpentry, wood machinery or fibrous plastering, and the ICRTS is an 18-month scheme for researchers in factual programming.

The number of new places available on the FT2 programmes may vary, but as a general indication, this was the situation in 2002:

- Technical Training Scheme – 12 places
- Set Crafts Apprenticeships – 4 places
- Researcher Training Scheme – 7 places

In May 2002, FT2 launched a new training initiative, the Feature Film Development Internships programme. This scheme runs for 62 weeks and provides full-time paid training in film script development. The scheme will be reviewed in 2004.

All schemes attract thousands of enquiries and applications. Successful candidates need to be very professional in their applications.

Qualifications required

Applicants should show demonstrable commitment to, and enthusiasm for, the industry. Good interpersonal skills are essential, as is the ability to comprehend and achieve the technical standards of the industry. Trainees will be expected to travel, live away from home and work long hours, and get up early in the morning! Many applicants for the Researcher Scheme are graduates, with proven relevant skills. Set Crafts trainees need a CITB NVQ level 2 or equivalent. Make-up and hairdressing trainees need NVQ level 2 in hairdressing and beauty therapy. Production trainees must be able to touch-type at 40 wpm.

Management

FT2 is managed by industry employers and unions: C4, PACT, APA, BBC, ITVA, BECTU and the MPA. *Skillset* supports FT2 through its Investment Funds. Contact:

The Administrator
FT2
4th Floor, Warwick House, 9 Warwick Street, London W1B 5LY
Tel: 020 7734 5141 Fax: 020 7287 9899
Website: www.ft2.org.uk
(Please look at the FT2 website before contacting the office.)

Cyfle

Cyfle, the national vocational training company for the film, television and interactive media industry in Wales, offers two vocational new-entrant training schemes.

The Cyfle full-time new-entrant scheme into film and television is currently 12 months long and offers 18 places in specific industry grades. Following an introductory course, the training is on-the-job with television, film and facilities companies throughout Wales. Trainees also attend specialist external training courses. An integral part of the scheme is attainment of the relevant *Skillset* NVQ: Cyfle is a *Skillset* NVQ Assessment Centre.

The second scheme, Dimension 10, is a full-time, six-month training programme for the interactive media industry, training ten people at a time. Industry-led, each trainee has exclusive use of a computer throughout the course. Trainees are paid a weekly training allowance on both schemes.

In August 2002, Cyfle launched a third programme, the Production Talent Development Scheme. Eleven applicants were selected for this 12-month work placement scheme. Over the next year they will be based with the 11 production companies who helped to select them. The scheme is part-funded by the European Social Fund and SC4. Cyfle manages and monitors the training and provides a training allowance.

Qualifications required

Cyfle's new-entrant training schemes are open to Welsh speakers, those learning Welsh, and non-Welsh speakers. Applicants should be able to demonstrate a burning commitment to working in the industry.

Management

Cyfle is funded by S4C and independent production companies. It also receives funding for new-entrant training from *Skillset*, Education and Learning, Wales (ELWa), the National Assembly for Wales and the European Social Fund.

Its Management Committee comprises representatives of S4C, TAC, BECTU, and *Skillset*. Contact:

Siôn Hughes, Chief Executive
Cyfle
Gronant, Penrallt Isaf, Caernarfon, Gwynedd LL55 1NS
Tel: 01286 671000 Fax: 01286 678831
Email: cyfle@cyfle.co.uk
Website: www.cyfle.co.uk

Scottish Screen

Scottish Screen fulfils a strategic role developing policy in training, skills and education, and also provides a range of training courses, events and seminars to support the development of new entrants and freelance and staff professionals based in Scotland. With the direct support of the local employers, trade associations and trade unions, Scottish Screen is also the approved *Skillset* Professional Qualification (SVQ/NVQ) Assessment Centre for Scotland. As such it plays a key role in the development of qualifications in secondary, Further and Higher Education.

Scottish Screen works with *Skillset* and other agencies to meet the skills gaps in the local industry and to develop models that anticipate future trends and needs. Contact:

Scottish Screen Training
2nd Floor, 249 West George Street, Glasgow G2 4QE
Tel: 0141 302 1700
Website: www.scottishscreen.com
Email: info@scottishscreen.com

Training in the nations and regions

In 2002 *Skillset* introduced an Approvals system for National and Regional Training Partners in response to a key recommendation of the 2001 AVITG report which highlighted the importance of matching education and training provision with industry needs. The *Skillset* industry seal of approval is a quality endorsement signifying that a training partner has met required organisational standards and demonstrated that they promote and deliver training standards that supply the industry with a highly and appropriately skilled workforce. An equivalent approvals system for Industry Training Providers was implemented in 2003.

National and regional training partners all have a slightly different focus, depending on the shape of the industry in their region. Some provide training; others help with training needs and analysis, and the recommendation of solutions. All are involved in three key areas:

- Providing access to relevant training
- Monitoring the changing needs of the industry in their region
- Devising strategies for further development.

Contact the national or regional training partner nearest to you to find out about specific new-entrant training opportunities, usually for very small numbers of people based in the relevant part of the country.

Contact details

Further information is available on the *Skillset* website, www.skillset.org.

Cyfle

Cardiff Office: 3rd Floor, Crichton House, 11–12 Mount Stuart Square, Cardiff CF10 5EE
Tel: 029 2046 5533
Caernarfon Office: Gronant, Penrallt Isaf, Caernarfon, Gwynedd LL55 1NS
Tel: 01286 671000
Website: www.cyfle.co.uk
Email: Cyfle@Cyfle.co.uk

EM Media

35–37 St Mary's Gate, Nottingham NG1 1PU
Tel: 0115 934 9090
Website: www.em0media.org.uk
Email: infor@em-media.org.uk

Media Training North West

Room GO82, BBC, Oxford Road, Manchester M60 1SJ
Tel: 0161 244 4637
Website: www.mtnw.co.uk
Email: info@mtnw.co.uk

Northern Film and Media

Central Square, Forth Street, Newcastle upon Tyne NE1 3PJ
Tel: 0191 369 9200
Website: www.northernmedia.org
Email: (first name of person and then) @northernmedia.org

Northern Ireland Film & Television Commission

3rd Floor, Alfred House, 21 Alfred Street, Belfast BT2 8ED
Tel: 028 9023 2444
Website: www.niftc.co.uk
Email: info@niftc.co.uk

Scottish Screen

2nd Floor, 249 West George Street, Glasgow G2 4QE
Tel: 0141 302 1700
Website: www.scottishscreen.com
Email: info@scottishscreen.com

Screen East
Anglia House, Norwich NR1 3JG
Tel: 0845 601 5670
Website: www.screeneast.co.uk
Email: info@screeneast.co.uk

Screen West Midlands
31–41 Bromley Street, Birmingham B9 4AN
Tel: 0121 766 1470 Fax: 0121 766 1480
Website: www.screenwm.co.uk
Email: info@screenwm.co.uk

South West Screen
St Bartholomews Court, Lewins Mead, Bristol BS1 5BT
Tel: 0117 952 9977
Website: www.swscreen.co.uk
Email: info@swscreen.co.uk

Screen Yorkshire
40 Hanover Square, Leeds LS3 1BQ
Tel: 0113 294 4410
(new website coming soon)

London/South-East: for this region, please contact *Skillset.*

TV training

The days of well-publicised annual training schemes have all but disappeared. The BBC – which, in the opinion of many, used to 'train for the whole industry' – has reduced its entry-level training provision over the past few years, concentrating instead on 'positive action' programmes or one-off initiatives which respond to current and future operational needs. Recent training schemes have included a New Media Trainee Scheme and training for Broadcast Engineers and Technicians. When they do occur, vacancies will be publicised in the national press, on Ceefax page 696, and on the BBC's website (www.bbc.co.uk/jobs/traineeships). Approximately 80,000 speculative enquiries are received by the BBC each year. Many thousands apply for the intermittently advertised 'flagship' training schemes, each offering only a small number of places.

Some ITV companies run local training schemes which are publicised within their own region. Those with satellite channels have found that the atmosphere and demands of low-budget production provide an excellent training ground for the new breed of multi-skilled and flexible production professionals. Occasionally, specialist training schemes (for journalists, in particular) will be publicised locally. ITV companies often have well-established links with a few colleges in their franchise area. Students from these colleges may benefit from visits, work experience and industry lecturers, and are in a good position to compete for relevant vacancies upon graduation. Other occasional initiatives include the annual Metroland Scheme for First Time Directors supported by Carlton Regional Programmes. This is usually advertised in the press in November.

C4 does not make its own programmes, but either commissions them from independent producers or buys direct from other organisations. The channel therefore relies on a trained pool of experienced and talented people to make the quality and standard of programming required for its schedule.

Channel 4 has devolved responsibility for cultural diversity across all departments as part of a major restructure in 2002. In addition, a new trainee scheme for Assistant Commissioners was set up, as well as work placements for new Researchers from ethnic minority backgrounds. It is worth checking the Channel 4 website regularly for such opportunities.

C4 funds training for people working within the independent sector via *Skillset*'s Investment Funds. This money enables freelancers already working in the industry to attend courses at subsidised rates. C4 also contributes, via the FTF, to *Skillset*'s industry-wide initiatives such as the Researcher and Set Crafts training schemes.

Every two years, C4 funds four places for people from an ethnic minority background on the FT2 new entrants scheme. The two-year training is broad-based, and consists of both college-based formal training and placements with independent production companies. The training will provide the necessary grounding for a potential career in the freelance and independent sectors in areas such as camera, editing, production assisting and sound. The training scheme is advertised in the national and ethnic press.

five does not organise any production training, but occasionally offers placements and has recently run a successful Broadcast Management Trainee scheme. BSkyB does not offer any training places at the time of writing. Whenever a 'household name' broadcaster advertises a training scheme it attracts vast numbers of applicants, many exhibiting considerable relevant experience, so competition is fierce. However, the bulk of these (one personnel manager said an estimated 90%) are merely 'having a try'. If you want to be treated seriously, make sure that you apply in a very professional, targeted way and follow the detailed guidelines which often accompany these application forms.

Channel 4/BFI Animator in Residence (AIR) Scheme

These three-month residencies – offering advice from a professional producer, a materials budget and a grant – are open to talented and technically proficient recent graduates with an original idea for a three-minute animation. Successful applicants are chosen by a panel of producers, writers and animators, and the residency can lead to a commission from C4. Contact:

The AIR Scheme Administrator, BFI/NT
South Bank, Waterloo, London SE1 8XT
Tel: 020 7815 1376
Website: www.a-i-r.info

Michael Samuelson VFG Lighting

Michael Samuelson VFG Lighting run a highly regarded new-entrant scheme for people who want to become professional lighting electricians. Graduates of the scheme work throughout the film industry, and often travel abroad. Up to ten trainees are selected each year. Applicants must have a relevant electrical qualification (e.g. City and Guilds 236 part 1), good communication skills, enjoy the film industry and be prepared to gain additional qualifications up to NVQ level 4. It's an intensive course, involving long hours on film sets, and can lead to an exciting and well-paid career. Recruitment takes place in May each year and trainees start in July. For further details, or to apply, please contact Tony Wilcox at:

Michael Samuelson VFG Lighting
Pinewood Studios, Iver Heath, Bucks SL0 0NH.
Alternatively, telephone the Assessment Centre on 020 8795 7000.

Further sources of industry training

The training sector is a business in itself, with many industry professionals now spending the bulk of their time providing skills training and industry knowledge to a diversity of students. Here is a cross-section of the training available.

Industry organisations and associations

The BBC

BBC training courses, both generic and specialist, are open to anyone. Some are subsidised for freelancers through the Freelance Training Fund (*see* also page 222). They cover a wide variety of relevant areas, including:

- An Introduction to Television
- An Introduction to Production
- Television Production Skills
- Working on Location
- Post-production Techniques
- Radio Production
- Digital Audio Skills
- Television Systems
- Technology Updates
- Computer and Network Technology
- Transmission
- Presentation
- Investigative Journalism on the Net
- Producing Images for the Web

For more details, contact:

BBC Training and Development
Wood Norton, Evesham, Worcs WR11 4YB
Website: http://www.bbctraining.co.uk

BKSTS: The Moving Image Society

BKSTS produces a series of relevant courses, some of which are designed for new entrants or individuals with limited working experience. These include:

- Film Foundation Course
- SFX Foundation Course
- An Introduction to Studio Lighting and Camera Techniques

The society also publishes a useful booklet about choosing a relevant course.
www.bksts.com

Women in Film and Television

Women in Film and Television (WFTV) is a membership organisation open to women with at least one year's professional experience in any aspect of either industry. WFTV exists to protect and enhance the status, interests and diversity of women working at all levels in both film and television. Although not a conventional training organisation, the events it organises can provide valuable industry knowledge and contacts.
www.wftv.org.uk

CSV Media

CSV Media runs numerous courses, especially for people currently under-represented in the industry. Courses – which are free to successful applicants – cover a range of TV and radio production skills.
www.csv.org.uk

BECTU

The main trade union for the industry provides opportunities for graduates and new entrants to gain knowledge from industry professionals through the Graduate Membership Scheme, and works with training providers to meet members' skills needs.
www.bectu.org.uk

Film Education

Film Education produces educational TV programmes and runs a series of useful workshops, events and in-service training for schools and colleges.
www.filmeducation.org

National Council for the Training of Journalists
The NCTJ accredits courses at universities and colleges, and also runs a variety of short courses – including several on the law.
www.nctj.com

National Union of Journalists
The NUJ offers a range of professional development opportunities for members.
www.nuj.org.uk

New Media Knowledge (NMK)
Owned by the University of Westminster, NMK runs a programme of events, seminars and training courses for digital media.
www.nmk.co.uk

PACT
PACT produces a voluntary code of practice for training and work experience; this outlines good practice for independent producers.
www.pact.co.uk

Short course training providers
The *Skillset*/BFI handbook, *Media and Multimedia – Short Courses* will provide a good overview of training providers in your region. The following will give you an idea of the variety on offer:

The National Short Course Training Programme – based at the *National Film and Television School* – has a well-established short-course programme aimed mainly at people who are currently working in the industry. Some courses may be ideal for 'topping up' the basic introductory skills learnt on many media courses. Contact at:

NSCTP
Beaconsfield Film Studios, Station Road, Beaconsfield, Bucks HP9 1LG
www.nftsfilm-tv.ac.uk

Ravensbourne College Short Course Unit – offers a range of craft skill short courses for broadcasting and production, many of which attract self-funded students who wish to enhance skills or become multi-skilled using industry-standard equipment. Contact at:

Walden Road, Chislehurst, Kent BR7 5SN
Website: www.rave.ac.uk

Note: universities and colleges are increasingly providing specialist short courses. Check with the relevant departments.

WAVES – the national centre for training women in the audio-visual media culture, with the intention of helping them to make their own work and gain industry employment. Practical and theoretical courses exist, and WAVES has access to industry-standard production equipment. Contact at:

4 Wild Court, London WC2B 4AU

YCTV – Youth Culture TV – a lively charity, with its own TV studio, provides TV production training for people aged between 11 and 20, including masterclasses by industry professionals. Contact at:

Ladbroke Hall, 85 Barlby Road, London W10 6AZ

The Workshop Sector – listed in the *BFI Film and TV Handbook* and on the *Skillsformedia* website www.skillsformedia.com, these organisations are usually non-profit-making. Funded by a range of sources (which may include the BFI, unions, local authorities or the National Lottery) they can provide excellent 'hands on' experience, which may lead to recognised qualifications.

First Film Foundation – set up to help aspiring writers, directors and producers make their first film, this charity offers practical help, as well as educational and promotional programmes. Publishes *First Facts*, a guide to training schemes, funding initiatives and organisations to help new talent. Contact at:

9 Bourlet Close, London W1W 7BP
www.firstfilm.co.uk

Specialist support
Film Education – a registered charity supported by the film industry in the UK. It aims to develop the use of film in the school

curriculum and to facilitate the use of cinemas by schools. It publishes a range of excellent (and free) teaching materials, produces relevant TV programmes, organises screenings, and runs a range of workshops, events and INSET. Contact at:

Film Education
Alhambra House, 27–31 Charing Cross Road, London WC2H 0AU
Tel: 020 7976 2291
Website: www.filmeducation.org

The Film Council – responsible for developing a coherent strategy for film culture and the British film industry, the Film Council has allocated £1 million a year for training. In the first three years the fund will support training in two key areas: scriptwriters and development executives; and business executives, primarily producers and distributors. Details can be found on the website: www.filmcouncil.org.uk.

Media Desk UK – a five-year programme of the European Union to strengthen the competitiveness of the film, TV and new media industries. Media supports nearly 50 of the top European training courses in screenwriting, business management and new technologies. Media desks operate in England, Scotland, Wales and Northern Ireland. Contact details and information can be found on the website: www.mediadesk.co.uk.

skillsformedia – jointly owned by BECTU and *Skillset, skillsformedia* is the UK industry careers advice service for anybody who wants to get into, or get on in, the media. Comprises a website (www.skillsformedia.com) packed with careers and training information; an online advice service; a UK helpline, in partnership with learndirect (08080 300 900); individual advice sessions with trained media careers advisors who have extensive industry experience themselves; and CV and marketing workshops.

Open Learning courses
BBC Television Training supplies a variety of production training videos to education providers, for use by registered students.

Training in specific skills

Because the industry is now dominated by freelancers, much of the craft training that used to come with the job is now the responsibility of the individual. One example of this is make-up and prosthetics. Specialist workshops and masterclasses are run by Woodbridge Productions Ltd, PO Box 123, Hounslow TW4 7EX. A series of training videos are also available.

Organisations that exist to help writers for the screen include:

ARISTA – runs workshops for producers, writers and script editors who already work in the industry, to develop scripts and enable teams to work effectively. Contact at:

11 Wells Mews, London W1P 3FL
Tel: 020 7323 1775
Website: www.aristadevelopment.com
Email: arista@aristotle.co.uk

Performing Arts Labs – run development workshops for exceptionally talented professional writers who want to write for film. Selection is by nomination from past lab participants, or other industry practitioners. Details can be found on the website: www.pallabs.org/labs/screenwriters.

Screenwriters' Workshop – runs courses and events for aspiring and established screenwriters, often involving industry practitioners. Contact at:

114 Whitfield Street, London W1P 5RW
Tel: 020 7387 5511
Website: www.lsw.org.uk

Attending professional/trade organisation events

A series of seminars, workshops, events and conferences is run each year by industry organisations committed to providing training and development for people already in the industry. Some events are suitable for, and open to, individuals at the start of their careers. Some are free, although most cost a few pounds (usually with reductions for full or student members). They are generally accepted to be good value.

More information on these events can be obtained from the following:

BKSTS – The Moving Image Society – runs courses on the practical skills of production, including some introductions and overviews useful for newcomers to the industry. Most courses and seminars are concerned with technical areas, including sound, editing and camerawork. Contact at:

5 Walpole Court, Ealing Studios, Ealing Green, London W5 5ED
Tel: 020 8584 5220
Website: www.bksts.com

The Radio Academy – runs the industry's annual conference, plus seminars and workshops. Contact at:
5 Market Place, London W1N 7AH
Tel: 020 7255 2010
Website: www.radioacademy.org

International Visual Communications Association – the IVCA has a well-developed Training Forum and Business Media Network which advises on training needs and opportunities for film, video, interactive media and business events. It provides a wide range of educational opportunities for its members, including monthly business training lunches, conferences, seminars, and new technology events which assist in skills development. The IVCA also supports the NSCTP and *Skillset.* Contact at:

Business Communication Centre, 19 Pepper Street, Glengall Bridge, London E14 9RP
Tel: 020 7512 0571
Website: www.ivca.org

New Producers Alliance – a membership organisation which offers development events for aspiring producers, directors and script-writers. Contact at:

9 Bourlet Close, London W1W 7BP
Tel: 020 7580 2480
Website: www.newproducer.co.uk

The Producers Alliance for Cinema and Television – PACT provides a training and consultancy service for members, mainly concerned with negotiating deals, getting contracts and building better businesses. Seminars, conferences and training books provide independent producers with legal and business information. PACT also offers a range of support services for new and aspiring producers. Contact at:

45 Mortimer Street, London W1N 7TD
Tel: 020 7331 6000
Website: www.pact.co.uk

The Royal Television Society – organises a wide range of events for the television industry, including special early evening events, conferences, lectures and awards. It sponsors Student Television Awards and welcomes full members and e-members. E-membership is free at the time of writing. For more information contact the RTS at:

Holborn Hall, 100 Grays Inn Road, London WC1X 8AL
Tel: 020 7430 1000
Website: www.rts.org.uk

Gaining specialised technical knowledge
Manufacturing and facilities companies often run courses. Designed primarily for established technicians and engineers who already have a familiarity with the appropriate equipment, they are often useful and good value. Such courses are probably of most interest to people transferring technical skills into the industry, or wishing to be able to offer a multiplicity of skills. In addition to courses, manufacturers often produce technical manuals and training videos, which can be purchased.

Applying for a course
Once you have read all the available literature about the course that interests you, and checked out as many facts as possible against your own priorities, it's time to apply.

The majority of applicants for popular courses will not get past the first hurdle. Why not? Because they are unprofessional in their approach, failing to convince the selectors that they have thought seriously about the industry (or clearly established the area to which their personal skills are best suited).

Find out what the course requires from you. Most will ask for a short, targeted CV and a sample of your work. This could be a short film or tape, a script, still photos – anything that you consider will emphasise your skills. Increasingly, it is important to focus your application on a particular specialism, especially for the industry-based schemes.

If your application impresses the selectors, you will probably be interviewed. As the highly regarded courses are all oversubscribed, you will be tested at this stage on your commitment to working in the industry, and to the course content. The emphasis on personal 'survival' skills is increasingly explored, to check out your likelihood of managing effectively as a freelancer in a tough marketplace. Think about how you organise your time, budget your money, and how you might demonstrate your ability to communicate with a wide range of people.

Access is becoming easier for people without formal academic qualifications. Interviewers will look for evidence that such candidates will 'fit in' and contribute effectively to a course.

Getting the money together

Some of the courses that you will see advertised are very expensive. Remember that high cost doesn't guarantee high quality, and some excellent training courses (even some which lead to relevant qualifications) may be heavily subsidised by a variety of funding bodies. The *Skillset* Freelance Training Fund supports a cross-section of training courses that offer a limited number of subsidised places to established industry practitioners – and there may also be training subsidies available from your regional training partner. **Please note that *Skillset* does not provide any individual funding** – so don't send letters asking for individual support, it will be a waste of your time and effort. Call *skillsformedia*'s free helpline for advice on funding on 08080 300 900.

For many people, though, training will need to be funded by a student loan, or a career development loan. Some 'New Deal' students are attending college courses supported by government funding. Keep up with similar government initiatives through your careers office or local Small Business Service. The Department for Education and Skills publishes a useful booklet, *Money to Learn: Financial Help for Adults in Further Education and Training*, which details possible sources of funding (available from the DfES publications centre, 0845 602 2260, or via the website www.lifelonglearning.dfes.gov.uk/moneytolearn).

If you are applying for a course, and feel that self-financing is out of the question, ask the course administrators for information about how previous students found their funding – they may have useful local contacts. Some may give a small number of free places to unemployed people, or people with useful administrative or IT skills who are prepared to help out.

There are two directories available in public libraries which are worth looking at, if you cannot raise money from more obvious sources: *The Directory of Grant Making Trusts* and *The Charities Digest*. These provide a great deal of useful information, but many of the grants mentioned are for fairly small amounts of money.

In conclusion

If you are determined to enter the TV, radio, film, video and inter-active media industry, it is not an impossible task. The best advice is to be *focused* – analyse your own skills honestly, find out as much as you can about the different aspects of the business, and then decide which is the best and most realistic area for you to target. Next, do everything you can to enhance your 'employability' in your chosen area of initial work. Practical skills are the most useful at this stage. These, in combination with boundless enthusiasm, complete flexibility and an obsession with the industry, may just do the trick.

Training opportunities for disabled people

Training opportunities within the industry for disabled people, or those with particular resource needs, are improving. Many disabled students have successfully completed both long and short courses in TV, radio, film, video and interactive media, or have obtained training places with employer organisations.

Colleges and other training providers

Many colleges are still very inaccessible both physically and in terms of the curriculum resources they offer (for instance, information and teaching materials in large print or on tape). However, some colleges and training organisations have built up valuable experience working with disabled people, and even those with limited access facilities will often go to great lengths to try to meet their needs.

If you are a disabled student or trainee with particular resource needs, you should seek as much information as possible about college sites or training locations, as well as course support facilities, before accepting a place. It is also important to visit the site before-hand if you can, and to talk to tutors to discuss your learning needs. Some universities and colleges have access support units or a designated Disability Advisor whose contact details are often on the establishment's website. Be as clear as possible about what you need from the outset, in order to avoid wasted energy spent on resolving access problems after you have started the course.

If you have an opportunity to go on a short, introductory course in video or other aspects of the media before committing yourself to a vocational course, do take advantage of this. Such courses are particularly useful if you are unsure about your career interests or want to explore your own abilities and limitations. Courses targeting disabled people may be advertised locally, or in the specialist disability arts or general disability press.

The broadcasters

The BBC

The BBC actively welcomes applications from disabled people. BBC opportunities are advertised in the broadcast and disability press, online and on Ceefax page 696. Vacancies can be viewed at www.bbc.co.uk/jobs, and there is a Disability Employment Advisor in BBC Recruitment who can advise on disability support services. You can also write directly to Human Resource departments in your own BBC region.

There are opportunities for work placements, such as the 'Extend' scheme which provides work placements for disabled people in a range of host departments. Details of this and other entry opportunities can be found on www.bbc.co.uk/howdoIgetin.shtml, or contact the Diversity Unit on 020 8576 1208.

ITV/five
Individual companies do target disabled people from time to time, and advertisements will appear in the media press and sometimes in disability publications. You can also write directly to Human Resource department directors at your nearest television company. A majority of the large broadcasters are members of the Broadcasters' Disability Network, which is part of the Employers' Forum on Disability. These companies have a particular commitment to seeking and supporting disabled employees, and under the BDN umbrella have produced their own Action Plans launched as part of a Manifesto of key commitments in May 2002.

Channel 4
Channel 4 is also a member of the Broadcasters' Disability Network. However, virtually all programmes for Channel 4 are made by independent production companies, so the opportunities for production jobs within the channel are very limited. There have been training initiatives in the past involving placements with independent production companies, and the Human Resources department should be contacted for up-to-date information. The channel also employs a Disability Advisor, and has a disability database on which disabled people with a variety of skills and talents can place their names. This internal database is used by Channel 4 and the independent companies which it commissions.

Production database
Hopes for a disability database for the industry have not so far been met. However, an initiative by the Broadcasters' Disability Network to sponsor 100 disabled industry workers on productionbase.co.uk is being developed. This is a subscription database widely used by the industry.

Workable
The organisation Workable has a Creative Industries section (previously known as 'Mediable' and 'Artable'). It aims to give disabled graduates work experience in the broadcasting and arts industries, and has already established contacts with major broadcasters.

Broadcast Journalism bursaries

RADAR (the Royal Association for Disability and Rehabilitation) has occasionally offered bursaries in broadcast journalism to disabled people, but it is not a yearly scheme. Write directly to them for up-to-date information.

Disability Support Funding

Employees and freelance workers are eligible for equipment and other assistance under the Employment Service's Access to Work scheme (ATW). Details are available from the local Disability Employment Advisor (DEA) who is a member of a Disability Service Team, and can be contacted through your local Jobcentre or Jobcentre Plus.

If you are not employed and want to do a training course, but need aids, equipment or other help similar to that provided under Access to Work, then you need to seek help from your local Learning and Skills Council (previously TECs). Individual charities and trusts may also be able to help: local libraries hold reference books listing these.

Students on accredited courses may also be eligible for the Disabled Students Allowance. The organisation Skill: The National Bureau for Students with Disabilities has helpful publications and up-to-date advice on DSA. Some of these are listed below, together with Skill's address.

Skillset itself does not fund individual trainees on courses, but does support courses that target or include disabled students. Courses or workshops that aim to attract disabled students are likely to have better support resources than others, but may be short in duration or only of the 'taster' variety. This can be frustrating for people wishing to enter the industry. Nevertheless, they are often fully funded and can offer invaluable experience. Such targeted courses are usually advertised in the specialist disability press and on local networks, as well as in the more mainstream advertising outlets.

Impact of the Disability Discrimination Act 1995

The right of access to training is covered under the Disability Discrimination Act. Under Part II of the Act, employers of more than 15 people (a figure that includes contract and part-time workers) have a duty to ensure that employees are not discriminated against in access to training during their career. Under Part III of the Act, service providers such as training organisations, large and small, should ensure that training courses are accessible to disabled people.

The Special Educational Needs and Disability Act 2001 (effective from September 2002) removes some of the problems and ambiguity in education and training provision caused by the very limited inclusion of education in the original DDA. The new Act effectively amends the DDA and in the Post-16 sector improvements in access are to be phased in from September 2002, 2003 and 2005.

Previously colleges and universities funded by Further Education or Higher Education Funding Councils needed only to provide an updated yearly Statement detailing the kind of access and support they offered to disabled students, but there were no rights of access for students under the DDA. The responsibilities of independently funded vocational schools and colleges that did not have to produce statements – for instance the National Film and Television School – fell into a grey area.

The new legislation makes the expectation of access to education and 'training' at all levels very clear, but this is a complex area and much depends on the development of case law. The Disability Rights Commission is an invaluable source of advice and key government publications about the DDA. Skill: The National Bureau for Students with Disabilities is also a useful source for disability and education publications and advice.

Publications

Information
A Guide to the Disability Discrimination Act 1995 for Institutions of Further and Higher Education (updated in 2002)
Financial Assistance in Further Education
Students with Disabilities in Higher Education: A Guide for All Staff by Corlett, S. and Cooper, D. (Aimed at teaching staff but information also useful for students)

All the above available from:

Skill: National Bureau for Students with Disabilities
Chapter House, 18–20 Crucifix Lane, London SE1 3JW
Office: Tel: 020 7450 0620 (voice and text)
Tel: Information Service (1.30–4.30 Mon–Fri) 0800 328 5050 (voice)
0800 068 2422 (text)
Website: www.skill.org.uk

Disability Discrimination Act 1995 publications
For a full government publications list and advice contact:

Disability Rights Commission
DRC Contact Centre, Freepost MIDO 2164, Stratford Upon Avon,
CV37 9BR
Helpline: Tel: 08459 622 833 Text: 08457 622 644 Fax: 08457 778 878
Email: enquiry@drc-gb.org
Websites: www.drc-gb.org
            www.disability.gov.uk

Disabled workers in the industry
Adjusting the Picture: A Producer's Guide to Disability
Employers' Forum on Disability and ITC
(Includes positive role models)
Copies from Broadcasters' Disability Network at EFD or ITC (EFD
address below), or access via websites www.employers-forum.co.uk
and www.itc.org.uk.

Declarations of Independence: War Zones and Wheelchairs
Hockenberry, John
Viking, 1996
(Autobiography of American wheelchair-using broadcast journalist)

Framed: Interrogating Disability in the Media
(*Part 3, Opening Doors: Performance, Production and Training*)
Pointon, A. & Davies, C. (eds)
BFI Publishing 1997
(Disabled people's accounts of entering the theatre and broad-
casting)

See it My Way
White, Peter
Little, Brown, 1999
(Autobiography of blind UK journalist, radio/television presenter and producer)

Disability press (for advertisements about courses and training schemes)

Disability Now
Scope, 6 Market Road, London N7 9PW
Tel: 020 7619 7323 (voice) 020 7619 7331 (fax) 020 7619 7332 (text)
Advertising: 020 7619 7336
Email: editor@disabilitynow.org.uk
Website: www.disabilitynow.org.uk
(Monthly, national reach)

Disability Times
84 Claverton Street, London SW1V 3AX
Tel: 020 8566 1204 (voice) 020 8566 1208 (fax) Advertising 020 8579 6002 (voice)
(Monthly – with link to Disability Update on C4 teletext 466)

DAIL Magazine (Disability Arts in London)
The Diorama Arts Centre, 34 Osnaburgh Street, London NW1 3ND
Tel: 020 7691 4202 (voice) 020 7619 4201 (text) 020 7916 5396 (fax)
Email: enquiries@dail.dircon.co.uk
Website: www.dail.dircon.co.uk
(Monthly, free to disabled people in the London area. National reach)

Etcetera (weekly on-line newsletter)
NDAF (National Disability Arts Forum)
MEA House, Ellison Place, Newcastle upon Tyne NE1 8XS
Tel: 0191 261 1628 (voice) 0191 261 32237 text 0191 222 0573 fax
Email: ndaf@ndaf.org
Website: www.ndaf.org
(Free online only bulletin includes jobs, training and funding opportunities in arts and media areas)

Useful addresses

AbilityNet
Helpline Tel: 0800 269 545
Email: enquiries@abilitynet.org.uk
Website: www.abilitynet.co.uk
(Expert advice in disability and computing)

Access to Work Scheme
Contact Disability Employment Advisor (DEA) via the nearest Jobcentre or Jobcentre Plus.
Website: www.Jobcentreplus.gov

British Council of Disabled People
Litchurch Plaza, Litchurch Lane, Derby DE24 8AA
Tel: 01332 295551 (voice) 01332 298288 (text), 01332 295580 (fax)
Email: general@bcodp.org.uk
Website: www.bcodp.org.uk
(Umbrella of organisations controlled by disabled people)

British Deaf Association
1–3 Worship Street, London EC2A 2AB
Tel: 0207 588 3520 Fax: 020 7588 3142 Text: 020 7588 3528
Website: www.bda.org.uk
(Campaigning organisation for British sign language users; also organises yearly Deaf Film Festival)

Broadcasters' Disability Network
Employers' Forum on Disability
Nutmeg House, 60 Gainsford Street, London SE1 2NY
Tel: 020 7403 3020 (voice and text)
Email: efd@employers-forum.co.uk
Website: www.employers-forum.co.uk

CACDP (Council for the Advancement of Communication with Deaf People)
Block 4, Science Park, Durham University, Stockton Road, Durham DH1 3UZ
Tel: 0191 383 1155 (voice) 0191 383 7915 (text)
Website: www.cacdp.demon.co.uk

(Publishes annual Register of Sign Language Interpreters and minimum rates)

Centre for Accessible Environments
Nutmeg House, 60 Gainsford Street, London SE1 2NY
Tel: 020 7403 3020 (voice/text)
Email: info@cae.org.uk
(Advice, publications on environmental access and register of access auditors)

Disabled Living Foundation
380–384 Harrow Road, London W9 2HU
Tel: 020 7298 6111 Helpline: 0870 603 9177
(Exhibition and advice on aids and equipment – appointment only)

Disability Wales
Wern Ddu Court, Caerphilly Business Park, Van Road, Caerphilly, CF83 3ED
Tel: 02920 887325 (voice/text) fax 02920 888702
Email: info@dwac.demon.co.uk
Website: www.dwac.demon.co.uk

LDAF (London Disability Arts Forum)
The Diorama Arts Centre, 34 Osnaburgh Street, London NW1 3ND
Tel: 020 7916 5484 (voice) 020 7691 4201 (text) 020 7916 5396 (fax)
Email: l.daf@virgin.net
Email: dff@virgin.net (for Disability Film Festival organisers)
Website: www.dail.dircon.co.uk

Mental Health Media (for Mediafirst)
356 Holloway Road, London N7 6PA
Tel: 020 7700 8171 (voice)
Website: www.mediafirst.org.uk
(Mediafirst promotes media and video journalism for people with learning difficulties)

RADAR (Royal Association for Disability and Rehabilitation)
12 City Forum, 250 City Road, London EC1V 8HF

Tel: 020 7250 3222 (voice) 020 7250 4119 (text) 020 7250 0212 (fax)
Email: radar@radar.org.uk
Website: www.radar.org.uk
(General information and monthly bulletin)

RNIB (Royal National Institute for the Blind)
105 Judd Street, London WC1H 9NE
Tel: 020 7388 1266 Text: 0845 758 5691 Fax: 020 7388 2034
Helpline: 0845 766 9999
Email: rnib@org.uk
Website: www.rnib.org.uk
(Information on audio-description, access/mobility, legal issues)
RNIB Customer Services, Peterborough, 0845 702 3153
(Aids, equipment and transcription service information)

RNID (Royal National Institute for Deaf People)
19–23 Featherstone Street, London EC1Y 8SL
Tel: 020 7296 8000 (voice) 020 7296 8001 (text)
Information line: 0808 808 0123 Text: 0808 808 9000
Email: informationline@rnid.org.uk
Website: www.rnid.org.uk and www.rnid.org.uk/equipment
(General advice, interpreters' service and information on aids and
equipment)

Scope
6 Market Road, London N7 9PW
Tel: 020 7619 7100 Fax: 020 7619 7399 Helpline: 0808 800 3333
Email: cphelpline@scope.org.uk
Website: www.scope.org.uk
(Employment support particularly for people with cerebral palsy)

Scottish Connections Disability Information and News
(via Making Connections Unit – website only)
Website: www.mcu.org.uk

Workable
123 Minories, London EC3N 1NT
Tel/text: 020 7553 0002 Fax: 020 7553 0008
Email: info@workableuk.org

Website: www.workableuk.org
(Contact: Creative Industries section dealing with employment
and training placements with media organisations – initiatives
previously known as 'Mediable' and 'Artable')

Skillset Professional Qualifications for industry practitioners

Once you start to gain experience in this industry, you will have to
think strategically about your future development and
marketability. As the industry becomes more competitive and
sectors converge, people who can assure potential employers of
their competence will be in a far stronger position than those with
vague CVs. The most effective way to do this is by completing a
Skillset Professional Qualification.

Skillset is the Sector Skills Council for the audio-visual industries.
It works with all parts of the industry (employers, trade associations,
unions, industry bodies, individuals, and training and education
providers), as well as government, to find out what the skills issues
of the industry are and what needs to be done to address them. Part
of this work involves the setting of occupational standards, and from
these standards *Skillset* Professional Qualifications have been
developed, enabling people working in the industry to prove and
enhance the skills that they have. Already, more than 3000 industry
practitioners have registered for a full cross-section of the *Skillset*
Professional Qualifications (NVQs/SVQs).

Why is there a need for standards and professional qualifications?

Changes in the TV, radio, film, video and interactive media industry
have brought the issue of training needs and skills shortages to the
top of the agenda for many industry strategists. Results published
from several extensive surveys – commissioned by *Skillset* – show
that although some work areas are oversupplied, others are
currently experiencing a lack of suitably trained practitioners, and
several work areas can expect skills shortages. At present, many of
these skills are supplied by an ageing workforce of people who were
systematically trained in the 'old days' of the BBC and ITV
companies when people were employed as staff. Now, entry into the
industry is much more haphazard and there are not always suitably

qualified replacements when the older generation start to leave. This emerging skills gap could damage the excellent reputation that the UK industry has. In response to this, *Skillset* has embarked upon the mammoth task of providing development pathways – through vocational training – to supply a skilled workforce which can respond effectively to the ever-changing demands of this competitive and increasingly high-technology environment.

At the time of writing, around 40 sets of occupational standards have been approved for this sector, against which a range of nationally recognised qualifications have been developed – from make-up and costume, to production research and interactive media. Standards for other areas are being developed and updated all the time: look at the *Skillset* website for details.

What are Skillset *Professional Qualifications?*

Skillset qualifications can only be awarded to professionals working in the industry, or those on new entrants schemes linked to the industry. They are based on the specific skills and competences needed to do a wide range of jobs across the industry. They concentrate on the real skills that people use everyday in doing their jobs.

High-level performance standards have been produced and agreed by professionals in their area of expertise. In order to gain a highly valued qualification which will be respected by future employers, individuals have to provide evidence to show that their skills meet these standards. All of *Skillset*'s Professional Qualifications are practically based, current and highly relevant. For example:

- Camera Assistance – level 2
- Camera Operations – level 3
- Camera Direction – level 4

The standards agreed for every skill area are relevant and up-to-date, with the criteria regularly reviewed to ensure that the skill requirements reflect the needs of a changing industry. This is particularly reassuring for individuals who need to feel confident that the time and money invested in their personal development will lead to a well-respected qualification. *Skillset* Professional Qualifications are particularly appropriate for people who will work across a range of sectors, or offer an assortment of skills.

These nationally recognised qualifications have all been formally accredited by the Qualification and Curriculum Authority (QCA), and the Scottish Qualifications Authority (SQA), and are accepted as absolute guides to practical competence in specific occupational areas as assessed by industry practitioners. The standards and qualifications have the support of many leading industry figures and they are now widely used by recruiters and training and development specialists to plan interviews and assess an individual's training needs.

Skillset Professional Qualifications are perhaps most valuable for the growing number of industry freelancers. When they approach a potential employer, it is a huge advantage to show that they have a guaranteed level of competence. In an industry where there is little room for 'passengers', producers and directors are very wary of making a mistake when building their team. In the past, this has meant that, unless you were already known to the recruiter, there was very little chance that they would risk taking you on. Now *Skillset* Professional Qualifications are helping a wide cross-section of people to develop their experience in all sectors.

a practical assessment of competence

Skillset qualifications are all about *the ability to do a real job*, so assessment takes place (as much as is possible) during real productions. Nine Assessment Centres have been established throughout the UK: some are in single large companies, such as the BBC; others are managed by the national and regional training partners (*see* also pp. 227–9); and another group has been provided by industry training providers such as FT2, Cyfle and Scottish Screen. Where appropriate, most offer the opportunity for assessment to internal and external freelancers. The individual Assessment Centres are key partners in helping *Skillset* to continue to develop these relevant qualifications. *Skillset* will provide you with information about the different qualifications and advise you about the appropriate Assessment Centre – see the website: www.skillset.org. By contacting the Assessment Centre you will be able to discuss your requirements and options with an industry specialist. If you do decide to embark upon a *Skillset* qualification, you will immediately become involved in a structured – but very flexible – process.

You will be allocated an assessor (who will always be someone currently working in your skill area), and briefed about what evidence and skills you will be expected to deliver for assessment. Assessors have been carefully selected as industry experts with up-to-date experience. They have all successfully completed a special training programme, and are all committed to the maintenance of high standards in their individual areas. The process will then start properly:

- You will be assessed on your competence in your present job.
- A series of meetings will be agreed with your assessor, who will help and advise you on how to build the appropriate 'portfolio of evidence' which will include relevant evidence and 'references' to support previous experience.
- When you feel ready, your assessor will come and observe you doing the relevant job. If there are any gaps in your experience and training (e.g. Health & Safety requirements), he or she will advise you on where to get appropriate training. Once you have shown practical evidence of skills equivalent to the compulsory and optional units for the qualification you have selected, you will be awarded the certificate.
- At regular intervals, the centre will be visited by an external verifier – also a practitioner in the industry – who will ensure that national standards are maintained.

Many experienced people within the industry are enthusiastic about achieving a qualification that formally recognises their competence. Documented past experience and peer testimonials are collected and presented to the assessor as 'evidence' for a specific qualification. This route to assessment is now available in all centres.

What is the relationship between the Skillset standards and training courses?

Hopefully, a very close one. In future, many of the best-regarded courses will be mapped to the standards and will give trainees the opportunity to acquire skills which relate to *Skillset* Professional Qualifications, and ultimately a full level of qualification. Unfortunately, at present some colleges and training centres are liable to give the false impression that the training they offer is more valuable than it really is. To ensure that your precious time and money isn't wasted, don't be afraid to ask questions of the course organisers – for example: 'Is the training based on *Skillset* standards for this employment area?'

The best way to get an insight into the skills required at each level is to look at the summary of *Skillset* standards and qualifications for the occupational area and level that interests you. The 'route-maps' are easy to read. For example: *Editing level 3* is for people who already work in a relevant editing media area, either in film or electronic post-production. Candidates are required to complete six units (three compulsory, one Health & Safety unit and two options). The following is an example of a mandatory unit for camera assistance:

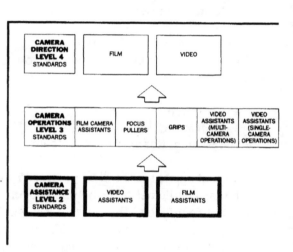

THE STANDARDS AND QUALIFICATIONS FOR CAMERA ASSISTANCE LEVEL 2

RELATED QUALIFICATIONS WITHIN CAMERA

Standards should not simply be looked at in isolation but considered in the context of the level of qualifications and related qualifications which may provide opportunities for career development.

CHOOSING THE RIGHT CAMERA ASSISTANCE ROUTE AT LEVEL 2

There are 2 recognised routes through Camera Assistance at Level 2. In total 5 units are required to complete this qualification.

Film Assistants will take C3, C4, X1, X2 and C6. Video Assistants will take C1, C2, X1, X2 and C5.

'How useful will this training be in helping me find work?'
Remember that people organising training courses are selling their product to you. Don't accept bland generalisations such as 'the majority of our graduates find work in the industry': ask around. Find out how the training is regarded by the sort of organisations you would like to work for. And, wherever possible, talk to previous course members. As a general rule, if the training provides you with the knowledge and skills to help you work towards a *Skillset*

Professional Qualification, that is the best indicator that the course content is relevant to the modern TV, radio, film, video and interactive media industry.

How long will it take me to gain a Skillset Professional Qualification?

There are no fixed timetables. Factors such as the level you wish to attain, the ease with which you can reach the standards for individual units, and your previous experience will all affect the length of time you can expect it to take. Unlike a conventional exam, *Skillset* Professional Qualifications are not gained by studying a formal syllabus; your 'syllabus' of practical, relevant experience will be agreed with your assessor. And the more detail you can present to show relevant past experience, the quicker the assessment process will be. You can also choose the order in which you decide to present units for assessment.

How much will this cost me?

You will need to plan to pay fees for your qualification, which will cover:

- Registration
- Certification
- Assessment (for external candidates)

Details of current fees will be provided by the Assessment Centre. External candidates may be charged on a different scale from internal candidates. The quoted cost will be for assessment and certification only. If you need additional training or experience to reach the required skill standards, you may need to pay for a specific course.

Who awards the qualifications?

Skillset Professional Qualifications are awarded by EAL (EMTA Awards Ltd). All the qualifications have been accredited by the Qualifications and Curriculum Authority (QCA) and the Scottish Qualifications Authority (SQA). Details of every award will be retained in a permanent national archive.

Designed to benefit all concerned

There is already plenty of evidence that the introduction of *Skillset* Professional Qualifications can lead to a 'win-win' situation for all concerned. In a predominantly freelance industry, they are proving a positive help to producers and production managers as they build teams of suitably qualified people. Recruiters are using the standards as the basis of 'person specifications' to check out at an interview, and heads of training and development are using the standards to identify individual skills shortages in their workforce.

The individuals

Skillset Professional Qualifications will both help you to develop relevant skills and give you formal recognition for your achievements. They should help you to obtain suitable work within your sector of the industry and also, when appropriate, in other sectors.

The employer

Recruiting people with *Skillset* Professional Qualifications can substantially reduce the risk involved in employing 'untried' people. Each qualification guarantees a specified level of competences, including aspects of Health & Safety which are becoming increasingly important for insurance requirements. For longer-term employees, investment in relevant industry training can only benefit the organisation, enhancing employee relations and contributing to quality creative output.

The industry

Skillset Professional Qualifications are beginning to deliver a more committed and flexible workforce, opening the way for predominantly freelance employees to keep abreast of new trends and technologies. They will provide consistently high-quality standards in a safety-conscious environment.

Skillset Professional Qualifications are open to anyone working within the TV, radio, film, video and interactive media industry. There are no minimum entry qualifications, and diversity policies are explicitly and implicitly embodied in the standards.

To find out more about *Skillset* Professional Qualifications, visit the website: www.skillset.org, or write to:

Skillset
Prospect House, 80–110 New Oxford Street, London WC1A 1HB
Tel: 020 7520 5757
Email: info@skillset.org
Or contact the Awarding Body:

EAL (EMTA Awards Ltd)
Customer Services, 14 Upton Road, Watford, Herts WD18 0JT
Tel: 01923 652 400
Email: customercare@emta.org

Getting in and Getting on in the TV, Radio, Film, Video and Interactive Media Industry

It is estimated that 60,000 people try to enter the audio-visual industries every year… and only a few thousand will actually find jobs. Within this chapter, we hope to give you some 'insider' information that should help your chances of success. We've spoken to a diversity of employers, who have been happy to share advice; and we have also gathered invaluable information from a range of *Skillset* research reports which have all been published since the first edition of this handbook.

The third industry census – conducted by *Skillset* to gain a 'snapshot' of people working in the industry on one day (26th May 2002) – provided a range of statistics which should be of interest to anyone planning to enter the industry. Key findings included the following:

- It was estimated that around 150,000 people were working on Census Day in the different industry sectors, with around a further 150,000 freelancers part of the workforce but not working on that day.
- Around 50% of the total workforce is freelance but the vast majority works in sectors such as film and commercials production.
- Around two-thirds of the industry work in London or the South East.
- Overall, women make up around two-fifths of the workforce.

However, there are also major differences in the proportions of women working in different occupational groups, down at only around one in ten in camera, lighting, sound, special effects and broadcast engineering. There are a few occupational groups where women comprise the majority of the workforce. They include make-up and hairdressing (93%), costume and wardrobe (82%), and production (55%).

- Between 2000 and 2002, there has been a substantial increase in the representation of ethnic minorities in the industry, rising from 5.4% to 8.6% among employees, and from 6.4% to 7.3% among freelancers. The increase is most marked in broadcast TV and radio, where for example, levels among employees have increased from 6.3% to 7.9% and 6.9% to 7.8% over two years.

All of this information provides useful food for thought: further information on the census is available from *Skillset* (access the website on www.skillset.org).

The *Skillset* Freelance Survey published in January 2002 supplements this knowledge. On any one day it estimated that 35% of the active workforce would be freelance (indicating, unsurprisingly, that not all 'active' freelancers work all the time). The average age was 39, with 6% younger than 25. The survey showed that younger elements of the freelance workforce are increasingly highly qualified, with media studies degrees well in evidence. Crucially, only 4% of the freelancers surveyed had found their work through advertisements.

When asked about their original entry routes into the industry for the *Skillset* workforce development plan, freelancers gave the following information (*see* table on p. 261).

The same research study gathered detailed information about qualifications (*see* table on p. 262).

Levels of postgraduate qualification are also relatively high, with at least one-fifth of freelancers in each sector holding a postgraduate degree. In some cases the proportion is considerably higher, such as:

- Animation (42%)
- Feature film (32%)
- Cable and satellite (31%)

Sector	Advertisement	From an Employer	Contacted Company	Trade Union	Agency/Diarist	Friend/Relative	Word of Mouth	Careers Service	Trainer/HE/FE
Animation	12	6	53	0	12	24	6	0	0
Broadcast Radio	31	8	13	0	4	19	12	12	0
Broadcast TV	24	13	32	1	4	21	10	3	4
Cable/Satellite	23	17	34	0	4	25	10	3	4
Commercials	12	17	31	3	3	29	12	3	2
Corporate Production	26	12	33	2	3	22	11	4	4
Facilities	22	19	28	3	0	22	9	6	3
Feature Film	14	19	26	4	6	32	9	1	3
Independent Production	19	14	31	2	3	27	11	1	5
New Media	17	19	38	2	4	19	13	4	6

Original entry routes into the industry for freelancers (nov 2000 – percentage [%])

Sector	P/G degree in Media Studies	P/G degree in other subject	U/G degree in Media Studies	U/G degree in other subject	Relevant technical qual.	Other technical qual.	NVQ	Modern Apprenticeship
Animation	30	12	41	24	12	6	6	0
Broadcast Radio	17	8	21	33	33	21	13	0
Broadcast TV	14	12	23	33	26	12	10	2
Cable/Satellite	18	13	28	46	34	8	12	0
Commercials	13	7	30	33	22	7	8	1
Corporate Production	14	14	28	33	26	11	13	1
Facilities	15	15	30	37	30	30	11	7
Feature Film	21	11	23	32	24	14	6	3
Independent Production	13	12	30	35	19	10	10	1
New Media	14	16	43	27	27	14	11	0

Freelancers in each sector holding qualifications (percentage [%])

- Facilities (30%)
- New media (30%)

Technical qualifications (which may be held in conjunction with degrees or other qualifications) are also widely held across the audio-visual industries, but with more variation by sector than graduate qualifications.

Sectors using higher levels of graduate and postgraduate freelancers tend to use proportionately fewer people with technical qualifications. Thus, for example, 12% of freelancers in animation hold or are studying for relevant technical qualifications, compared to 33% in broadcast radio and 26% in broadcast television, where the use of graduates is lower.

However, although 50% of the workforce is freelance, the other 50% isn't... and getting in and getting on for most people requires a mix of talent and common sense. Within this chapter, we aim to provide useful guidelines – whether you plan to be employed or self-employed.

Skillset Professional Qualifications are open to anyone working within the TV, radio, film, video and interactive media industry. There are no minimum entry qualifications, and Equal Opportunities policies are explicitly and implicitly embodied in the standards. To find out more about *Skillset* Professional Qualifications, *see* Chapter 9, pp. 251–8, and visit the website www.skillset.org or email them on info@skillset.org.

There is a big difference, however, in trying to get into a hugely oversubscribed and demanding area, and being more strategic in identifying what different employers are looking for in other areas (which may well open doors into the original area within a fairly short time). People throughout the industry commented on the advantages given to individuals that were 'already there'. So the careers advisors were probably right... if you keep your options open, you will improve your chances of getting in. Getting on will then be up to you!

Planning your strategy

Everyone knows that the traditional media industry is difficult to get established in. If you have already talked to a careers advisor, it's more than likely that you have been given sensible advice about 'keeping your options open' and 'doing your research thoroughly'. For many people with a passion for media, this barrier merely confirms their intention to keep on trying.

In the most oversubscribed areas, especially junior programme- or film-making jobs, the recruiters felt that 'up to 90%' of applications were 'a waste of time'. Yet in other, less obvious areas, they said: 'It's difficult to attract reasonable applicants, and we have to resort to agencies.' Throughout the traditional industry there are areas of skills shortage where good candidates can virtually name their price. If people do as careers advisors suggest, and research their options thoroughly, it may be possible to create a satisfying 'win-win' situation.

So, before you start out on the inevitably time-consuming, frustrating – and often expensive – pathway into the industry, stop for a moment and think:

- What do I have to offer? Be realistic about your current skills, aptitudes and experience.
- When am I prepared to offer these things?
- Where do I want to work? Flexibility is the best policy at the start of careers in this industry.
- What sort of lifestyle do I want – now and in the future?

When you have answered these questions honestly and realistically, the next step is to do the research to establish who might be interested in what you have to offer. Then, as the marketing people say, offer yourself:

- In the right way
- At the right time.

It sounds simple, doesn't it? So why do so many thousands of people receive disappointing news each week? Many *Media Guardian* ads now include a rather depressing statement, along the lines of 'successful candidates will be notified by x date' – meaning that unsuccessful ones will not merit any communication at all. This is perfectly understandable. Quite apart from the stationery and stamps, the labour costs required to respond may be more than the company can justify.

To avoid this fate, ensure that you are well informed, extremely realistic, and knowledgeable about the work area that you decide to focus on. Then, you just have to persuade someone – very effectively – to give you a break. In this chapter, we give you some pointers to help you approach the task of finding that all-important first job in a professional manner.

Consider your skills

Before you start to think about individual jobs, or potential employers, you need to think about what you have to offer the industry. Remember that, in these increasingly cost-conscious times, employers are looking for people who can make a contribution from day one – and not just people who would like to work in the industry 'because it looks interesting'.

Think about what you do well, and how you could present evidence of this effectively at an interview. Make a list of the skills you would be able to take to a job at the moment, and think of three examples to support each one. Here are some examples:

I could help out in a film or TV production office:
- I have good IT skills
- I'm not afraid of figures
- I have customer service experience and am used to using the telephone.

I'd like to join a games production team:
- I have strong analytical skills
- I enjoy working in a creative team
- I love playing computer games.

I'd like to be a runner in a facilities house:
- I am good at establishing relationships with people
- I enjoy dealing with 'customers'
- I have a range of technical skills and interests.

I'd like to be a research assistant:
- I'm very well organised, and can manage my time effectively
- I can file and access information from a variety of sources
- I am confident about using the telephone.

Think about the things you could be better at

What sort of skills could you develop or 'polish' to make you more attractive as a candidate? Some of the most employable individuals can offer a portfolio of sought-after 'transferable skills' which, at first, may not seem entirely relevant to the work you want to do.

In addition to the specialised practical skills required by particular jobs (such as camera operation or sound balancing), employers are increasingly impressed by skills in some of the following:

- Word processing
- Spreadsheet production
- Report writing
- Web design
- Practical problem-solving
- Team membership
- Customer service
- Sales and marketing ability
- Financial awareness
- Languages
- Time management
- Presentation
- Database management
- Presentation tools
- Internet research
- Image manipulation
- Project management
- Client relationship management
- Quality assurance
- General business awareness

Build up a picture of yourself at the moment, and consider how to fill the gaps. In particular, think about your constraints, which are the things that hold you back. Some are real, and need to be accepted – if you don't like heights, don't be an electrician! Some are temporary ('I can't type at the moment'), and some are almost certainly imaginary ('they wouldn't be interested in me...'). Knowing about your constraints can improve your chances of making a good career decision, and appearing as a serious candidate. People often feel that by 'promising to do anything' they will impress. Don't promise anything that you can't deliver… it's a very small world, and it won't do your reputation any good.

Many jobs in TV, radio, film, video and interactive media involve long – and often unpredictable – hours, often with periods away from home. This means that anyone who has to care for young children or elderly relations, or has to be anywhere at fixed times during the week, may find it difficult to balance all the demands. Most freelance jobs do not provide a regular income, and substantial financial commitments (such as a mortgage) can be a real worry. This may be a good reason to delay the start of your freelance career until you have saved a protective 'cushion' of money from other work – consistent advice from feature-film professionals at the time of writing. Think about the things that may prevent you from doing – and enjoying – some jobs, and target the ones which will meet your needs, even if initially they appear less 'glamorous'.

skillsformedia – *careers and training advice for the industries*

skillsformedia is a partnership initiative between *Skillset* and BECTU, supported by the major broadcasters, which provides an on- and offline careers development and training advice, information and guidance service for students, new entrants, and people already working in the industry. It offers independent, confidential advice to help you get the media career you want.

The online service: www.skillsformedia.com provides information, advice and links to a wide range of careers information resources, including case studies, practical hints and tips and job profiles. The site has two main navigation routes:

- 'Getting In': aimed predominantly at new entrants
- 'Getting On': aimed at industry professionals seeking to update skills, change direction, or gain promotion.

Other services offered by *skillsformedia* to clients throughout the UK include:

skillsformedia Helpline: Careers information and advice by phone – call 08080 300 900 to speak to a specialist media advisor. The line is open from 8.00 a.m. to 10.00 p.m, seven days a week, and is free.

The service is provided in partnership with learndirect, the national learning advice line.

skillsformedia Direct: Individual in-depth career management advice for experienced media practitioners.

skillsformedia Express: One-on-one careers advice for graduates and new entrants.

www.skillsformedia.com: The industry-backed portal for information and advice about media careers, qualifications and training. Free email careers advice is available from a specialist media advisor (currently employed in the industry), through the website.

skillsformedia Workshops: Marketing and business development workshops run by media experts.

skillsformedia is the only industry-specific careers advice service, owned and managed by the industry. All *skillsformedia* advisors also currently work within the industry in addition to their advisory responsibilities, and the information and advice provided by the service is based on up-to-date industry research. *skillsformedia* works in partnership with *Skillset's* network of regional and national training agencies to ensure that advisors can provide information about training and opportunities throughout the UK.

What could skillsformedia do for you?

In addition to helping new entrants into the industry, *skillsformedia* advisors work with experienced practitioners to offer a range of relevant services, including:

- Helping individuals to identify skills gaps and training needs
- Developing marketing skills
- Assessing and developing CVs
- Short, medium and long term career planning.

How much does it cost?

skillsformedia is subsidised by industry and government, allowing some services to be provided free. There is a charge for individual services.

For more information, call freephone 08080 300 900, or visit the website www.skillsformedia.com to find out more about this exciting (and much needed) initiative.

Skills sought throughout the industry

Skillset Professional Qualifications are now well established as reliable indicators of required competences and skills in a wide cross-section of industry jobs (*see* also Chapter 9, pp. 251–8). Find out about the qualification routes for any jobs that you are interested in.

However, above and beyond the specific skills required by any one job, there are a number of generic skills which literally cross the industry. The most important is the ability to '*establish and maintain good working relationships*'. The industry is built on effective and increasingly multi-skilled teamwork, so that the ability to 'get on' with colleagues from a diversity of backgrounds – sometimes almost instantly – is a feature of successful industry practitioners.

Other essential skills include:

- Creativity
- Good communication skills
- Sensitivity to situations
- Ability to work safely under pressure
- Problem-solving/lateral thinking
- Reliability
- Tenacity
- Common-sense
- And, as the global industry develops – language skills, and knowledge of 'territories'

Most jobs, especially in production areas, demand long and frequently unsociable hours. Quite a lot of jobs also require stamina, and reasonable mobility and fitness. There are opportunities for disabled people, however – for further information, *see* Chapter 9, pp. 241–51.

Different styles of employment

Throughout this handbook, we refer to the 'employers' in general, but of course, when you start to seriously look for jobs, it's important to understand the incredible diversity of organisations that could give you the break you need. Beyond the household names of the BBC, ITV and major film companies there are literally thousands of small and medium sized employers (SMEs) who can provide work experience and career opportunities for people with appropriate skills and attitude. Independent production companies, satellite and cable channels, digital radio stations, interactive producers and games developers... and these are just the tip of the iceberg. Consult the trade directories to get more information.

Surely the growth of employment areas across the industry is good news for anyone at the start of their career? The answer is both yes and no. If your idea of a job involves a permanent contract, with holidays, sickness pay and a pension, it may be a good idea to explore other career options now. Such jobs do exist throughout the industry, but they are increasingly rare in film- or programme-making and in 'creative' areas. Companies tend to give full-time deals only to people whom they need all the time – and that usually means the 'core business' team of management, administration, finance, marketing and (increasingly) legal affairs. Small companies seldom 'employ' anyone, choosing instead to pay for help as and when it is needed.

Throughout the industry, people are employed on a variety of terms and conditions.

Permanent 'staff' jobs

These come with an annual salary, sick leave, paid holidays and pension rights. As mentioned above, people with permanent 'staff' jobs are usually 'core' to each business, including managers (sometimes producers), finance people, sales and marketing professionals, and technical or administrative support staff. Some journalists may also be in staff jobs. The new media world offers many opportunities for this type of work.

Fixed term/renewable contracts

These usually have some of the 'normal' benefits associated with full-time employment, such as sick leave. The length of employment may (sometimes deliberately) reduce statutory rights, such as claims for redundancy.

'Useful' people, who have skills and experience which allow them to move from one project to another (or sometimes to handle several at any one time) are most likely to be on renewable contracts. Presenters, producers, researchers, production managers, and design and make-up staff are all good examples. Big companies now often offer a range of employment benefits, such as holidays and pension rights, to staff in this category.

Working freelance

The majority of people working on the production side of television, film, video and interactive media are self-employed, responsible for their own tax, National Insurance and pension contributions. The biggest surprise to many people interested in film- or programme-making is that they will almost certainly need to be self-employed for at least part of their career. Freelancers are employed by the business decision-makers when – and only when – they are needed. They have no security of employment, and may be contracted for anything from a few hours to many weeks. Most freelancers work on a self-negotiated 'day rate'; this may be very high or very low, depending on reputation and experience. BECTU (the Broadcasting, Entertainment, Cinematograph and Theatre Union) and PACT (the Producers Alliance for Cinema and Television) have an agreement which establishes minimum rates.

Please refer to the BECTU website for up-to-date information on agreements and rates of pay throughout the industry (www.bectu.org.uk/resources/agree/index.html or www.bectu. org. uk/resources/rates/index.html) but remember that these may not be adhered to by all employers – or by the freelancers themselves. The majority of freelancers are employed for less than half the year, and one-third earn less than £20,000 per year. Read the section on necessary skills (*see* Chapter 1, pp. 5–7) to see if you could cope with this sort of existence.

skillsformedia is a careers guidance service which has been established to help freelancers build and manage effective careers (including changing areas) throughout the industry. The service is described in detail in this chapter (*see* pp. 267–9), and there is more information on www.skillsformedia.com.

Hybrid/portfolio contracts

This is where freelancers are part employed and part self-employed – a situation that is becoming increasingly common throughout the industry. People move between sectors, or may even supplement their industry income with work in an entirely different employment sector.

Annualised hours

This refers to when a 'permanent' employee is contracted for a specified number of days each year. Overtime is only paid once the specified limit has been passed.

In the 'old' days of television, some categories of staff – especially in the technical areas – could earn substantial additional income by working overtime on a regular basis. Annualised contracts (which may affect people such as camera operators, sound recordists, electricians, VTR engineers and some journalists) give management in big companies much more control than in the past. Sometimes, for instance, it is much cheaper to employ a freelancer than to pay overtime to an employee. Individuals who are on this sort of arrangement may find themselves working very hard indeed for a few months, and then getting 'garden leave' in which they are free to freelance for other companies.

Getting in – entry-level jobs

Getting into the new media sector

This fast-expanding sector offers a diversity of career opportunities to people with a wide range of skills and qualifications. People who are changing career from areas of traditional media can be very successful candidates. There are lots of jobs available and – in contrast to many areas described in this handbook – recruiters often find difficulty attracting enough suitably qualified applicants. Described in more detail in Chapters 7 and 8, there are several ways of getting into this sector, including responding to media advertisements, applying through the Internet, registering with specialist recruitment agencies – or making direct approaches to target companies. We spoke to several people who had been offered first jobs after a period of successful work experience.

Getting an entry-level job in the film- or programme-making sector

Most jobs in this industry are never formally advertised, although there are some notable exceptions – especially with regard to specific training schemes. As anyone will tell you, it's a 'contacts business'. Once people know about the skills, knowledge and experience you can contribute, they are more likely to consider you seriously for a job.

Most companies (even the smaller ones) prefer people to 'prove themselves' in a junior capacity, a process which may involve long or unsociable hours and which is often poorly paid. There are divided views on this practice, with some employers seeing the experience as an 'apprenticeship' or learning experience which can 'showcase' the individual for greater things. The alternate view is that the industry is capitalising on its popularity by offering jobs at 'slave labour' rates. It's up to you to decide... certainly, people are not expected to stay in these entry-level jobs for a great length of time. One Soho facilities house commented that, 'Within six months we know whether we want them to join the (well-paid, specialist) team.'

So – don't be too ambitious when approaching potential employers for that all-important first job. One of the big complaints is that many media graduates, perhaps spurred on by their lecturers, believe that they are qualified as film- or programme-makers just by doing the course. They either apply for jobs that are too big, or, if they've taken a very junior job, can't wait to move on. Be warned – some of the most successful programme-makers in the business served long apprenticeships (very long sometimes... especially in the film industry) before they got the opportunity to directly apply skills gained in film school or in junior production jobs. Most will say that they benefited from the experience.

Look out for these types of jobs, or approach potential employers direct:

- Technical Assistant (e.g. camera or sound)
- Trainee VT/Film Editor
- Assistant Floor Manager
- Runner/Gopher/3rd Assistant Director

Many people will start as runners – being useful (and reliable) in supporting a production team. Increasingly infrequent training schemes in television companies offer chances to a few highly motivated individuals to enter production and journalistic areas. The employers and unions also manage industry-based, new-entrant freelance training schemes. Enthusiasm and demonstrable commitment to the industry are the key qualities sought. Those who are successful generally have relevant experience and are confident that they understand the fundamentals of the work as a result of practical involvement. Many have considerable general work experience and are in their mid-20s when they enter the training schemes. Several entry-level initiatives are well established in the film industry, including FT2 (*see* pp. 223–5). Securing a place on one of these schemes will provide invaluable experience – *see* Chapter 9 for more information.

Entry-level jobs, when advertised, often specify quite modest essential qualifications and experience, but shortlisted candidates will often exhibit well above the minimum requirements. Many people applying for permanent or longer-contract jobs will already have substantial work experience, usually as a freelancer.

Other entry-level jobs

The media industry is a successful, global business, and the majority of advertised jobs will relate to the business of TV, radio, film, video and interactive media. Programmes are the 'product', and a range of interesting, often well-paid work is generated by the behind-the-scenes support necessary to ensure that the companies generate income to survive – and make more programmes. Such work is usually offered on a permanent or renewable contract basis.

Examples include:

- Airtime sales assistant
- Rights assistant
- Business affairs (legal) assistant
- Technical scheduling assistant
- Administrative and secretarial jobs
- Accounts /contracts assistant
- Film booking assistant

Gaining a foothold in one of these areas can take you to the heart of the business. In large companies there will almost certainly be further career opportunities advertised internally, although it's very difficult to cross to the programme-making side. In independent and corporate production companies, secretarial and administrative staff gain a unique insight into the day-to-day workings of the business. Some will become researchers and eventually producers or business development specialists.

Finding out about opportunities

Every hopeful candidate will look for advertisements in the media pages of the national press. What can you do to find out about less-publicised opportunities?

A good first step is to look for advertisements in the specialised trade and technical press, for example *Broadcast, Audio Visual, The Press Gazette, Screen International* and *Campaign* (a comprehensive list is included in Chapter 11, *Finding Out More*). Many of these journals will be available in your local reference library, and the majority have websites.

All BBC jobs are advertised in the national and local press as well as in specialist journals. Visit Ceefax page 696 and www.bbc.co.uk/jobs. For general recruitment enquiries contact:

BBC Recruitment
PO Box 7000, London W1A 8GJ
Tel: 0870 333 1330
Email: recruitment@bbc.co.uk

You will need to be consistent in your approach. Adverts only appear once, and as many of the jobs will not be advertised at all, to find out about them you will need to be told about possibilities or approach potential employers direct.

Making contacts and keeping informed

It's a contacts business, and if nobody knows that you exist you will not be offered a job – regardless of your skills, talent and incredible personality. Start making contacts by attending short courses, conferences – anything, in fact, that is relevant to your field of interest. Approach people in the industry – by name – and ask how they reached the positions they now hold, and for their advice on your career planning. This is often very effective, but only if you've already done your research on your interviewees' careers, and on their employing organisation.

Be proactive. A number of industry organisations will welcome people *before* they actually start their professional careers, including the following:

Broadcasting, Entertainment, Cinematograph and Theatre Union (BECTU) – joining BECTU will help you find out more about the industry, and provide you with contacts and information through their New Entrant/Graduate Membership scheme.
Website: www.bectu.org.uk

Royal Television Society (RTS) – a free e-membership linked to industry events featuring hot topics and programme-makers is available via www.rts.org.uk/emembers.

The Guardian, EITVF (Edinburgh International TV Festival), TVYP (TV for Young People) – the annual TV festival includes a series of special events and workshops for pre-selected young people planning to work in the industry.
Website: www.geitf.co.uk

New Producers Alliance (NPA) – a membership organisation for aspiring producers, directors and scriptwriters.
Website: www.npa.org.uk

First Film Foundation – a charity which exists to help new British writers, producers and directors to make their first film.
Website: www.firstfilm.co.uk

The Moving Image Society (BKSTS) – a long-established industry organisation which offers a diversity of valuable training and networking opportunities to people at the start of their careers.
Website: www.bksts.com

The Radio Academy – the professional membership organisation for the radio industry.
Website: www.radioacademy.org

Contact details of all these organisations may be found in Chapter 11, *Finding Out More*, or Chapter 4, *The Film Industry*.

Find out about who is winning awards... or enter yourself

The awards business has become an industry in itself, with some accolades being more highly valued than others. Watch the trade press to see who is winning in the relevant categories. Each year there are a number of student awards; doing well in a particular category may improve your chances of getting an interview, or even a job. Some of the most successful recent entrants into the film and commercials sector have been 'cherry picked' after student film festivals.

Keep up with what's going on

Watch all types of television, go to films, read the magazines, listen to BBC and commercial radio, visit the relevant websites and then talk to people about your views. Find out what is in production at any time, and arrange to visit a film or TV set. Anything that will add to your knowledge, and further demonstrate your commitment, will eventually help you make the break.

Approach things critically – not just at face value – and think about all the components that make up the finished whole. As well as the creative and technical aspects, consider the budget, financing, marketing, publicity, and potential for international sales of any production.

Work experience

This is where the need for tenacity begins to show itself! Once you have a fair picture of the skills you can offer, then offer them for a short period of media work experience. Contact one of the 'desks' in a local radio station offering ideas for features, and a willingness to do the necessary legwork... work as a volunteer with a community radio project... write to a cameraperson whose work you admire and offer to carry their equipment around for a few days. Turn up at the shoot of a film and offer to make excellent coffee. Be useful, don't get in the way, and keep your eyes and ears wide open. You'll learn a lot. Some students on relevant vocational courses will have work placements as a compulsory element of training, which is a huge advantage. Companies all have different policies about offering work experience – find out before you apply. The BBC has now centrally co-ordinated all work experience requests and offers: www.bbc.co.uk/workexperience BBC Work Experience, PO Box 27118, London W1A 6ZL, or call a *skillsformedia* advisor on 08080 300 900 for general work experience advice.

One problem with work experience is that it can make you more confident about how the business works than you can justify – you may still need considerable training before you would be considered for even a junior job. A bigger problem is that because so many people are prepared to work for no pay – even for periods between three and six months – some employers are tempted to take advantage of this free labour. Use the work experience to benefit you and the employer who has provided you with the opportunity to learn more – but beware of being exploited! If you are in doubt about what you are being asked to do or how much you are being offered to do it, you can always check with the relevant trade association or trade union. Both PACT and BECTU have codes of practice relating to this area.

One television Producer/Director – Chrissy Yeates, who has considerable experience of managing people during work placements – gave this advice: *'You're in! Get noticed!'* In other words, if you get a placement, cash in on your success. Experience and contacts are the key to a job in this industry, so these crucial few weeks could be the launch pad of your career. Here are some of her tips for getting it right with a TV company. The same principles apply across the industry.

First impressions count

You're now a member of a busy team. Everyone will make quick decisions: first, about whether they'll enjoy having you aboard; and second, whether you're going to be of any use to them! Win them over by being friendly and enthusiastic. Tell them you're keen to help out, and you'll find that they'll return the favour by helping you to make the most of your time with them. You're also on to a winner if you:

- Brief yourself – find out about the show or department you're working in *before* you arrive.

- Offer to help – don't wait to be asked.
- Listen carefully to instructions – ask if you don't understand.
- Work quickly – everyone has tight deadlines.
- Stay alert.
- Obey orders – especially on shoots and in studio.
- Know when to shut up – many careers have stopped before they have started as a result of questions at inappropriate moments.
- Check before you act on a bright idea.
- If in doubt, make tea – you're guaranteed friends for life!

You're on to a loser if you:

- Arrive late.
- Run down the show or film you're working on.
- Look bored.
- Think and act like you know it all.
- Interrupt or get in the way.
- 'Bunk off'.
- Go home before you've finished an urgent job.

Real live winners
Students who make an impact during work experience can go on to be offered a trainee job. People like:

- *Anna* – managed to find a large house with a swimming pool, to film in when the original shoot location was cancelled at the last minute.
- *Rick* – sorted and filed hundreds of newspaper cuttings. A boring job, but the researchers are still using his system.
- *Mel* – came up with great ideas which were included in a discussion programme for young people.
- *Spencer* – saved the day when the wrong paint was delivered to a shoot. He rushed out into the rain to B&Q to get the right colour.
- *Catherine* – spotted that the team were working through lunch and organised sandwiches and drinks to keep them going.

Real live losers
They will remain nameless, but needless to say, we never heard from them again! Their mistakes included:

- Not listening to the Director and walking into shot during a complicated take – repeatedly.
- Going missing on location! The shoot was held up while the Producer ascertained where this trainee was, for safety reasons. He'd bunked off to meet his mate at HMV.
- Chatting to a presenter as they tried to write their script just before going on air.
- Never offering to make the tea!

Work experience in film and video

Gaining useful work experience in other areas of the industry will also help. The advice given above can also be applied to film, video and interactive media. In Chapter 4, *The Film Industry*, advice from 'people who've made it' should prove useful to you (*see* pp. 150–1).

Getting the most out of work experience

There's more to this type of work experience than keeping your boss happy – it should help you decide if television, radio, video, film or interactive media are for you, and which type of job would suit you best. *Treat your placement as a fact-finding mission:*

- Get a notebook before you go, and draw up a list of *what you want from a job in the industry*. Do you want glamour, excitement, to meet the stars, to be a star, travel, a good salary, to be creative, to change the world? Would you work shifts, weekends, long hours? When you're there, do a reality check. Give each thing on your list marks out of ten based on what you observe and what people say. Does the job measure up to your expectations?
- *Keep a diary* of your experiences. Note the highs and lows of the day for you. Which bits of the job do you like most and least? What new skills have you acquired? Whose job do you like the look of, and why?
- *Notice who does what.* What skills are they using? How do they deal with problems? How do the teams work together? List any questions you might have and then…
- *Interview people.* Arrange a convenient time when they've got a few minutes to spare. Prepare your questions in advance. They could include: What was their first job and how did they get it? What is their job description? What are the perks and the

drawbacks of their job? Ask them to assess your performance and give you ideas for areas you could improve. Would they give you a reference?

- Using your diary, *update your CV* with all the skills you've acquired or improved.
- *Ask around* to see if there are any opportunities for work experience that may tie in with your holidays.
- *Write a behind-the-scenes report* for a school or college magazine, e-zine or website – get it published and add this to your CV!

Don't forget to keep in touch with your new contacts. A thank-you note to key people is always appreciated. A letter to update them on how you are getting on once or twice a year is a good way of reminding people how brilliant you are! Many people get runner jobs as a result of successful work experience.

Applying for that first job

Start marketing yourself

Now that you feel confident about your skills, and know enough about the various areas of opportunity to focus on one, it is time to develop a personal advertising campaign. You'll need a CV, and some tangible evidence of your talent. This could be any of the items listed below:

- Highlights of audiotaped interviews
- A 'taster' of a show you have presented
- A short showreel of different techniques
- A relevant collection of your film, TV or radio reviews
- A portfolio of still photos – beautifully presented!
- A short video or film (most people won't watch more than ten minutes)
- Scripts for radio or TV commercials
- Or anything else you feel shows off a relevant practical skill.

Developing a CV

A CV is a portrait of you, at any moment in time. Depending on who will receive it, you can decide which aspects of your skills, abilities, personality and experience should be highlighted, which areas are less important to the employer, and which are actually irrelevant and should be taken off the document. It doesn't need to be very long – one side of A4, well laid out, is often the most effective size – but it does need to be *relevant*.

The key to producing an effective CV is to write it for the recipient, anticipating the questions that he or she is likely to be asking about any applicant. For instance:

- Could this person do the job?
- Would this person do the job?

In other words, are you showing in the CV that you have considered the industry, the job, the type of people that you would be working alongside – and matched yourself against the 'person specification' of skills and experience that a recruiter will have in mind?

Think about what an employer will be looking for – for instance, the skills and abilities often quoted by people who recruit runners include:

- Commonsense
- A pleasant personality
- Practical skills
- Good communication skills
- Sensitivity
- Lots of energy
- Experience of teamwork – and not just sports teams!
- Curiosity
- Attention to detail
- Lateral thinking
- Knowing when to shut up
- Not afraid of getting your hands dirty
- Not too grand to make the sandwiches, wash up, etc.
- And, of course – *a passion for the industry.*

So how do you apply for a job as a runner or any other entry-level job? Think of all the things you have done that will convince the reader of your CV that you may be worth a try… a vacation working in a restaurant or hotel could easily be just as relevant at this stage as academic qualifications.

There are no rules about CVs – they are personal documents, and in an industry that contains a wealth of talent, some of them are very individualistic indeed! But the best ones share common factors, being:

- Concise
- Relevant
- Well laid out.

Above all, they should make the reader want to meet the person and find out more.

Once you've got a CV, maybe in two or three different versions, you can either send it off to advertised vacancies – if the company doesn't specify its own application form – or make direct approaches to people whom you feel/hope may be interested in you. In both cases, you should also send a 'covering letter'. This need only be simple, hand-written or preferably typed (keyboard skills are a real advantage), giving information about where you saw or heard about the opportunity, and why you feel you would be particularly suited to it. Don't repeat information given on your CV, and make sure that your grammar and spelling are correct.

If you are asked to complete an application form – especially for training schemes – apply the same principles. Before answering any question, take time to think: Why are they asking this? How does it relate to the job? How can I get over all the important information about my skills and experience within the confines of this (sometimes very short) form? Employers don't like extra pieces of paper, and they all object to questions answered with 'see attached CV'. Only send what you are asked to provide. Take your chosen examples of work to the interview unless specifically asked to enclose them with your application.

Although it is tempting to send CVs/letters by email, there is a real risk that they may be deleted by a busy employer. A hard copy, delivered by mail (or by hand if you're close enough), may be safer – and more effective.

Knock on doors

Because most jobs aren't advertised, most will not offer formal interviews – so many people will get first jobs by turning up and being ready and willing in the right place at the right time. In small companies especially, where the work comes and goes, it is worth calling in occasionally to see if they need any help. This is relatively easy in Soho, if you're London-based, but much harder if you are trying to get to the film studio or on location. People do, though, and jobs often get offered on a first-come-first-served basis.

The London Film Commission operates a runners database, which provides details to producers who are looking for help. Many people find that their reference library is an excellent networking venue, too.

At the interview

Relax! If you've got to this stage, something that you have done so far is of interest to them. Listen to the questions and think – how does this relate to the job? Answer with something relevant. You may be desperate to tell them about your film/book/project, but it's best to sit on it until asked. Remember that they're looking for someone to join a team, and the 'fitting in' factor is one of the most important things that they're trying to assess. A dose of modesty at this stage (especially if you've won an award, for example) can be very refreshing. However much you think you know before you join the industry, don't push it around. It can be very embarrassing to find out that you still have a lot to learn.

Once you're in, you've crossed the threshold, and your chances of progressing from an entry-level job are quite high. But before you get promoted, you will need to do that entry-level job quite brilliantly... and spend any free time you may have gaining skills, knowledge and generally making yourself indispensable.

Recently, we've talked to lots of recruiters within a major ITV group. Here is a synopsis of the advice they offered to staff who were already in the company, and looking to progress. It should be especially useful for people looking for second and third jobs in the industry. The same principles apply to anyone wishing to develop their role in film, video, interactive media or other areas of broadcasting.

Progressing within the industry

Making the most of yourself at interviews

When a job is advertised, the manager of that position is looking to find, keep and develop an appropriately skilled and motivated person who will help them achieve goals in line with the business. (This principle applies in equal measure to the 'talent' areas of TV.) He or she will want to do this in the most cost-effective way and, in theory, should prefer to choose an internal candidate. It doesn't always work like that for a multitude of reasons, including the fact that many internal candidates fail to impress due to lack of preparation and enthusiasm. However, internal candidates *are* at an advantage. If you can show that you match the basic skill requirements, you should get an interview, and it will be up to you to convince the recruiter(s) that you are the best candidate.

Here are some ideas to get you started. If you want to find out more there are some good books around (visit your local library) and some useful websites – search under 'interview skills'.

Before the interview

Preparation is more than half the battle. Spend time – and not just the night before – researching the following:

- *The type of job you are being interviewed for* – talk to people who already work within the employment area(s), including (if possible) the current job-holder and his or her boss.
- *The department, and how it fits within the company* – what is the purpose of the job? How does it fit into the company's business strategy? Remember that the cultures of different companies vary enormously.
- *Issues within the sector* – keep up-to-date with issues that affect the fast-changing television sector, and practise talking about your views and ideas with others.
- *Watch the output, and the competition* – it's incredible how many candidates appear for interviews with lame excuses about their lack of preparation in these key areas.

Above all, you should have thoroughly researched yourself, and be able to talk confidently and honestly about what you could contribute to the job. Here is some more good advice:

- *Be punctual* – pleading overwork is far from impressive.
- *Dress for the part* – many people, especially in programme-making areas, give an impression that the interview is 'just another part of the day' and wear their everyday clothes. You don't have to wear a suit (although it may be wise for some jobs), but do look as if the interview is an important occasion.
- *Treat the interviewer as an external interviewer* – many internal candidates fall into the trap of over-familiarity, assuming that the interviewer already knows about their competences, and that the interview is just a 'chat' – it isn't.
- *Take advantage of the situation* – even if you do not get offered the job, an interview is a wonderful opportunity to find out about the interviewer's work, and express enthusiasm for the future.
- *Research the interviewer's style* – contrary to suspicions, interviewers are merely human, and every one will have their own style, likes and dislikes. Find out as much as you can before the interview.
- *Put yourself in the interviewer's shoes* – there are few management decisions more visible than a poor appointment. Prepare well, and try to understand (and respond to) their agenda.
- *Come brimming with good ideas* – especially in programme-making areas, you should expect to be asked to contribute and justify ideas based on a thorough knowledge of the departmental output.
- *Mention your future aspirations* – send out an enthusiastic and strategic message about what you hope to contribute.
- *Understand something of the whole business* – for example, many programmes will be commissioned to attract or keep a target audience for advertisers. Familiarity with ratings, etc. will also help.
- *Be prepared to talk about your weaknesses as well as your strengths* – we all have them, but if they are relevant to the job in question you will have to provide well-thought-out proof that you can improve. For example: 'I know that I'm not brilliant at meeting deadlines, but this is what I've been doing recently to improve my time management, and it's having a noticeable effect.'
- *Be honest* – sometimes it's very amusing to listen to people 'overselling' their contribution to a project... but if you don't get

caught out in the interview, you're likely to be quickly shown up in the job.

- *Retain eye contact* – interviews are 'conversations with a purpose'. In a good interview, much of the signalling and communication will take place through eye contact.
- *Smile* – it's hard work interviewing people, and much more enjoyable to meet someone who looks pleased to be there.
- *Be aware of your body language* – look interested and 'engaged' in the conversation. Ask questions, be enthusiastic. Many interviewees are either too keen, or too 'laid back'. Try to achieve a professional-looking balance between the two extremes.

And finally, some pointers about what you should definitely not do:

- Don't say 'I don't have time to watch TV/listen to radio/go to films' or 'What programmes do you make?'
- Don't expect the interviewer to know everything about you just because you are an acquaintance.
- Don't be overconfident – a dose of modesty is very attractive.
- Don't interrupt, or fail to pick up the body-language signals which suggest that you should stop talking.

On a positive note – the interviewer would far rather you were suitable. External candidates are always 'riskier' appointments.

Getting on as a freelancer

If you decide that the freelance life would best suit you, you will need to put considerable effort into making yourself attractive to prospective employers. Freelancers are effectively small businesses, and you will need to organise yourself well if you are not to run into problems with the taxman. You may also be interested in gaining *Skillset* Professional Qualifications in your chosen area, to enhance your skills – and credibility with employers. A saying within the industry is, 'You're only as good as your last piece of work.' Getting on as a freelancer requires determination, personal marketing, reliability – and luck.

Whichever route you choose into this exciting industry – **Good Luck!**

11

Finding Out More

Every year, the audio-visual industries attract large numbers of people who simply want to 'work in the media'. If you are serious about wanting to work in these high-profile industries, you will take the time to find out exactly what goes into making the programmes that end up on our screens and radios. There are many sources of information to help you understand the technology, skills, and complex planning that go into creating and delivering the products that we see and hear. It takes time to acquire a genuine understanding and to work out where you might fit into what are, above all, collaborative media. But the chances are that the more you discover, the more you will want to know about these fascinating and fast-moving industries. Keep researching, keep asking questions, keep learning – in time the knowledge you acquire will help you to make real progress in your area of choice. There is always more to learn. This chapter provides some suggestions for further reading and exploration, including:

- Specialist books
- Trade press and newspapers
- Websites
- Organisations and societies that represent your area of interest.

The industry itself has recognised that there is a need for more advice and information for people starting out on their media careers. The result is *skillsformedia*, an advice service that aims to provide up-to-date and relevant information, based on the latest research, about the skills needs of the audio-visual industries, and the training and opportunities that exist to meet those needs. The *skillsformedia* website www.skillsformedia.com is probably the best starting point for anyone who wants to find out more.

Trade associations, guilds, unions, societies and support organisations

The different sectors of this industry are supported by a network of associations, trade unions, societies and guilds which act on behalf of their membership. Many are keen to help people at the start of their industry careers. A selection of general interest is listed below:

Advertising Producers' Association

26 Noel Street, London W1V 3RD
Tel: 020 7434 2651
Website: http://www.a-p-a.net
Represents the interests of producers of commercials, and has negotiated agreements with relevant unions. It has an online database of vacancies.

Amalgamated Engineering and Electrical Union (AMICUS)

Hayes Court, West Common Road, Bromley, Kent BR2 7AU
Tel: 020 8462 7755
Website: www.aeeu.org.uk
A large multi-industry union which includes approximately 1000 members involved in film and TV production.

British Film Commission (BFC)

10 Little Portland Street, London W1W 7JG
Tel: 020 7861 7860
Website: www.bfc.co.uk
Now part of the Film Council, the BFC is supported by government funding. It promotes the UK as an international production centre, and provides support for those filming in the UK.

British Film Institute (BFI)

21 Stephen Street, London W1T 1LN
Tel: 020 7255 1444
Website: www.bfi.org.uk
The BFI's mission is to develop greater understanding and appreciation of film, television and the moving image. There is an extensive online database which includes training courses.

Broadcasting, Entertainment, Cinematograph & Theatre Union (BECTU)

373–377 Clapham Road, London SW9 9BT
Tel: 020 7346 0900
Website:www.bectu.org.uk

BECTU represents all technical production and support staff in broadcasting, film and independent production, both permanently employed and freelance. The union negotiates collective agreements for these sectors and offers members a range of professional, legal and financial benefits and services. It publishes a regular journal Stage, Screen & Radio, *and runs a New Entrants/Graduates scheme. This discounted scheme provides all the benefits of union membership, plus opportunities to showcase work and to establish contacts in the industry.*

BECTU campaigns vigorously for diversity and equality of opportunity. The union offers support networks for women, black and disabled members.

In partnership with Skillset, *BECTU owns and manages* skillsformedia, *the UK media industry's careers advice service.*

British Academy of Film and Television Arts (BAFTA)

195 Piccadilly, London W1J 9LN
Tel: 020 7734 0022
Website: www.bafta.org

BAFTA promotes high creative standards in film, TV and interactive media production, and gives awards for excellence in a range of areas. It has an extensive programme of lectures, seminars and events. Membership applicants must have a minimum of three years' professional experience in the film, TV or interactive entertainment industries.

British Interactive Media Association (BIMA)

Briarlea House, Southend Road, South Green, Billericay CM11 2PR
Tel: 01277 658107
Website: www.bima.co.uk

The trade association representing the interactive media industries in the UK. It has a searchable online database of members, provides industry news, arranges meetings, and provides opportunities to attend seminars and events run by industry organisations.

BKSTS – The Moving Image Society
5 Walpole Court, Ealing Studios, Ealing Green, London W5 5ED
Tel: 020 8584 5220
Website: www.bksts.com
Email: info@bksts.com
Organises regular meetings and demonstrations of new equipment and techniques, and runs training courses. BKSTS also organises a biennial conference and specialist seminars which include special effects and wildlife film-making. It regularly reviews the relevant training offered to newcomers to the industry. Student membership is a good way to make contacts in the industry.

British Society of Cinematographers (BSC)
PO Box 2587, Gerrards Cross, Bucks SL9 7W2
Tel: 01753 888052
Website: www.bscine.com
Representing British cinematographers, BSC lists all its members online with contacts and filmographies. Arranges meetings, film shows and provides news and information about industry events.

Broadcasting Standards Commission (BSC)
7 The Sanctuary, London SW1P 3JS
Tel: 020 7808 1000
Website: www.bsc.org.uk
The BSC is the statutory body for both standards and fairness in broadcasting. It acts to:
- *produce codes of conduct relating to standards and fairness*
- *consider and adjudicate on complaints*
- *monitor, research and report on standards and fairness in broadcasting.*

Commercial Radio Companies Association
The Radiocentre, 77 Shaftesbury Avenue, London W1D 5DU
Tel: 020 7306 2603
Email: info@crca.co.uk
Website: www.crca.co.uk
The trade body for UK commercial radio, it organises training for radio producers and workshops for presenters.

The Cinema & Television Benevolent Fund
22 Golden Square, London W1F 9AD
Tel: 020 7437 6567
Website: www.ctbf.co.uk
Email: charity@ctbf.co.uk
The trade charity of the film, cinema and television industries.

Community Media Association
The Workstation, 15 Paternoster Row, Sheffield, S1 2BX
Tel: 0114 279 5219
Website: www.commedia.org.uk
Email: cma@commedia.org.uk
AND/OR Resource Centre, 356 Holloway Road, London N7 6PA
Tel: 0207 700 0100 X 234
Email: cmalondon@commedia.org.uk
Provides training for many industry hopefuls and holds conferences and events.

CSV Media
237 Pentonville Road, London N1 9NJ
Tel: 020 7278 6601
Website: www.csv.org.uk
Email: information@csv.org.uk
Part of the national charity Community Service Volunteers, CSV Media specialises in social action broadcasting, media support services and media training. Offices in Scotland, Wales and N Ireland.

Cyfle
Cardiff Office: 3rd Floor, Crichton House, 11–12 Mount Stuart Square, Cardiff CF10 5EE
Tel: 029 2046 5533
Caernarfon Office: Gronant, Penrallt Isaf, Caernarfon, Gwynedd LL55 1NS
Tel: 01286 67100
Website: www.cyfle.co.uk
Email: Cyfle@Cyfle.co.uk
Provides industry training and new entrant schemes.

Directors Guild of Great Britain
Acorn House, 314–320 Gray's Inn Road, London WC1X 8DP
Tel: 020 7278 4343

Website: www.dggb.co.uk
Email: guild@dggb.co.uk
Represents the interests and concerns of directors in all media. It seeks to maintain high standards in the film, television and theatrical media.

EM Media
35–37 St Mary's Gate, Nottingham NG1 1PU
Tel: 0115 934 9090
Website: www.em0media.org.uk
Email: infor@em-media.org.uk
Provides a range of services, including industry training information and support, for the East Midlands region.

Film Council
10 Little Portland Street, London W1W 7JG
Tel: 020 7861 7861
Website: www.filmcouncil.org.uk
Email: info@filmcouncil.org.uk
The council aims to nurture excellence and innovation in the UK film industry and to promote diversity and social inclusion. It provides funding for film production, supports training to maintain and develop the skills base of the industry, and funds schemes to develop and encourage emerging film talent.

(The) Guardian Edinburgh International Television Festival (GEITF)
1st Floor, 17–21 Emerald Street, London WC1N 3QN
Tel: 020 7430 1333
Website: www.geitf.co.uk
Email: info@geitf.co.uk
August bank holiday get-together for leading industry figures. The Television and Young People scheme (TVYP) offers 150 places to 18–21 year olds to attend training days.

Guild of British Camera Technicians
GBCT Membership, c/o Panavision UK, Metropolitan Centre, Bristol Road, Greenford, Middlesex UB6 8GD
Tel: 020 8813 1999
Website: www.gbct.org
The Guild's aim is to further the professional interests of technicians working with motion picture cameras. Members must demonstrate competence in their field of work and be members of their appropriate union.

The Guild of TV Cameramen
April Cottage, The Chalks, Chew Magna, Bristol BS40 8SN
Website: www.gtc.org.uk
Holds specialist workshops and publishes Zerb *magazine twice yearly. Membership is available at associate, affiliate and student level.*

Independent Television Commission (ITC)
33 Foley Street, London W1W 7TL
Tel: 0845 601 3608
Website: www.itc.org.uk
Licenses and regulates commercial television services in the UK (excluding S4C in Wales). It produces regular publications including codes, guidance and research.

International Visual Communication Association (IVCA)
Business Communication Centre, 19 Pepper Street, Glengall Bridge, London E14 9RP
Tel: 020 7512 0571
Website: www.ivca.org
Email: info@ivca.org
IVCA is the professional trade association representing the interests and needs of the visual communications user or supplier. In particular, the association represents the non-broadcast film, video and AV market and the facilities industry. It has over 1500 members representing programme producers, commissioners, users, in-house units, facilities, manu-facturers, freelance personnel and students.

Media Desk UK
4th Floor, 66–68 Margaret Street, London W1W 8SR
Tel: 020 7323 9733
Website: www.mediadesk.co.uk
MEDIA is a five-year programme of the EU to strengthen the competitive-ness of the European film, TV, and new media industries. Media desks, or antennae, operate throughout Europe and can help track down contacts and resources, and advise on the European industry. MEDIA Plus is a five-year scheme for the provision of training to audio-visual industries professionals.

Media Training North West
Room GO82, BBC, Oxford Road, Manchester M60 1SJ

Tel: 0161 244 4637
Website: www.mtnw.co.uk
Email: info@mtnw.co.uk
Provides a range of services, including industry training information and support, for the North West region.

Music Video Producers Association (MVPA)
26 Noel Street, London W1V 3RD
Tel: 020 7434 2651
Website: www.mvpa.co.uk
Email: info@mvpa.co.uk
The MVPA represents production companies making music promos, and advises on agreements with record companies

National Union of Journalists (NUJ)
Headland House, 308–312 Gray's Inn Road, London WC1X 8DP
Tel: 020 7278 7916
Website: www.nuj.org.uk
Many journalists and researchers who work in TV and Radio or as freelancers belong to the NUJ, and most of the broadcasters have agreements with the union.

New Producers Alliance
9 Bourlet Close, London W1W 7BP
Tel: 020 7580 2480
Website: www.npa.org.uk
Email: queries@npa.org.uk
National membership and training organisation for independent film producers ranging from film students and first-timers to experienced feature film-makers. It publishes a directory of members and produces a monthly news magazine.

Northern Film & Media
Central Square, Forth Street, Newcastle upon Tyne NE1 3PJ
Tel: 0191 269 9200
Website: www.northernmedia.org
Email: (first name of person and then) @northernmedia.org
Provides a range of services, including industry training information and support, for the North East region.

PACT (Producers Alliance for Cinema and Television)
45 Mortimer Street, London W1W 8HJ
Tel: 020 7331 6000
Website: www.pact.co.uk
Email: enquiries@pact.co.uk
PACT serves the film and independent TV, animation and new media production sectors, and is the UK contact point for international co-production or co-financial partners and distributors. Members are given training opportunities and a range of business advice and services. The monthly PACT *magazine is a useful source of information about the independent sector. PACT also runs an industrial relations service which provides information on standard agreements and contracts, and negotiates with the relevant unions.*

(The) Production Managers Association (PMA)
Ealing Studios, Ealing Green, London W5 5EP
Tel: 020 8758 8699
Website: www.pma.org.uk
Email: pma@pma.org.uk
Provides training, job opportunities and support for experienced production managers working in film, television, corporate and multimedia production.

(The) Radio Academy
5 Market Place, London W1W 8AE
Tel: 020 7255 2010
Website: www.radioacademy. org
Professional membership organisation for the radio industry. Organises the industry's annual conference, the Radio Festival, plus seminars and workshops. Regional centres organise their own programme of events.

Radio Authority
Holbrook House, 14 Great Queen Street, London WC2B 5DG
Tel: 020 7430 2724
Website: www.radioauthority.org.uk
Licenses and regulates all independent radio. The Radio Authority Pocketbook, *which lists FM and AM stations, is available online.*

Royal Television Society (RTS)
Holborn Hall, 100 Gray's Inn Road, London WC1X 8AL
Tel: 020 7430 1000
Website: www.rts.org.uk
Email: info@rts.org.uk
Promotes the art and science of television broadcasting. The Society is at the heart of the British television world. It provides a unique forum where all branches of the industry can meet and discuss major issues. Organises conferences, lectures, workshops, masterclasses and award ceremonies. The RTS has regional centres, each running their own programme of events. It publishes a useful magazine – Television.

Scottish Screen
2nd Floor, 249 West George Street, Glasgow G2 4QE
Tel: 0141 302 1700
Website: www.scottishscreen.com
Email: info@scottishscreen.com
A Government-backed body, it develops, encourages and promotes every aspect of film, television and new media in Scotland. Training, events, news and links are available online.

Screen East
Anglia House, Norwich NR1 3JG
Tel: 0845 6015670
Website: www.screeneast.co.uk
Email: info@screeneast.co.uk
Provides a range of services, including industry training, information and support, for the East of England region.

Screen West Midlands
31–41 Bromley Street, Birmingham B9 4AN
Tel: 0121 766 1470
Website: www.screenwm.co.uk
Email: info@screenwm.co.uk
Provides a range of services, including industry training, information and support, for the West Midlands region.

Screen Yorkshire

40 Hanover Square, Leeds LS3 1BQ
Tel: 0113 294 4410
Website: new website coming soon
Provides media training information and support for the Yorkshire and Humber region.

Sgrin – Media Agency for Wales

The Bank, 10 Mount Stuart Square, Cardiff Bay, Cardiff CF10 5EE
Tel: 02920 333300
Website: www.sgrin.co.uk
Email: sgrin@sgrin.co.uk
The Welsh national information centre is committed to promoting and supporting film, television and new media production in Wales. It runs a number of annual schemes, co-funded by broadcasters and Arts Councils in Wales, which are open to a cross-section of new and experienced film-makers. The website is bi-lingual, Welsh and English.

South West Screen

St Bartholomews Court, Lewins Mead, Bristol BS1 5BT
Tel: 0117 952 9977
Website: www.swscreen.co.uk
Email: info@swscreen.co.uk
Provides a range of services, including industry training information and support, for the South West region.

Skillset

Prospect House, 80–110 New Oxford Street, London WC1A 1HB
Tel: 020 7520 5757
Website: www.skillset.org
Email: info@skillset.org
The Sector Skills Council for the audio-visual industries. Works with all parts of the media industries (employers, trade associations, unions, training and education providers) to find out what skills issues exist and to address them. Operates at a strategic level to improve training and education policy. Publishes research and information, and investigates employment and market trends. Sets industry standards for training and education providers. Involved in every aspect of the industry, Skillset is managed and funded by the BBC, Channel 4, five, S4C, ITV, Commercial

Radio Companies Association (CRCA), Sky, the Federation of Enter-
tainment Unions (FEU), International Visual Communications
Association (IVCA), the Producers Alliance for Film and Television
(PACT), the Film Council and the Motion Picture Association (MPA).
Skillset owns and manages skillsformedia, the industry careers advice
service, in partnership with BECTU.

skillsformedia

Prospect House, 80–110 New Oxford Street, London WC1A 1HB
Tel: 020 7520 5757
Website: www.skillsformedia.com
Email: info@skillsformedia.com
The UK media industry's careers advice service. Offers a range of services
including: individual careers advice; a national helpline 08080 300 900,
in partnership with learndirect; online advice; and specialist workshops.
The website is packed with information about careers, training and
resources, with links to other industry organisations, and real-life case
studies.

Student Radio Association

c/o: The Radio Academy, 5 Market Place, London W1W 8AE
Tel: 020 7255 2010 (ask for the SRA)
Website: www.studentradio.org.uk
Email: advice@studentradio.org.uk
Represents student radio stations, holds member conferences, and helps to
organise the Radio 1 Student Radio Awards.

Women in Film and Television

6 Langley Street, London WC2H 9JA
Tel: 020 7240 4875
Website: www.wftv.org.uk
Email: info@wftv.org.uk
Professional membership organisation for women working in the film,
TV and digital media industries. It provides a forum, offers a contacts
network, safeguards the interest of women, and champions their
achievements in the industry.

The Writers' Guild of Great Britain

15 Britannia Street, London WC1X 9JN
Tel: 020 7833 0777
Website: www.writersguild.org.uk
Email: admin@writersguild.org.uk

The union for professional writers working in TV, film, radio, theatre, books and multimedia. It has agreements with PACT, BBC, ITV, ITC, TWA and TAC. Provides support for members, organises events and publishes The Writers Bulletin *six times a year for members.*

Chapter 4, *The Film Industry* contains additional information about specific organisations relevant to aspiring film professionals (*see* pp. 157–60).

Useful magazines and journals

Many of these publications can be found in specialist libraries. Alternatively, large newsagents will order copies on your behalf.

Ariel
The BBC in-house magazine, also available in some libraries on subscription.

AV Magazine
Covers business-to-business use of audio-visual communications including presentations, video multimedia, video conferencing, film, business television networks, the Internet and live events.

Broadcast
An invaluable information source for anyone who is serious about the TV and radio industries. Published weekly.

Bfm-Black Filmmaker
Provides information and insights for film and TV enthusiasts.

The British Cinematographer (incorporating *Eyepiece*) (only available from BSC, or GBCT or order on 01753 650101)
A new magazine produced by the Guild of British Camera Technicians, full of information relevant to aspiring film-makers.

Campaign
The bible of the advertising industry. Useful for anyone interested in the commercial or corporate career areas.

Computer Arts
Monthly guide for graphic designers and digital artists with tutorials and software reviews.

Direct
The quarterly magazine for members of the Directors Guild of Great Britain – selected articles available online from www.dggb.co.uk.

Edge
Worldwide interactive entertainment and games industry news and previews (monthly).

Future Music
Guide to making music on PCs and Macs with reviews and tutorials for software applications.

Image Technology
Magazine of the Moving Image Society (BKSTS). Useful for anyone planning a technical career. (Available to non-members.)

Imagine (A-UK Publishing) Tel: 0117 902 9966
Magazine with news about the animation and digital media industries (formerly Animationuk).

Internet Magazine
For all net users, it includes articles and tutorials on Web Design.

London Film and Video News
Quarterly newsletter of the London Film and Video Development Agency which is distributed free to independent film and video organisations in London. Also available online at www.lfvda.demon.co.uk.

Media Week
Trade magazine covering the UK media industry.

Moving Pictures International
Major film industry soruce of festival and film market information.

New Media Age
UK business weekly with digital information and news covering the Internet, interactive TV, e-commerce and online publishing.

OffAir
The bi-monthly, members-only magazine of the Radio Academy.

The PACT Magazine
For members of the independent television producers' trade association (magazine-only subscription available).

Press Gazette
For all journalists. Introduced the Students Journalism awards in 2002.

The Radio Magazine
A weekly magazine focusing on radio issues.

Radio Times
Still widely accepted as the best source of scheduling information.

Screen International
Invaluable for aspiring film-makers, it contains interviews, features and reviews.

Stage, Screen and Radio
The BECTU journal, also available on subscription.

The Stage
Primarily for actors, but valuable for anyone interested in light entertainment.

Update
The newsletter of the IVCA, published six times a year for members who work in the corporate and non-broadcast production and facilities sector.

Television
The RTS journal which often contains articles by high-profile industry figures. Published ten times a year.

Television Lighting
Journal of the Society of Television Lighting Directors. Published three times a year.

Televisual
Widely accepted as the best source of information about the facilities sector. Publishes an 'awards list' of facilities houses every September. Monthly.

Voice of the Listener and Viewer
Published by the independent non-profit making association representing the citizen and consumer interest in broadcasting

Zerb
The magazine for members of the Guild of TV Cameramen. Published twice yearly.

Chapter 4, *The Film Industry* contains additional information about specialist film publications.

Useful reference books

Many of these are too expensive for an individual to purchase: visit a specialist or business library. Some texts are available on the Internet. All prices are at the time of writing.

Animation UK
A-UK Publishing, 2nd Floor, The Tobacco Factory, Raleigh Road, Bristol BS3 1TF
Tel: 0117 9029966
Website: www.animationuk.com
£20 *The directory of the animation industry.*

Blue Book of British Broadcasting
TNS (Taylor Nelson Sofres), 292 Vauxhall Bridge Road, London SW1V 1AE
Tel: 0207 963 7638
Publisher: TNS
£75 *A contacts book for radio, TV and satellite containing many thousands of names, addresses and phone numbers.*

BFI Film and Television Handbook
21 Stephen Street, London W1T 1LN
Tel: 020 7255 1444
Website: www.bfi.org.uk
£21.99 Combines hundreds of film and broadcasting facts and figures with an extensive directory of thousands of contacts and addresses.

Creative Handbook
Reed Business Information, Windsor Court, East Grinstead House, East Grinstead, West Sussex RH19 1XA
Tel: 01342 332028
Website: www.chb.com
Publisher: Kemps Publishing
£150 inc p&p   The Art Director's handbook – an excellent showcase of graphic arts and animation.

The CRCA Work Placement Digest
The Radiocentre, 77 Shaftesbury Avenue, London W1D 5DU
Tel: 020 7306 2603
Website: www.crca.co.uk
The Commercial Radio Companies Association has a free, downloadable database of radio companies that accept applications for work placements.

Directors Guild Directory
Acorn House, 314–320 Gray's Inn Road, London WC1X 8DP
Tel: 020 7278 4343
Email: guild@dggb.co.uk
Publisher: Directors Guild of Great Britain
£10 + £2.50 p&p A–Z of Britain's TV, film, radio and theatre directors.

The PACT Directory of Independent Producers
45 Mortimer Street, London W1W 8HJ
Tel: 020 7331 6000
Website: www.pact.co.uk
Publisher: PACT
£30 Full details of PACT members.

Directory of International Film and Video Festivals
The British Council, Films and Television Department, 11 Portland Place, London W1B 1EJ
Tel: 020 7389 3065
Website: www.britishcouncil.org
Publisher: British Council
Available from the British Council and online.

The IVCA Business Media Handbook
Business Communication Centre, 19 Pepper Street. Glengall Bridge, London E14 9RP
Tel: 020 7512 0571
Email: info@ivca.org
Publisher: IVCA
£37 *The essential guide to the corporate visual communications industry. Comprehensive industrial facts and figures, and information about the business benefits of visual communication media – combined with a guide to over 1000 companies and practitioners in corporate film, video, interactive media, the Internet, business television, business events, and hire and facility provision.*

Kays UK Production Manual
Pinewood Studios, Pinewood Road, Iver Heath, Bucks SL0 0NH
Tel: 01753 651171
Website: www.kays.tv
Publisher: Kay Media
£80 *Can be ordered online. With its* Crew Directory, *a comprehensive and reliable manual of people and organisations in the production side of the film, TV and broadcast industry. Contains thousands of names of addresses in over 250 classifications.*

The Knowledge
c/o CMP Information, Riverbank House, Angel Lane, Tonbridge, Kent TN9 1SN
Tel: 01732 362 666
Website: www.theknowledgeonline.com
Publisher: Miller Freeman Information Services
Book: £95; CD-Rom £95 A comprehensive guide to the products and services of the UK film, TV and video industry.

The Guardian Media Guide
Atlantic Books. ISBN 1843 540142
£17.99　*An invaluable source of reference, with a mass of information and contact details relevant for anyone working or planning to work in the industry.*

The Production Guide
33–39 Bowling Green Lane, London EC1R 0DA
Tel: 020 7505 8000
Website: www.productionguideonline.com
Subscriptions: Tower 01858 438847
Publisher: Emap Media
£80　*Annual details of technical contacts, services and equipment from the publishers of the weekly magazine* Broadcast. *Student price £40.*

Radio Authority Pocket Guide
Holbrook House, 14 Great Queens St, London WC2B 5DG
Tel: 020 7430 2724
Website: www.radioauthority.co.uk
Publisher: Radio Authority
Free reference booklet for the independent radio business. Also available online.

Radio Listener's Guide
PO Box 888, Plymouth PL8 1YJ
Tel: 01752 872 888
Website: www.radiolistenersguide.co.uk
£5.75　*Pocket guide to all the UK radio stations. Also available to order online.*

Royal Television Society Handbook
Holborn Hall, 100 Gray's Inn Road, London WC1X 8AL
Tel: 020 7430 1000
Website: www.rts.org.uk
Publisher: Royal Television Society
£10　*Guide to this society, with listings of its members.*

Television Business International Yearbook 2003
Informa UK, Sheepen Place, Colchester, Essex CO3 3LP

Tel: 01206 772224
Website: www.bookshop.informamedia.com
Publisher: FT Media and Telecoms
£350 Handbook for international TV executives.

The Art of the Deal (3rd edition)
Dorothy Viljoen: PACT
PACT, 45 Mortimer Street, London W1W 8HJ
Tel: 020 7331 6000
Website: www.pact.org.uk
£50 Comprehensive guide to business affairs for TV and film producers.

Other books of particular relevance to people who would like to find out more about working within the industry include:

Research for Media Production (2nd edition)
Kathy Chater: Focal Press £15.99 Website: www.focalpress.com

Television News (4th edition)
Ivor Yorke: Focal Press £22.99 Website: www.focalpress.com

Getting into Films and Television
Robert Angell: How to Books Ltd Website: www.getintofilm.com

Broadcast Journalism (5th edition)
Andrew Boyd: Focal Press: £22.99 Website: www.focalpress.com

The Camera Assistant's Manual (Film) (3rd edition)
David E Elkins: Focal Press: £29.99 Website: www.focalpress.com

Confronting Reality: An Introduction to Television Documentary
Richard Kilborn, John Izod: Manchester University Press: £12.99

Books are constantly being published about the media. Look at them in a library before spending your money – many lack up-to-date information. However, one book which, in our opinion, *does* provide a valuable overview of the industry is:

Lights Camera, Action!
Josephine Langham: BFI: £13.99 Website: www.bfi.org.uk

Focal Press publishes a large range of books used by practitioners throughout the industry, in addition to the titles mentioned here. Website: www.focalpress.com.

Specialist film publications – Chapter 4, *The Film Industry* contains additional information about specialist titles, which may be of interest to aspiring film professionals.

Specialist bookshops

Most large bookshops will have specialist cinema or broadcasting sections. You can use the Internet to search for industry titles.

The BBC World Service Bookshop
Bush House, The Aldwych, London WC2B 4PH (entrance in the Strand)
Tel: 020 7557 2576
Stocks BBC publications, videos, CDs and other related merchandise.

Mail order services are provided by:
The Cinema Bookshop
13/14 Great Russell Street, London WC1B 3NH
Tel: 020 7637 0206 Fax: 020 7436 9979

Offstage Theatre & Film Bookshop
37 Chalk Farm Road, London NW1 8AJ
Tel: 020 7485 4996 Fax: 020 7916 8046
Email: offstagebookshop@aol.com

Where the jobs are advertised

The majority of the jobs in this industry are not advertised. Personal marketing of skills and availability ensure that most work comes through direct or indirect contact. The larger companies all prefer to advertise opportunities to their existing staff before entering the open market, thus creating more junior vacancies which will often go to people who have made excellent speculative applications.

If you do respond to an advertisement, make your application as professional (and short) as possible. Some will ask for practical evidence of your skills. Ensure that your personal advertising campaign is targeted to the individual recipient – a very general CV and tape may get lost in the hundreds of applications generated by an 'interesting' job advertisement.

Some companies provide information about vacancies to Job Centres, university and college careers services, and also advertise in the local and ethnic press. It is worth looking for job advertisements in:

- *Ariel*
- *AV Magazine*
- *Broadcast*
- *Campaign*
- *The Daily Telegraph*
- *Evening Standard (London)*
- *The Guardian (Mondays)*
- *The Independent (Wednesdays)*
- *The Observer*
- *Screen International*
- *The Stage*
- *The Sunday Times*
- *Televisual*
- *Time Out*
- *The Times*
- *Press Gazette*
- And – especially for ITV companies – in the local press

Further sources of information

It is worth having a look at the websites of the main broadcasters for a wealth of information about careers, output, training and other opportunities.

Channel 4:	www.channel4.com
BBC:	www.bbc.co.uk
five:	www.channel5.co.uk

Specialist recruitment agencies

Specialist agencies, which can be invaluable in helping freelancers to find work, are listed in the major industry production resource directories, such as *The Production Guide*, *The Knowledge* and *Kays & Kemps Directories*. The unions and trade associations usually maintain an up-to-date list of relevant vacancies for their members.

Useful information for anyone with a disability is included in the specialist reference section of this book.

Global Media Recruitment Ltd:	www.globalmediarecruitment.com
Grapevine Jobs:	www.grapevinejobs.com
Switched On Production Consultancy:	www.switchedonjobs.com
Major Players:	www.majorplayers.co.uk
Media UK Internet Directory:	www.mediauk.com
Recruit Media (New Media):	www.recruitmedia.co.uk
Production Base:	www.productionbase.co.uk
Media Guardian:	www.mediaguardian.co.uk
Searchlight:	www.search-light.com
Mandy's Film and TV Production Directory:	www.mandy.com (worldwide)
Shooting People:	www.shootingpeople.org

Health & Safety issues

Health & Safety is a significant issue for many film- and programme-makers and their bosses. The Health & Safety Executive has published a series of factsheets of particular relevance to the film and TV industry, and also produced a book called *Health and Safety for Freelances*. The information line is 08701 545500. BECTU can also assist members with Health & Safety issues.

Places to visit

Absorbing the atmosphere of a production will help put your reading into perspective. Many radio and television companies are prepared to organise group visits. Sometimes, direct contact with a producer will result in a visit or short period of work experience. In addition, visits to the following places will be both informative and fun:

- The National Museum of Photography, Film and Television (Bradford) Website: www.nmpft.org.uk
- Backstage tours of the BBC (London) can be booked via the website www.bbc.co.uk/tours

Finding out about practical experience opportunities

Your Regional Screen Agency will have information about the range of opportunities available for 'hands on' workshop experience in your area. Details of each may be found via the Arts Council website: www.artscouncil.org.uk.

The national or regional training partners (described in Chapter 9, *Training and Education for the Industry* – see pp. 227–9) may also be able to guide you to local workshop providers. Their contact details can be found earlier in this chapter under 'Support organisations'.

Skillset research publications

Skillset, the Sector Skills Council for broadcast, film, video and interactive media, regularly conducts research about employment trends and training needs within the relevant industries (*see* also pp. 000–00). Information is available on their website, and copies of the publications may be found in specialist libraries, including the BFI and ITC libraries.

and finally

To survive and thrive in this industry, you will need to constantly absorb new information. Applying for internal vacancies once you have crossed the first big hurdle into a 'real' job, or finding the second big contract, will require at least as much effort. But if you are passionate about your work, and determined to do well, it should prove an enjoyable and rewarding experience.

Good luck!

Index

CPSIA information can be obtained
at www.ICGtesting.com
Printed in the USA
LVHW021037090619
620629LV00011B/352